WINNING THE CUSTOMER EXPERIENCE RACE

EDWIN MARGULIES

WINNING THE CUSTOMER EXPERIENCE RACE

The industry playbook to balance automation and human assistance

Copyright © 2025 by Nextiva. All rights reserved.

No part of this publication may be reproduced, distributed, or transmitted in any form or by any means, including photocopying, recording, or other electronic or mechanical methods, without the prior written permission of the publisher, except as permitted by U.S. copyright law.

This book is sold subject to the condition that it shall not, by way of trade or otherwise, be lent, resold, hired out, or otherwise circulated without the publisher's prior consent in any form of binding or cover other than that in which it is published and without a similar condition including this condition being imposed on the subsequent purchaser. Scanning, uploading, and distribution of this book via the Internet or via any other means without the permission of the publisher is illegal and punishable by law. Please purchase only authorized electronic editions. Do not participate in or encourage electronic piracy of copyrighted materials.

Your support of the author's rights is appreciated. Images are reproduced for education and commentary purposes. No infringement is intended by the author or publisher. All rights are reserved.

ISBN 979-8-9910452-3-0

Printed in the United States of America

First edition | 2025

Endorsements from Industry Experts

"Packed with real-world examples and sharp insights, *Winning the Customer Experience Race* is the must-have playbook for any organization ready to transform customer experience into a powerful, competitive edge. Discover how to stay ahead of the curve while striking the right balance with innovation in every customer interaction."

—Mark Harris, Chief Operating Officer, KinISO Software

"Whether you have started your automation journey or are just getting started, this book offers a smorgasbord of ideas, opportunities, and inspiration to improve your ability to deliver an exceptional customer experience. Every professional and leader in customer service and customer experience should mine the case studies in this book, not only from their own industry but also from other sectors. Doing so will undoubtedly help you differentiate your brand from your competitors."

—Adrian Swinscoe, best-selling author, *Forbes* contributor, and advisor

"Success in business requires that an organization's practices and processes be both effective and efficient—doing the right things in the right way. In these highly competitive times, success demands the wise application of automation from prospecting to client onboarding to relationship management. When it's time to consider and reconsider call center automation—and it's always time—this book is a great resource—logically organized, well written, and insightful. Kudos!"

—Ray Horak, industry expert and author of *Webster's New World Telecom Dictionary*

Contents

Acknowledgments	1
Foreword	3
Today's Savvy Consumer	4
Why You Should Read This Book	4
Thrive, Not Just Survive	5
About Us	6
Introduction	9
The Careful Balance	10
Approach To The Subject Matter	11
Should You Read The Whole Book?	12
Business Services	15
Key Automation Opportunities For Business Services	16
Top Challenges In Accounting, Legal, And Real Estate Services	17
Business Services Use Case Examples	19
Financial Services	41
Top Automation Targets In Financial Services	41
Challenges With Automation In Financial Services	44
Financial Services Use Cases	48
Healthcare	91
Top Automation Targets In Healthcare	92
Challenges In Healthcare	95
Top Automation Use Cases In Healthcare	100

Insurance Services — 129

- Top Automation Targets For Insurance Services — 130
- Challenges With Automation In Insurance Services — 132
- Top Automation Use Cases For Insurance Services — 133

Manufacturing — 157

- Top Automation Targets In Manufacturing — 158
- Top Challenges In Manufacturing — 163
- Manufacturing Use Cases — 167

Non-Profit and Education — 189

- Automation Targets For Non-profit And Education Sectors — 190
- Top Challenges In Non-profit And Education Sectors — 192
- Use Case Examples In Non-profit And Education Sectors — 194

Retail Goods And Services — 213

- Top Automation Targets In Retail — 214
- Challenges With Automation In Retail — 217
- Top Automation Targets In Retail — 220

Service Providers — 259

- Top Automation Targets For Service Providers — 259
- Challenges With Automation For Service Providers — 263
- Top Automation Use Cases For Service Providers — 264

Travel And Hospitality — 295

- Top Automation Targets In Travel And Hospitality — 296
- Automation Challenges In Travel And Hospitality — 300
- Top Automation Use Cases In Travel And Hospitality — 305

Final Thoughts — 327

- Conclusion — 330

About The Editor — 332

Acknowledgments

I THANK MARCO Burgarello for his meticulous production work and promotion efforts. Marco efficiently coordinates typesetters, artists, editors, writers, printers, and fulfillment vendors with professionalism and enthusiasm. Thank you, Marco, for your hard work and dedication.

The entire product marketing team at Nextiva contributed to the writing of this book. They conducted customer interviews, performed research, and created diagrams to enhance readability and engagement. I extend my gratitude to Bhavana Rana for her coaching of the team on industry specialization aspects. This included assistance with persona development, addressing industry challenges, and identifying key automation targets. Additionally, Bhavana contributed to the writing and editing of three chapters: Financial Services, Healthcare, and Retail.

I also extend my gratitude to Sarah Skidd for developing the business services use cases. Her writing skills made it a pleasure to collaborate with her. Thanks to Tyler Zeman for his work on the non-profit, education, and insurance chapters. Cara Plowman and Alexandra

Lueck partnered with Tyler on the non-profit and insurance use cases, respectively. Gabby Maurice contributed to the financial services chapter, while Tallon Brown focused on healthcare use cases. Both are prolific writers dedicated to the technical aspects of the Nextiva UCXM platform. I appreciate their collaboration.

I am grateful to Alexandra Lueck for her assistance with the insurance chapter and success stories. Her enthusiasm positively impacted the team. Thanks to Kate Hodgins and Dom Conway for partnering on the manufacturing use cases, with a special mention of Dom's IoT example. Lastly, my thanks go to Ben Kirchner for his work on the retail, travel, and hospitality chapters. I am proud of everyone's contributions and enjoyed collaborating on this project.

—Edwin Margulies, editor-at-large

Foreword

By TOMAS GORNY
CEO AND CO-FOUNDER OF NEXTIVA

BUSINESSES THAT NEGLECT customer experience risk extinction. In the '60s, companies on the S&P 500 list had a 35-year lifespan. By 2025, they've dropped to about 20 years. This is attributed not only to rapid technological evolution or increasingly demanding consumers but also to intensifying global competition and constantly shifting market preferences. The main point is that businesses need to adapt swiftly to stay relevant.

History has shown us that businesses that continually innovate, adapt, and engage with their customers don't just survive; they thrive. This book aims to guide you through the complexities of technological advancements and evolving customer expectations with clarity and precision. With customer experience now crucial in loyalty decisions, past achievements no longer guarantee success.

Consumers constantly ask, "What have you done for me lately?" In today's market, where alternatives are easily accessible, any mistake can drive customers to competitors. This applies across all industries, whether dealing with products or services. Every interaction, from sales conversations to product performance, is vital.

Today's Savvy Consumer

Consider your own experiences in retail, travel, hospitality, or tech, and you'll recognize how crucial your last interaction was with your favorite brand. A sour moment in a store, a less-than-spotless hotel room, or a lag in customer support can tip the scales, pushing you to reconsider your loyalty. This highlights a simple yet powerful truth: nailing that final interaction is key to keeping your customers close.

Thinking about our own shopping adventures, it's easy to see why. Whether we don the hat of a customer or a business professional, recent experiences heavily influence where our loyalties lie.

This discussion isn't just brain food for those of us in the biz; it's a prompt for any business to put delivering outstanding experiences front and center. After all, no one wants to be that business left behind. Navigating the right mix of tech and human touch isn't just best practice; it's critical for building and keeping customer loyalty.

Modern consumers are becoming increasingly demanding; they crowdsource their buying decisions, openly share opinions on social media, and are fickler than ever before. As a result, business owners and executives must prioritize driving efficiency by gaining real-time insights into customer behavior, enhancing team productivity, and enabling quick, informed decision-making.

This focus stems from the understanding that customer experience (CX) is vital in achieving competitive advantage and fostering brand loyalty. Consequently, it is essential to balance customer expectations with the needs of the organization for overall success.

Why You Should Read This Book

When you're deciding how to dive into a publication like this, you might be torn between reading it straight through from cover to cover or just cherry-picking the chapters that really speak to your specific interests. Each section is crafted with care, designed to spark creativity and offer up some real, practical insights for folks in different industries. But, even if it seems like some chapters might not be directly relevant to you, giving the whole thing a read can bring a bunch of benefits.

For starters, while every chapter zeroes in on topics tailored to sectors, the core ideas and concepts tend to have a broader appeal. Take a case study on automating retail processes, for example. This could light up some lightbulbs for solving similar puzzles in the healthcare world. Dipping into various chapters gives you a rounded view of how automation might be leveraged in all sorts of contexts, possibly leading to some fresh, innovative approaches you hadn't thought of before.

Then there's the fact that today's industries are all kind of woven together, with developments in one area often rippling through to others. Getting familiar with the challenges and wins in different sectors can help you see coming trends and shifts that could affect your own work. This kind of cross-industry insight is gold for strategic planning and staying ahead of the curve.

Plus, the book is built to be flexible. You don't have to plow through it in order; you can roam free, following your own interests and needs. This pick-and-choose style can make for a more engaging and personalized reading experience. You might start with a chapter that tackles a burning issue you're facing and then let your curiosity guide you through the rest. This way of jumping around can help tailor the journey to you.

Lastly, chatting about what you've learned with colleagues or partners can kick off some great conversations and brainstorming moments. Working through the book's concepts together can help you develop a solid plan for implementing automation in your business.

This shared understanding not only deepens everyone's grasp of the material but also ensures that the solutions you develop are well-rounded and effective.

Thrive, Not Just Survive

This book highlights how your business can not only survive but thrive despite overwhelming odds to the contrary. I invite you to explore its pages, taking note of how different industries are taking advantage of automation in its various forms and balancing it with good old-fashioned human help. This dual approach offers customers effective solutions and positions them ahead in the rapidly evolving technology landscape.

Above all, this is an idea book. I encourage you not only to read it but to share it with your business colleagues and make it required reading for your entire sales, marketing, development, and CX teams. Use it as a brainstorming tool. Use it to teach new employees how to come up with fresh ideas for pleasing customers.

In summary, while it's true that each chapter stands on its own, weaving through the entire publication can really deepen your understanding of automation and how it might fit into your world. Whether you go page by page or skip around, the key is being open to new ideas and figuring out how to make them work for your unique situation. Happy reading!

About Us

Nextiva aspires to be your technology partner as you strive for customer delight and satisfaction. We are committed to assisting you in leveling the playing field and enabling you to succeed through your dedication to exceptional customer service.

A key factor in the success of any significant automation project is the accuracy and accessibility of customer transaction data. This is an area where we provide strong support as a technology partner. The Nextiva Unified Customer Experience Management (UCXM) platform is the quintessential system of record for all customer interactions.

We position ourselves this way because possessing accurate data at the moment of customer interaction distinguishes a perfect encounter from a disappointing one. This system of transactional fidelity sets the tone for success in your pursuit of satisfied and loyal customers.

We hope you find this book insightful and that the automation ideas and use cases presented within inspire you to excel in serving your customers. The concepts discussed in this publication highlight how automation, when balanced with human touch, can lead to more effective and efficient customer solutions, keeping you ahead in the rapidly evolving technology landscape.

Nextiva is dedicated to fostering winning approaches with our customers and partners. We believe that working together on the insights gained from this book can lead to innovative solutions and a deeper understanding of how automation can benefit your business. Discussing these ideas with your colleagues and Nextiva can spark new strategies and ensure a well-rounded approach to implementation.

The team at Nextiva is committed to providing you with the appropriate technology and guiding you toward delivering exceptional customer experiences.

We look forward to embarking on this journey with you and are excited about the opportunities that lie ahead. By leveraging the insights from this book and the capabilities of the Nextiva UCXM platform, we are confident that you can achieve remarkable success and deliver outstanding customer satisfaction. Should you wish to discuss strategies for advancing your company despite challenges, please do not hesitate to contact me at tomas.gorny@nextiva.com.

Sincerely,
Tomas Gorny

Introduction

THIS BOOK IS meant to be a guide for those interested in enhancing the customer experience. It is particularly useful for solutions engineers, customer service professionals, and business owners. Here, we offer insights on using automation, contact centers, and customer experience (CX) technology across different industries. By exploring these ideas, readers will better understand how to improve customer interactions, including sales, service, and basic customer feedback.

Each chapter offers practical, actionable ideas, with illustrative examples and details on proposed solutions and their benefits. Use this as an "idea book," enabling new employees and seasoned professionals to share thoughts, brainstorm new concepts, and address the challenges posed by today's discerning and sophisticated consumers.

As you explore various industries, such as retail, travel, and hospitality, you'll notice a recurring theme regarding the balance between human assistance and automation. While automation can enhance customer journeys, human involvement is sometimes necessary to resolve in-store issues, provide a resolution path, or simply lend an empathic ear. Sadly, even a simple mistake can affect customer loyalty, emphasizing the importance of each and every interaction with a customer. Now, achieving the proper balance between automation and high touch is becoming increasingly important.

The Careful Balance

Here are a few insights from industry leaders and authors to illustrate the complexity of this balance we care so much about. Stewart Butterfield, CEO and co-founder of Slack, astutely observed, "There's a lot of automation that can happen that isn't a replacement of humans, but of mind-numbing behavior." This highlights the potential of automation to handle tedious tasks, freeing humans to engage in more meaningful and creatively fulfilling work.

Now consider what Nicholas Carr outlines in his piece, "The Glass Cage," regarding the balance required when implementing automation technologies. He cautions, "Automation has allowed us to become more efficient, accurate, and productive, but it also challenges us to critically examine the consequences of handing over control to machines." Carr's perspective invites organizations to consider the broader implications of automation, ensuring it enhances human capabilities without diminishing critical thinking and decision-making skills.

Bill Gates's insights are equally relevant here. He emphasized, "Automation applied to an inefficient operation will magnify the inefficiency. Automation applied to an efficient operation will magnify the efficiency." This underscores the importance of scrutinizing processes before applying automation; doing so correctly can significantly enhance effectiveness.

Given these perspectives, it becomes evident that the customer experience is crucial when evaluating an automation strategy. Identifying opportunities where technology can complement human efforts ensures a harmonious balance that elevates the overall customer experience. Striving for this equilibrium enables automation to enhance quality interaction and service rather than detract from it.

Approach To The Subject Matter

Each chapter of this book is structured to introduce automation and live assistance in various business sectors. Chapters are divided into three main parts:

- Top automation targets
- Current business challenges
- Industry-specific use cases

Top Automation Targets

The "top automation targets" section in each chapter identifies the most common areas where automation and AI can be beneficial. These targets are based on insights and observations from industry experts. Throughout the research, significant effort was made to identify the main automation targets for each industry. Some repetition may occur across chapters, which indicates that certain automation opportunities are relevant to multiple sectors.

Current Business Challenges

In each chapter, this "business challenges" section covers the key aspects of what keeps your fellow practitioners up at night. This section aims to resonate with you by addressing issues relevant to your industry.

To elaborate, the challenges discussed include operational inefficiencies, customer service hurdles, and technological limitations that hinder growth. By identifying and understanding these obstacles, businesses can develop targeted strategies to overcome them. This section also emphasizes the importance of a proactive approach to problem-solving.

In summary, each chapter's focus on current business challenges is a foundation for understanding the broader context in which automation can be applied. By addressing these challenges head-on, businesses can create a more solid groundwork for implementing effective and sustainable automation strategies.

Industry-Specific Use Cases

These sections outline current and potential automation and high-touch use cases. These examples aim to inform and guide you on effectively integrating automation into your operations. Here, you'll encounter use cases that might already be part of your toolbox, some that you've contemplated, and perhaps a few that stand out as something you'd like to explore further.

Before diving headfirst into adopting these new ideas, we emphasize the importance of thoughtful reflection and comprehensive discovery. In this light, we draw attention to a companion document, "Mastering the Customer Experience," also brought to you by Nextiva Press. This publication is a practical guide, providing step-by-step advice on undertaking a thorough discovery process to pinpoint the most apt use cases for your enterprise. "Mastering the Customer Experience" lays down a systematic approach to navigating your internal discovery journey. You'll hear more about it in the "final thoughts" section at the end of the book.

Should You Read The Whole Book?

When approaching this publication, you might wonder whether to read it entirely or focus on specific chapters. Each section offers practical insights for various industries. Even if some chapters seem less relevant, reading the entire publication can be beneficial.

Each chapter focuses on sector-specific topics, but the core ideas have broader relevance. For example, a case study on automating retail processes could also apply to a healthcare scenario. Exploring various chapters provides a comprehensive view of automation's potential across different contexts, potentially inspiring new approaches. Getting familiar with the challenges and wins in different sectors can help you see coming trends and shifts that could affect your work. This kind of cross-industry insight is valuable for strategic planning and staying ahead of the curve.

Lastly, discussing what you've learned with colleagues or partners can foster valuable conversations and brainstorming sessions. Working through the book's concepts together can help you develop a solid plan for implementing automation in your business. This shared understanding ensures that the solutions you develop are well-rounded and effective.

Please share this idea book with your colleagues and partners. Collaboration will keep your business competitive and responsive to customer needs. Happy reading!

Business Services

IN COMPETITIVE FIELDS like accounting, legal services, and real estate, improving CX is crucial for retaining clients and increasing revenue. Each industry has specific challenges that affect client interactions, from initial contact to service delivery and follow-up. By using automation and advanced technologies, businesses can streamline operations and improve client engagement, leading to more personalized and timely services.

Integrating automation also allows professionals to focus on tasks that require their expertise. For instance, in accounting, automating routine tasks such as journal entries and invoice processing helps ensure clients receive accurate financial insights on time. In legal services, automated document management and communication can give lawyers more time for complex cases. In real estate, automation can enhance lead management and property maintenance, creating a smoother client experience. Addressing these operational challenges can significantly improve the customer experience, leading to better client retention and increased revenue.

Key Automation Opportunities For Business Services

In today's dynamic business landscape, automation is essential for improving efficiency in industries like accounting, legal, and real estate services. These automation initiatives also enhance CX and can be effectively integrated with contact center systems to optimize the collaboration between human staff and technology.

In accounting, automation streamlines processes, directly benefiting clients. For example, automating journal entries reduces repetitive tasks, minimizes errors, and saves time, ensuring clients receive precise financial statements promptly. AI-driven invoice processing automates invoice extraction, validation, and payment, boosting productivity and ensuring timely financial reports that offer real-time insights for better decision-making. Automated compliance management helps businesses meet regulatory standards, reduce non-compliance risk, and provide clients peace of mind.

Integrating automation tools with contact center systems enables real-time updates and prompt responses to client inquiries. By combining automated processes with human expertise, companies can ensure complex issues are tackled by skilled professionals while routine tasks are efficiently handled by machines, enhancing service quality.

The legal sector also reaps significant benefits from automation, leading to a better client experience through faster and more precise services. AI-powered document management systems streamline legal documents' creation, review, and management, significantly reducing workloads. Automating routine client communications, like follow-up emails and appointment scheduling, allows legal professionals to concentrate on more intricate tasks and respond promptly. Workflow automation further enhances efficiency in billing, scheduling, and case management.

Additionally, AI tools speed up legal research by quickly analyzing relevant case law and statutes, equipping lawyers with the insights to serve their clients effectively.

By integrating automation with contact center infrastructure, legal firms improve CX by providing timely and accurate client information. AI can manage initial inquiries while routing more complex concerns to human agents, balancing technology and personal interaction.

In real estate, automation is crucial for managing various operational tasks, positively affecting client satisfaction. Lead management systems that utilize CRM software automate lead generation, tracking, and follow-ups, ensuring no potential client is missed. Property management benefits from automated solutions for maintenance requests, tenant screening, and rent collection, enabling property managers to operate efficiently. Robotic process automation (RPA) can streamline lease contract processing and tax billing tasks. In contrast, marketing automation aids real estate businesses in managing property listings, email campaigns, and social media outreach.

These automation tools provide quicker responses and more personalized services for real estate clients. Integrating automation with contact center operations ensures that client inquiries are addressed swiftly, with complex issues elevated to human agents for resolution, leading to a seamless service experience.

Overall, these automation strategies are designed to fit each industry's unique needs and workflows, resulting in improved efficiency, increased accuracy, and heightened client satisfaction. Automation in accounting enhances compliance and precision in financial management while accelerating document handling and research in legal services. In real estate, it optimizes client engagement and operational tasks, ensuring responsive and effective service. By aligning advanced automation tools with contact center infrastructure, businesses across these sectors can streamline operations, reduce manual workload, and deliver exceptional service to clients, achieving an effective equilibrium between automation and human interaction.

Top Challenges In Accounting, Legal, And Real Estate Services

Automation is crucial in improving accounting, legal, and real estate services efficiency. While it enhances customer experience (CX) and can work well with contact center systems, each sector faces unique challenges in CX.

Managing Client Expectations And Communication

A significant challenge in accounting is managing client expectations and communication, particularly during busy times like tax season. Clients look for timely updates on their financial status and tax returns. Automating routine updates can help ensure clients receive real-time notifications. However, it is important to balance these automated communications with personalized interactions. Clients often prefer the reassurance of human communication, especially for complex financial matters. Therefore, creating a smooth transition from automated systems to human agents for more personalized service is essential for maintaining client trust.

Ensuring Timeliness And Precision In Case Management

Legal services must ensure timely and precise management of cases and client communications. Clients expect updates on their cases and accurate handling of legal documents. While automation can streamline document management and routine communications, it's essential to integrate these solutions with contact center operations. This integration allows clients to escalate complex issues quickly to human agents while routine tasks are handled automatically. Balancing efficiency with the nuanced understanding of human interaction is crucial for maintaining client satisfaction in legal services.

Managing A High Volume Of Client Inquiries

Real estate services often face the challenge of handling a high volume of client inquiries, especially during peak seasons. Prospective clients need prompt responses and personalized service when searching for properties. Automation can help manage inquiries through CRM systems and automated follow-ups, but it's important to ensure human touchpoints are available. Automated systems should handle initial inquiries and seamlessly direct more detailed questions to human agents, ensuring clients feel valued throughout their interactions.

Client Engagement And Retention Across All Sectors

Maintaining client engagement and retention is a common challenge across accounting, legal, and real estate services. Clients expect consistent, quality service and personalized attention. Automation can enhance engagement by providing timely updates and personalized communications. However, it's important to integrate automated processes with contact center systems so clients can easily reach human support when needed. Balancing efficient automated communications with accessible human interaction is key to fostering long-term client relationships.

Data Security And Privacy Concerns

Ensuring data security and privacy is another significant challenge in these industries. Clients trust service providers with sensitive financial, legal, and personal information. Automated systems must prioritize protecting this data, and integration with contact centers must be secure to prevent breaches. Compliance with industry regulations and establishing client confidence in data security are critical. Implementing secure automated solutions alongside human oversight can help address these concerns while improving overall CX.

These challenges underscore the need for a balanced approach that utilizes both automation and human expertise to enhance customer experience across accounting, legal, and real estate services. By effectively integrating automation tools with contact center infrastructure, businesses can streamline operations, reduce manual workloads, and provide strong service to their clients.

Business Services Use Case Examples

In today's business service industries, integrating automation and artificial intelligence with live assistance in contact centers is becoming increasingly vital for enhancing customer experiences. Various strategies can be employed to streamline processes and improve client engagement across different sectors.

For example, companies can implement screening chatbots on their websites to effectively identify high-potential cases. This approach not only simplifies the client intake process but also enables the allocation of scheduling links exclusively to these promising cases, benefiting both clients and the firm.

Moreover, utilizing omnichannel automation for case status updates is an innovative way to enhance transparency. By disseminating current case statuses through multiple platforms—such as websites, phone systems, and text messaging services—firms can significantly reduce the need for manual intervention, thereby improving operational efficiency.

In the realm of legal class action outreach, omnichannel automation can play a crucial role in raising awareness among potential clients. By sending automated texts, voicemails, and emails, firms can effectively document opt-in and opt-out decisions, gather necessary inputs, and issue timely reminders, all of which contribute to a more organized and effective communication strategy.

Real estate firms can also benefit from these technologies. Implementing a web chatbot to manage the influx of prospective client inquiries ensures that potential clients are matched with agents who are knowledgeable about their specific areas and price points, ultimately enhancing both the quality and quantity of leads generated.

In property maintenance, automated systems that leverage interactive voice response (IVR), text messaging, or web chatbots can facilitate the submission of maintenance requests. This innovation allows renters to send in their requests, often accompanied by images. Supervisors can then review these submissions and send scheduling links to the most suitable technicians, ensuring prompt and effective resolutions.

For accounting firms, especially during tax season, clients often experience heightened anxiety regarding their tax returns and refunds. By integrating contact center software with the firm's system of record and sending automated status alerts via email, SMS, and voicemail, firms can keep clients informed. This not only alleviates client concerns but also reduces the workload on accountants, thereby safeguarding the firm's reputation and enhancing client satisfaction.

In the following use case examples, we will explore these applications of automation and AI in greater detail, examining their implementation and impact on customer experience across various business services.

Legal Intake Screening Via Chatbot

Legal firms often face a significant problem with the high volume of prospective case inquiries that do not align with their areas of expertise. This situation leads to wasted time during intake interactions, as staff spend valuable resources addressing cases that are ultimately not a good fit. Consequently, the overwhelming number of intake activities places undue stress on the firm's personnel.

One effective solution to this problem is utilizing a screening chatbot on the firm's website. This chatbot serves as the primary pathway for intake screening, efficiently identifying high-potential cases. Only these high-potential cases are provided with a scheduling link within the chatbot, streamlining the process for clients and the firm.

This approach offers numerous benefits. Firstly, the chatbot effectively screens out zero-potential cases, allowing the firm to avoid wasting time and resources on inquiries that don't match its expertise. This ensures that staff time is spent more efficiently on relevant cases and has a higher likelihood of success.

Secondly, by providing scheduling links only to high-potential cases, the chatbot eliminates the time-consuming process of manually scheduling intake meetings. This streamlined approach ensures that calendars are filled with high-potential cases, maximizing productivity and allowing the firm to handle more cases within the same timeframe.

Thirdly, with the chatbot handling initial screenings and scheduling, staff can focus on more meaningful interactions, reducing overall stress and workload. This enables the firm to concentrate on the most promising opportunities, enhancing its ability to provide high-quality service to clients who truly need their expertise.

Additionally, the use of a chatbot creates a more organized and systematic intake process, which can lead to better data management and tracking. The automated system can log all interactions and maintain a record of inquiries and screenings, making it easier to review

Figure 1: Legal intake screening via chatbot

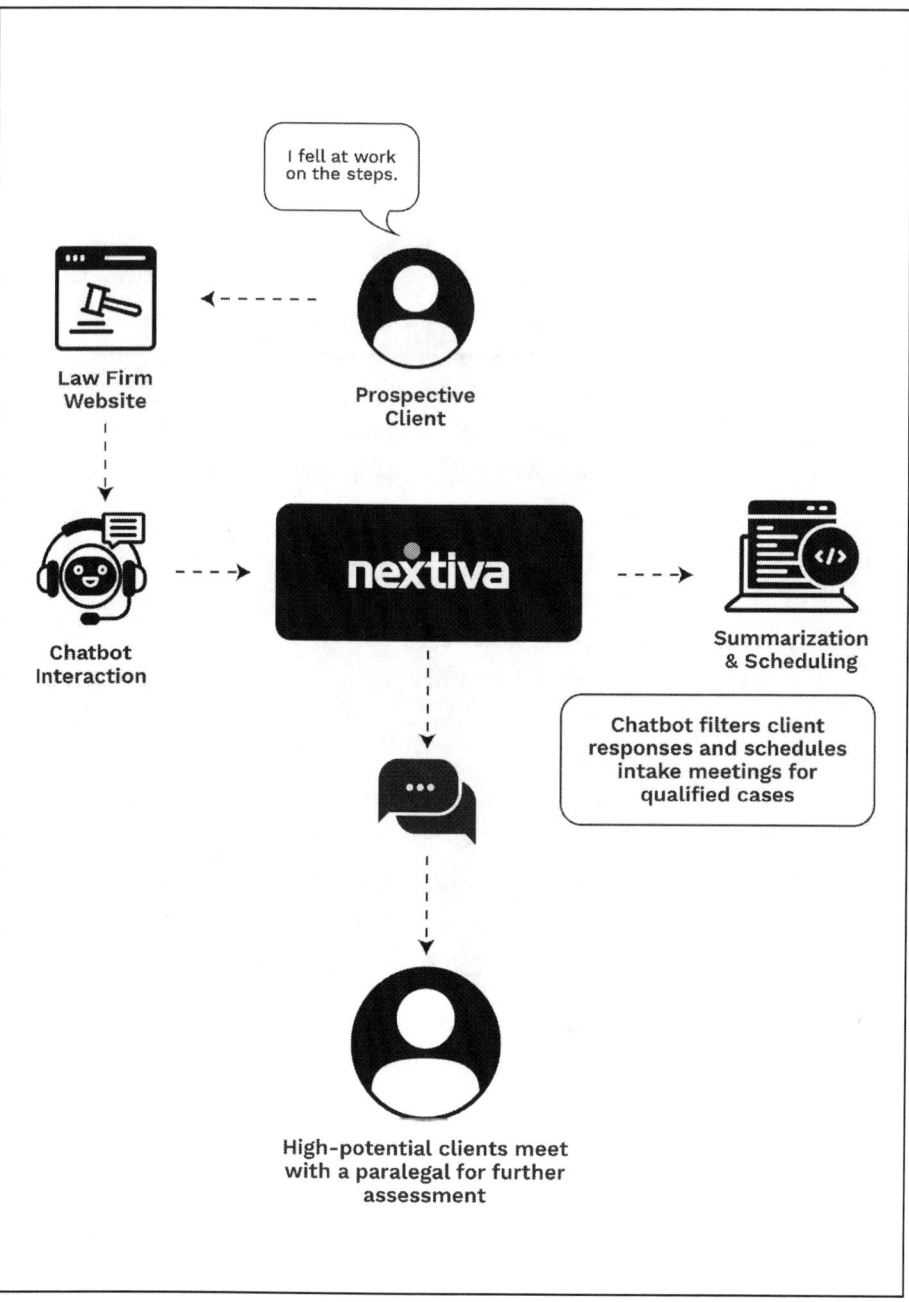

Table 1: Benefits of legal intake screening via chatbot

Intake screening capability	Chief benefits
Screening chatbot on the firm website to handle intake interactions	Effectively screens out zero-potential cases, ensuring staff time is spent on relevant inquiries
Efficient scheduling	By providing scheduling links only to high-potential cases, the chatbot removes the time-consuming process of manually scheduling intake meetings; this streamlined approach ensures that calendars are filled with high-potential cases, maximizing productivity
Automate initial screenings	Allows staff to focus on more meaningful interactions, reducing overall stress and workload
Organized and systematic intake process	Leads to better data management and tracking, making it easier to review and analyze intake activities
24/7 operation	Provides potential clients with immediate responses and assistance outside of regular business hours, improving client experience and increasing the firm's accessibility
Reduced stress via self-service aid	With the chatbot handling initial screenings and scheduling, staff can focus on more meaningful interactions, reducing the overall stress and workload on personnel
Improved focus	The firm can concentrate on the most promising opportunities, enhancing their ability to provide high-quality service to clients who truly need their expertise

and analyze intake activities. This can help the firm identify trends, improve processes, and make data-driven decisions.

Furthermore, a chatbot can operate 24/7, providing potential clients with immediate responses and assistance outside of regular business hours. This not only improves the client experience by offering timely support but also increases the firm's accessibility, potentially attracting more high-potential cases.

By implementing this screening chatbot, legal firms can achieve a more efficient and focused intake process, leading to better resource allocation and improved client satisfaction. The benefits of this approach are multifaceted, encompassing time savings, increased productivity, reduced stress, improved data management, and enhanced client service.

Case Status Via Omnichannel Automation

Legal firms often face the challenge of managing a high volume of client requests for status updates, which consumes significant amounts of valuable staff time. This distraction prevents staff from focusing on complex tasks that require their expertise and can overwhelm them with the sheer volume of inquiries.

An effective solution to this issue involves implementing omnichannel automation for case status updates. This automation can be integrated across various platforms, such as the firm's website, phone systems, and text messaging services. By linking these channels with the firm's backend systems, the current case status can be automatically relayed to clients without requiring manual intervention from staff.

The benefits of this approach are substantial. First, it eliminates wasted time on mundane tasks, freeing up staff to concentrate on more complex and important work. Second, it ensures that staff time is used efficiently and reserved for tasks that truly need their expertise. Additionally, by automating status updates, the firm can eliminate communication errors and create a reliable paper trail, which enhances accuracy and accountability.

Moreover, providing clients with real-time status updates through their preferred communication channels improves client satisfaction and trust. Clients appreciate timely information and transparency,

Figure 2: Case status via omnichannel automation

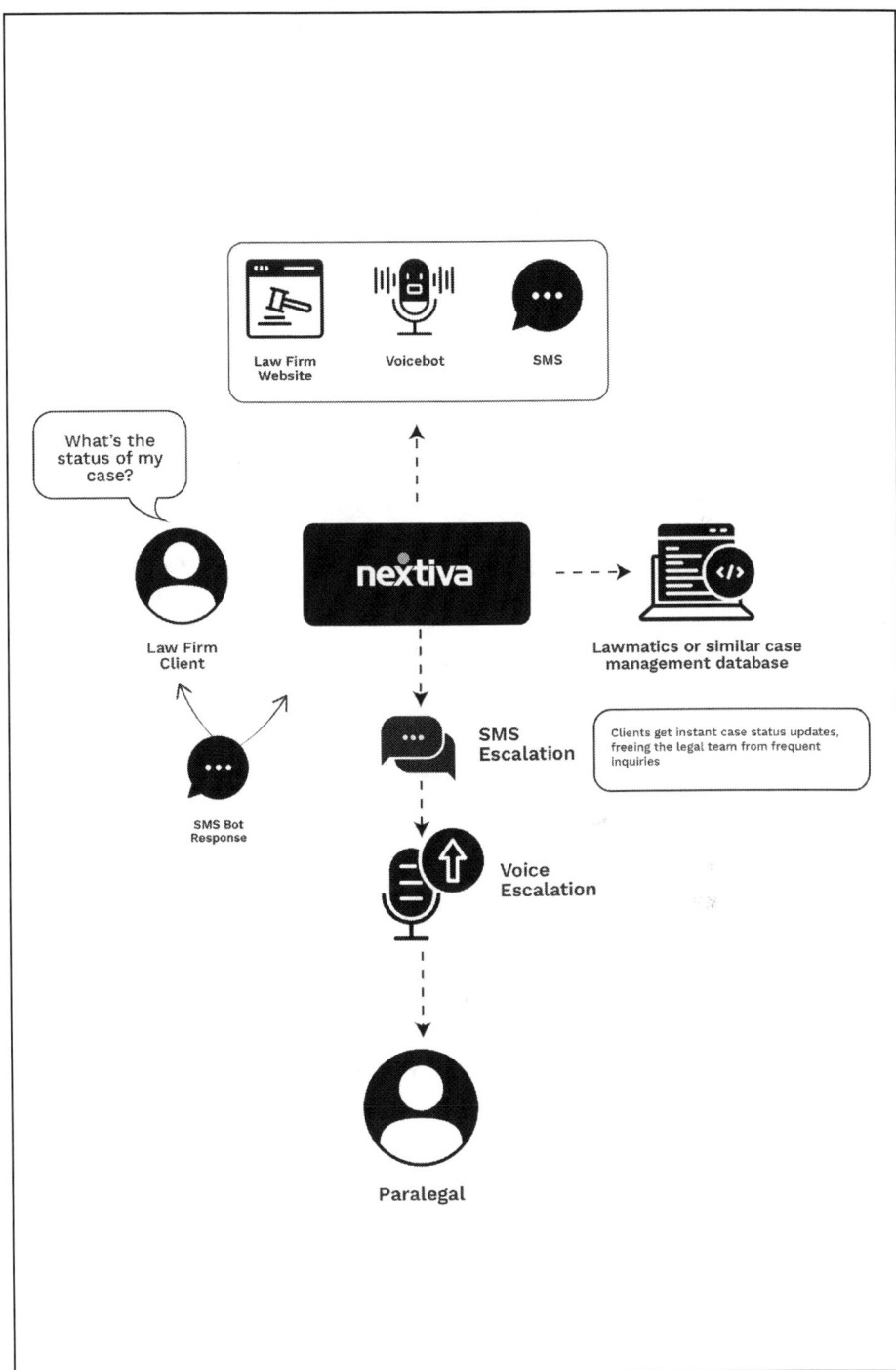

leading to stronger client relationships and higher retention rates. Automation also allows for personalized updates, catering to each client's specific needs and preferences, enhancing the overall client experience.

By implementing omnichannel automated updates, legal firms can significantly improve their operational efficiency, reduce stress on their staff, and ensure timely and accurate information delivery to their clients. This approach optimizes resource utilization and fosters a more client-centric service model, driving better outcomes for both the firm and its clients.

Table 2: Benefits of case status via omnichannel automation

Omnichannel automation capability	Chief benefits
Omnichannel automation to handle case status updates	Elimination of time wasted on mundane tasks
Automated scheduling links	Efficient use of staff time—links only to high-potential cases through the chatbot, ensuring calendars are filled with meaningful tasks
Automate initial screening	Reduced stress on staff; allow staff to concentrate on more valuable interactions and reduce their workload
Automate status updates	Elimination of communication errors; ensure accuracy and create a reliable paper trail for better accountability
Updates on preferred channels	Improved client satisfaction, enhancing transparency and trust
Tailored updates	Personalized client experience based on each client's specific needs and preferences
Timely information delivery	Stronger client relationships and higher retention rates; foster better client relationships

Class Action Outreach Via Omnichannel Automation

Legal firms often face the challenge of raising awareness among a large group of class members in a class action lawsuit. This task is complicated by the numerous requirements that class members must meet, making it difficult to gather input from a large group. Also, law firms struggle to track who has submitted what, where, and when, leading to inefficiencies and potential errors.

One effective solution to this problem is to use omnichannel automation for communication. By sending automated texts, voicemails, and emails, the firm can efficiently raise awareness and document opt-in/out decisions. For those who opt-in, the firm can gather the required input and documentation and send reminders via voice, text, and email, ensuring that all necessary information is collected promptly.

The benefits of this approach are numerous. Firstly, it eliminates wasted time and money on outbound awareness efforts, allowing staff to focus on more critical tasks. Secondly, it creates a single source of truth to document outreach efforts and track input and documentation, reducing the risk of errors and ensuring that all data is easily accessible.

Thirdly, class members can participate through their preferred communication channels, whether text, voicemail, or email, making engaging and providing the necessary information easier.

Moreover, this approach improves overall efficiency by automating repetitive tasks and reducing the staff's manual workload. It also enhances data accuracy and compliance by ensuring all communications and responses are properly logged and tracked. The system helps keep class members informed and engaged throughout the process by providing timely reminders and updates, leading to higher response rates and more successful outcomes. Lastly, this method fosters a better client experience by offering convenience and flexibility, which can enhance the firm's reputation and client satisfaction.

In summary, implementing omnichannel automation for class action outreach enables legal firms to efficiently manage large volumes of communications, streamline the intake process, and ensure that all necessary documentation is collected accurately and promptly. This

Figure 3: Class action outreach via omnichannel automation

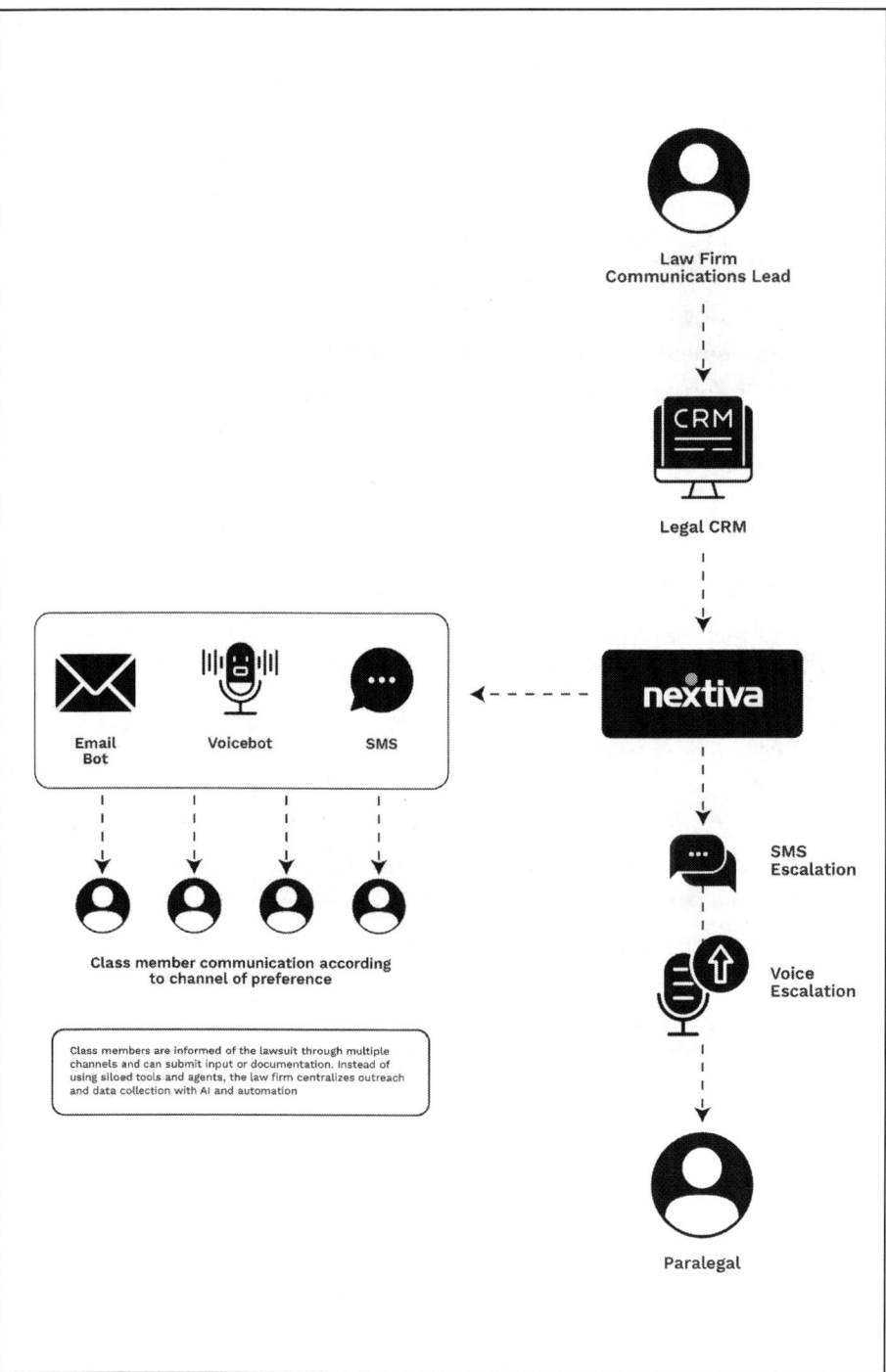

Table 3: Benefits of automated class action outreach

Automated class action outreach capability	Chief benefits
Use omnichannel automation for communication by sending automated texts, voicemails, and emails	Eliminates time and money wasted on outbound awareness efforts
Document opt-in/out decisions through automated communications	Creates a single source of truth to document outreach efforts and track input and documentation
Gather required input and documentation and send reminders via voice, text, and email for those who opt-in	Ensures that all necessary information is collected promptly
Allow class members to participate through their preferred communication channel	It makes it easier for class members to engage and provide the necessary information
Automate repetitive tasks to reduce the manual workload on staff	Improves overall efficiency and allows staff to focus on critical tasks
Provide timely reminders and updates	Keeps class members informed and engaged, leading to higher response rates
Log and track all communications and responses	Enhances data accuracy and compliance

approach saves time and resources and enhances the effectiveness and success of class action lawsuits.

Agent Search Via Chatbot

Real estate firms often face significant challenges in managing a high volume of prospective client inquiries. These clients are motivated to buy or sell property and seek agents familiar with their area and price point. However, finding an agent who offers the required services and has expertise in a specific neighborhood and price range can be difficult.

Real estate brokers, motivated to attract new clients, aim to differentiate themselves by offering a seamless and detailed agent search process. Unfortunately, brokerage admins often struggle to refer leads to the best-fit agents, leading to lost leads and dissatisfaction among agents who do not receive enough or suitable leads.

Real estate agents are motivated to get new clients and meet their quotas, and they seek to provide clients with an excellent buying or selling experience. However, they often waste time on leads that aren't a good fit and do not receive enough leads from their brokerages.

The solution to these challenges is to use a web chatbot to increase the quantity and quality of leads. The chatbot makes the search process efficient and effective, providing clients with an easy way to find agents based on their specific criteria.

The benefits of this approach are numerous. Prospective clients can quickly find an agent that fits their needs, ensuring they get the proper support for buying or selling property. Brokerages can

Table 4: Benefits of agent search via chatbot

Agent search via chatbot capability	Chief benefits
Use a web chatbot to increase the quantity of leads by making the search process efficient and effective	Prospective clients can quickly find an agent that fits their needs
Use a web chatbot to increase the quality of leads	Brokerages can increase revenue without additional headcount
Standardized means to collect essential data	Reduces errors in intake typing (from the professional) as the potential client is more likely to get their own data correct
Automate initial screenings and scheduling with the chatbot	Agents hit their quotas by serving clients they prefer to work with

Figure 4: Agent search via chatbot

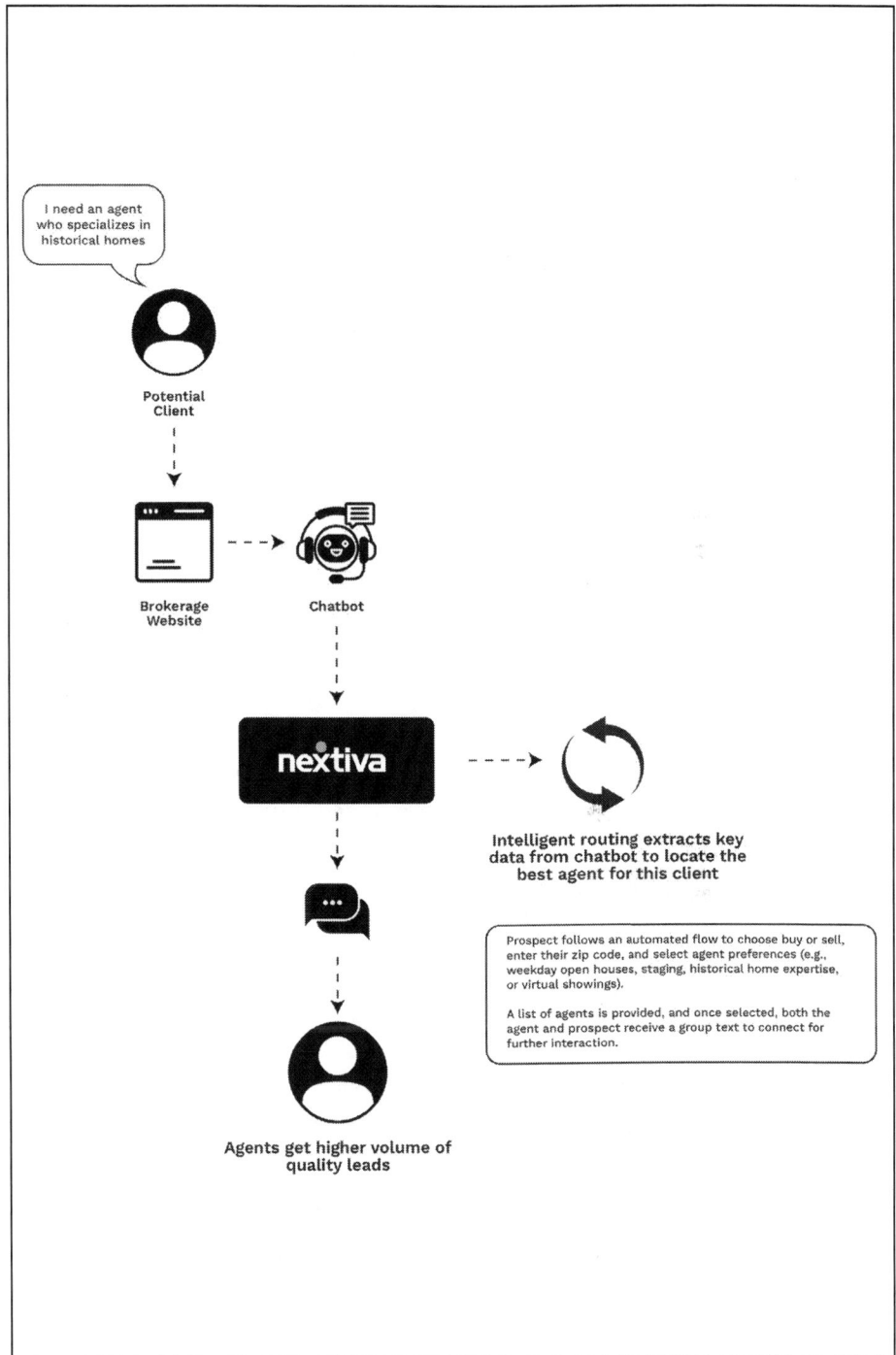

increase revenue without needing additional headcount, and they can gather valuable data on what prospects are looking for in an agent. This data can help brokerages recruit agents who meet these criteria. Additionally, agents can hit their quotas by serving clients they prefer to work with, improving their job satisfaction and performance.

By implementing this screening chatbot, real estate firms can achieve a more efficient and focused lead management process, leading to better resource allocation and improved client satisfaction. The benefits of this approach include saving time and resources, increasing productivity, reducing stress, improving data management, and enhancing client service.

Automated Maintenance Requests

Renters often face issues like a dripping faucet and want a quick resolution from the apartment maintenance team. Their primary task is to schedule a maintenance technician. Still, they encounter challenges such as slow responses from property management and no easy way to send photos or videos of the issue.

The motivation for the property management maintenance supervisor is to meet company service level agreements (SLA) for service requests by providing efficient service and reducing complaints. However, with many apartments to manage, numerous requests and manual processes lead to a backlog. Additionally, renters often forget about appointments because no reminders are sent.

Field maintenance technicians are motivated to provide quality service and complete repairs in one trip. Their top tasks include being on time for appointments, communicating delays, assessing and completing repairs, and documenting repairs with renter signoff. However, they often don't have the necessary supplies because the information the renter supplies is inadequate, slowing down the process.

Implementing an automated system using interactive voice response (IVR), text, or a web chatbot can address these challenges. Renters can click through prompts to submit requests, including images. Supervisors review requests and send renters scheduling links connected to the best-fit technician. The system automatically attaches

Figure 5: Automated maintenance requests

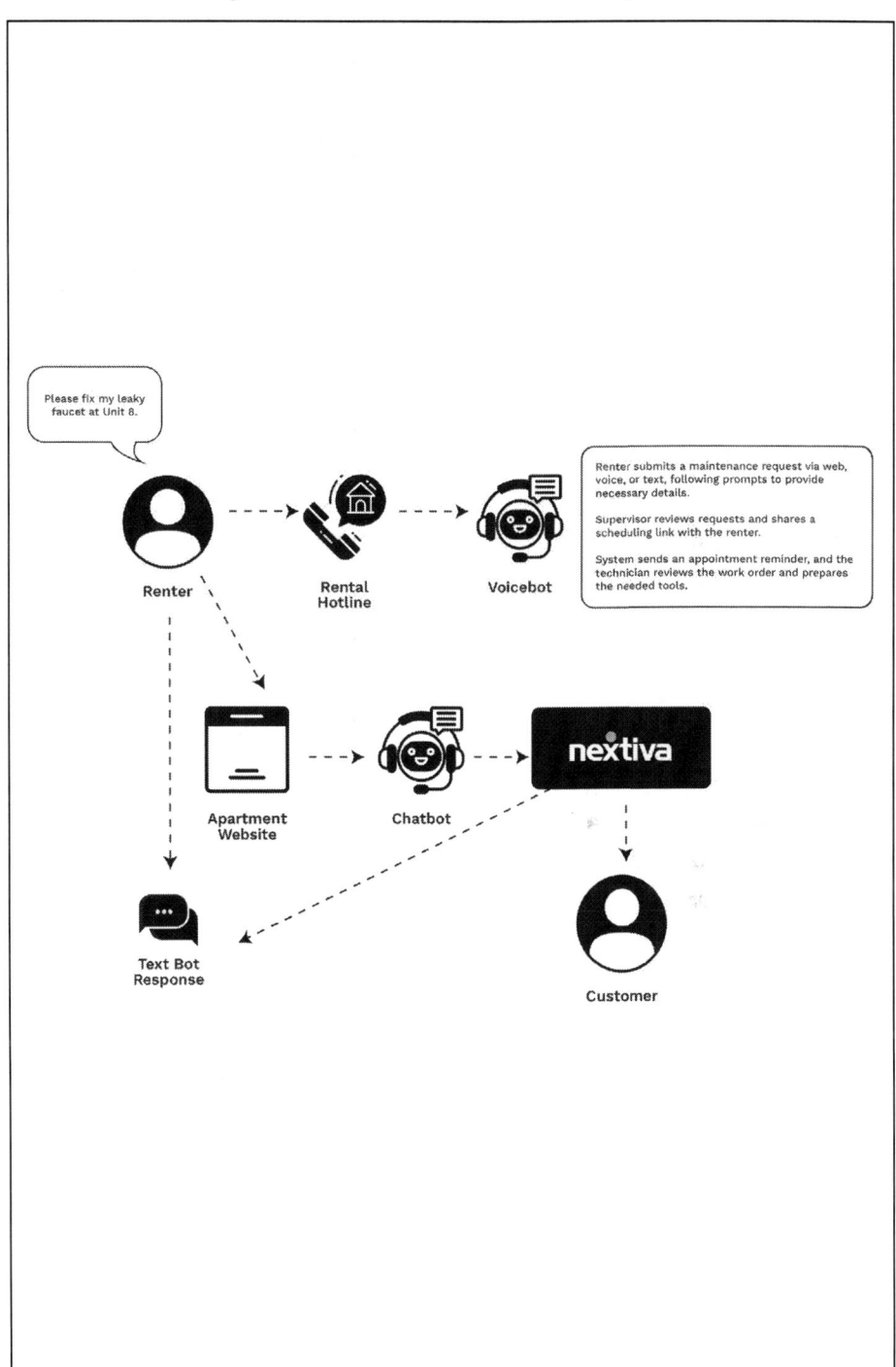

work orders to calendar events, ensuring technicians can prepare the necessary supplies. It also sends appointment reminders to renters.

This approach offers several benefits. Renters get their issues acknowledged and scheduled quickly. Supervisors save time by viewing all requests in one place for quick assessment. Technicians increase one-visit resolutions because the renter remembers the appointment, and the tech has the necessary tools. Additionally, the supervisor has

Table 5: Benefits of automated maintenance requests

Automated maintenance request capability	Chief benefits
Use IVR, text, or web chatbot for renters to submit requests, including images	Renters get their issues acknowledged and scheduled quickly
Supervisor reviews requests and sends scheduling links to renters connected to the best-fit technician	Supervisors save time by viewing all requests in one place for quick assessment
System automatically attaches work orders to calendar events	Technicians increase one-visit resolutions because the renter remembers the appointment, and the tech has the necessary tools
Automatic appointment reminders to renters	Renters remember their appointments, reducing no-shows
Automated paper trail	Memorializing requests, appointments, and work orders ensures accurate reporting to upper management
Reduction of manual tasks	Renters benefit from faster service, improving satisfaction and reducing repeat requests
Technicians' preparation	Maintenance team is better prepared with necessary supplies so repairs can be made quicker at lower first-time fix rates

a paper trail for requests, appointments, and work orders, ensuring accurate reporting to upper management.

Furthermore, automated requests enhance efficiency by reducing manual tasks and ensuring accurate and timely communication. Renters benefit from faster service, which improves satisfaction and reduces repeat requests. Property management can better allocate resources, leading to cost savings and improved service levels. Technicians are better prepared, leading to quicker repairs and higher first-time fix rates. Overall, this system streamlines the maintenance process, making it more effective and efficient for all parties involved.

Omnichannel Status Alerts On Tax Returns

During tax season, accounting clients often experience anxiety about whether their tax returns have been submitted and when they will receive their refunds. They find it challenging to get ahold of their accountants for status updates, leading to frequent check-in requests. Accountants motivated to provide excellent service without burning out face a heavy workload and struggle to respond to all client status requests or proactively reach out with updates. This high volume of client inquiries can negatively impact the firm's reputation if clients feel neglected.

Firm owners are driven to maintain their reputation as leading tax return service providers by ensuring their accounting staff has adequate time to perform crucial tasks without distractions. They also aim to provide excellent service to all clients. However, the high volume of check-in requests from anxious clients and the resulting burnout from overworked accountants pose significant challenges.

To address these issues, integrating contact center software with the accounting firm's record system can be highly effective. Automated status alerts can be sent to clients via email, SMS, and voicemail drop, informing them about their tax return and refund status.

This solution offers numerous benefits. Clients receive timely tax returns and refund status updates, reducing anxiety and improving their overall experience. Accountants can focus on critical tasks without being overwhelmed by status inquiries, leading to better productivity and job satisfaction. Additionally, providing excellent service

Figure 6: Omnichannel status alerts on tax returns

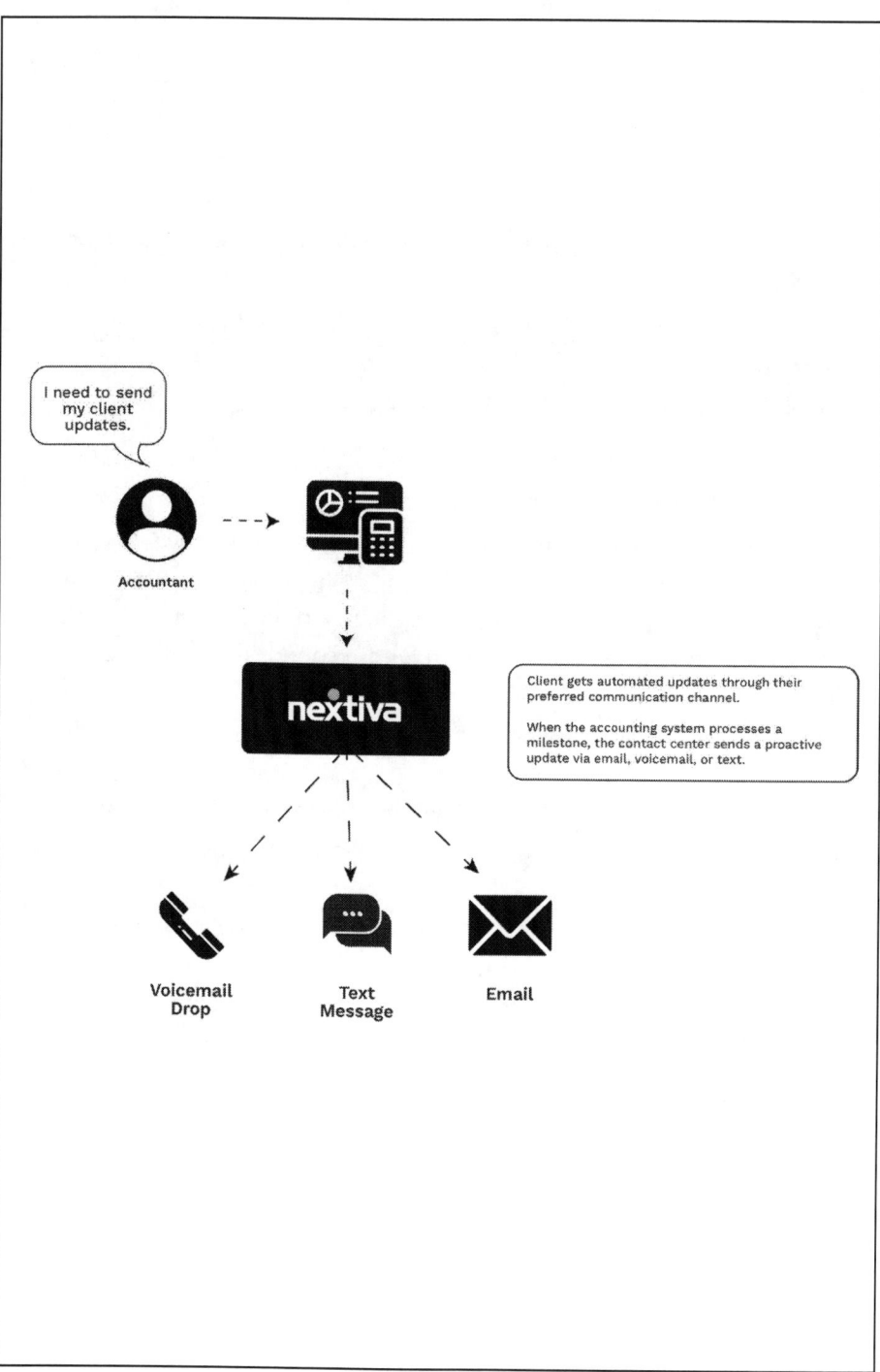

Table 6: Benefits of automated tax return status alerts

Automated tax return status alerts benefits	Chief benefits
Integrate contact center software with the accounting firm's system of record	Clients receive timely updates on their tax return and refund status, reducing anxiety and improving their overall experience
Send automated status alerts to clients via email, SMS, and voicemail drop	Accountants can focus on critical tasks without being overwhelmed by status inquiries, leading to better productivity and job satisfaction
Provide automated and consistent communication	Helps maintain the firm's reputation as a leading tax return service provider
Use of automation to optimize resource allocation	Reduces the need for manual updates and ensures compliance and accurate record-keeping

through automated and consistent communication helps maintain the firm's reputation as a leading tax return service provider.

Further benefits include enhanced operational efficiency and better resource allocation. Automated status alerts ensure clients are consistently informed, reducing the need for manual updates and freeing up accountants to concentrate on more complex tasks. This system also helps maintain accurate communication records for compliance and audit purposes. Overall, it enhances client satisfaction, boosts employee morale, and strengthens the firm's market position.

Free Estimate Chatbot

Accounting clients are motivated to find a reliable and reputable accounting firm that can handle their financial needs at a reasonable price. They seek a free estimate to determine whether the firm can meet their specific requirements, and their main tasks include managing their finances, particularly tax preparation. However, clients often face the challenge of wasting time on firms that may not be able to provide the necessary services at an acceptable price.

Intake professionals are motivated to ensure accountants do not waste time on clients who are unlikely to sign on. They intend to filter out tire kickers and process only the best-fit clients to pass on to the accountants, ensuring potential customers feel confident about choosing the right firm. However, it is time-consuming to speak with a high volume of people to assess if they qualify for a free estimate.

Accounting firm owners are motivated to ensure their staff can focus on best-fit clients. Their intent is to filter out unqualified leads and maintain high productivity levels by reducing the time spent on unqualified prospects. For example, if the firm has no experience in handling 501(c)3 non-profits or limited liability entities, this can be easily caught and filtered out during an automated or semi-automated qualification process. Additionally, they want to ensure clients are satisfied with the services provided. The challenge lies in firms wasting a lot of time on tire kickers, and highly paid staff spend too much time on non-billable hours assessing client fit.

The primary problem is that accounting firms waste considerable time providing free estimates to prospects who are a poor fit. Prospective clients also do not want to waste their time meeting with firms that are too expensive or do not offer the specific services they need.

To address this issue, the solution involves automating the assessment process to qualify for a free estimate. Adding an AI-powered chatbot to the firm's website allows the chatbot to ask intake questions and route qualified prospects to a live agent if they meet the necessary criteria.

The benefits of this solution are significant. The firm can significantly reduce the time wasted on free estimates for clients who are a poor fit. Prospective clients can quickly determine if the firm suits their needs, saving both parties time and effort. Additionally, the firm can maintain high productivity levels by focusing on qualified leads, leading to better client satisfaction and more efficient use of resources.

Moreover, this approach allows firms to allocate their staff more effectively, enhancing overall operational efficiency. Automated assessments ensure that only serious and qualified prospects are passed to

Figure 7: Free estimate chatbot

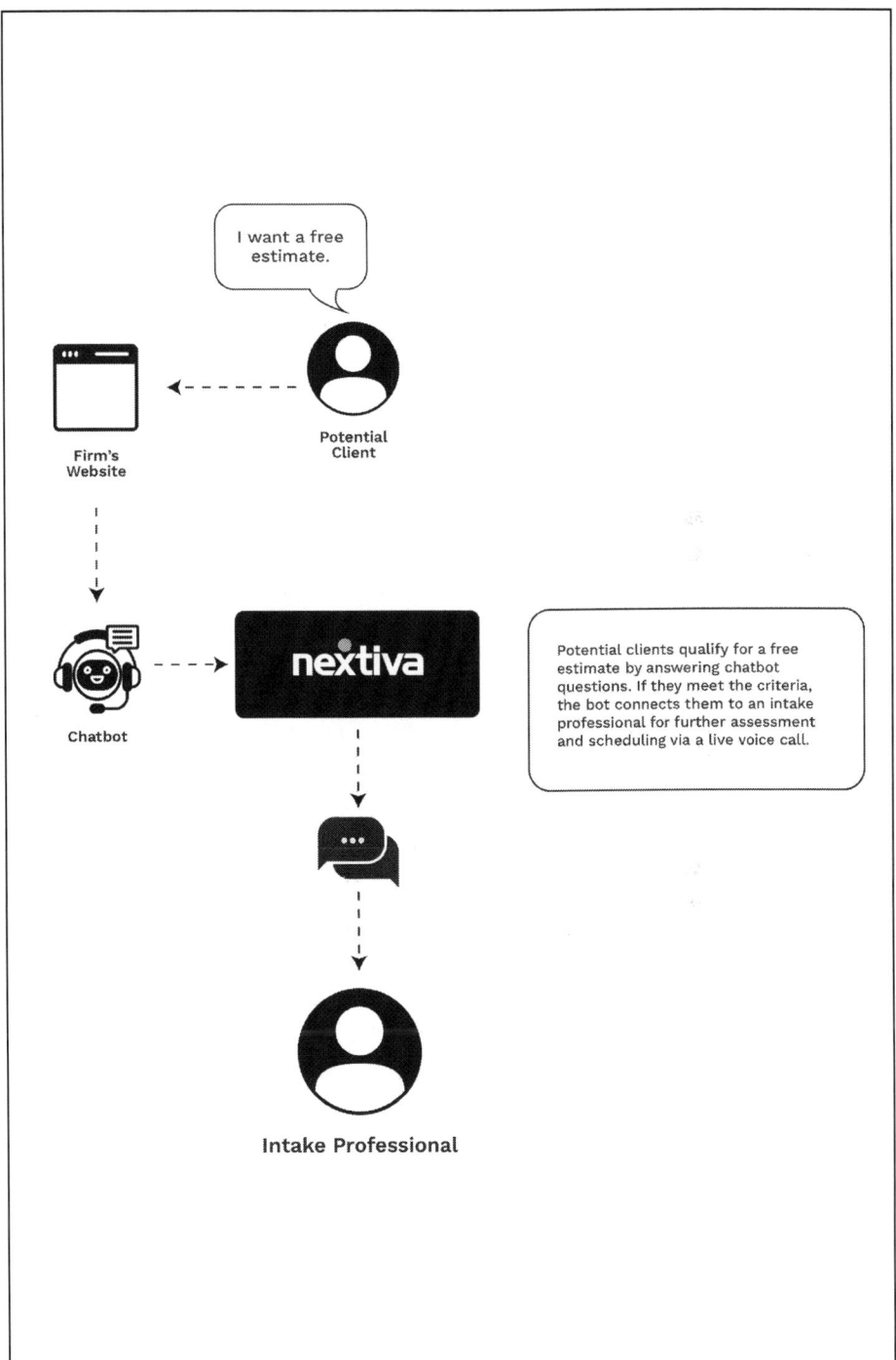

accountants, reducing the burden on highly paid staff. This also helps maintain a high level of service quality, as accountants can dedicate their time to clients who are a good match. The streamlined process enhances the client experience, increasing satisfaction and retention rates.

Table 7: Benefits of free estimate chatbot

Free estimate chatbot benefits	Chief benefits
Automate the assessment to qualify for a free estimate	Firm significantly reduces time wasted on free estimates provided to clients who are a poor fit
AI-powered chatbot for intake questions	Route to a live agent if qualifications are met; prospective clients can quickly discover if this firm is right for them
Automated assessments to filter serious and qualified prospects	Ensures staff can focus on qualified leads, maintaining high productivity and client satisfaction
Use of AI to streamline the intake process	Enhances overall operational efficiency and reduces the burden on highly paid staff; offer means that clients can determine if they fit with the firm; improves client experience, leading to higher satisfaction and retention rates

Financial Services

IN THE FINANCIAL services industry, combining contact center technology with live assistance and AI can improve client service. These technologies allow financial institutions to deliver personalized customer interactions. By using automation and CX technologies, banks can automate customer touchpoints and provide recommendations based on individual financial history and needs, enhancing the overall client experience.

Top Automation Targets In Financial Services

In the financial services industry, AI and automation are being integrated into customer experience management and contact centers, changing how organizations operate and serve their clients. Key areas of implementation include AI-powered chatbots for automating customer inquiries, which enhance response times and customer satisfaction, and robotic process automation (RPA) for handling repetitive tasks like data entry and transaction processing, thus reducing errors and improving efficiency.

Knowledge management systems facilitate the handling, storage, and retrieval of documents, ensuring compliance with regulatory requirements, while omnichannel platforms consolidate various communication channels to provide a unified customer experience. Additionally, AI-enhanced transaction routing directs customer transactions to the most appropriate agents based on their needs and the agent's expertise, thereby improving service quality and efficiency.

These areas highlight some of the leading automation and contact center solutions being applied in the financial services sector. Nonetheless, it is important to recognize that these do not encompass all the explorations within the industry. The sector is continuously evolving, with numerous other innovative technologies and strategies being developed to enhance customer experience and operational efficiency.

Automation Of Customer Inquiries

AI-powered chatbots in financial services can transform customer support by handling a wide range of inquiries, from account information to transactions. This automation improves response times and customer satisfaction, offering instant assistance without the need for human agents.

This boosts customer experience and frees human agents for complex tasks. Chatbots learn from interactions to improve efficiency over time. Additionally, data from these interactions provides insights into customer behavior, enhancing service offerings.

Process Automation

Robotic process automation (RPA) in financial services can automate repetitive tasks such as data entry, transaction processing, and compliance checks. This automation reduces errors and increases efficiency, freeing up human employees to focus on more strategic and complex tasks. For example, RPA can handle large volumes of transaction data quickly and accurately, ensuring that records are updated in real-time without the risk of human error. Compliance checks, critical in the financial industry, can also be automated to ensure they are carried out consistently and accurately. By automating these routine processes, financial institutions can save time, reduce costs, and improve the accuracy and reliability of their operations. Furthermore, the scalability of RPA allows businesses to handle increased workloads during peak times without compromising on performance or quality.

Knowledge Management

Knowledge management systems in financial services automate document handling, storage, and retrieval. They manage large data volumes, making it accessible to employees. Customer service agents can quickly access client history for personalized service.

These systems ensure proper indexing and storage of records, reducing the risk of loss. They also help comply with regulatory requirements by ensuring documents meet standards and are available for audits. Improving document management efficiency and accuracy enhances operational capabilities and customer service in financial institutions.

Omnichannel Transaction Management

Omnichannel platforms integrate various communication channels like phone, email, chat, and social media to provide a seamless customer experience. In the financial services industry, these platforms ensure customers can interact with their financial institutions through their preferred channels, maintaining consistency and continuity across all touchpoints. For example, a customer might start a query via chat and then continue the conversation over the phone without having to repeat themselves.

This integration improves the customer experience and allows businesses to maintain a comprehensive view of each customer's interactions, enabling more personalized and effective service. Additionally, omnichannel platforms can utilize data from all channels to gain insights into customer preferences and behaviors, helping financial institutions tailor their services to meet customer needs more effectively.

AI-Enhanced Transaction Routing

AI-enhanced transaction routing can analyze incoming transactions of all kinds and route them to the most appropriate agent based on the customer's needs and the agent's expertise. This ensures that each transaction is handled by the best-suited agent, improving efficiency and customer satisfaction.

For instance, AI can analyze a transaction request and determine that a particular agent has the most relevant expertise to handle it, routing the request accordingly. This not only speeds up the resolution process but also ensures that customers receive the highest quality of service.

Additionally, by analyzing transaction patterns and agent performance, AI can continually optimize routing decisions, improving efficiency and service quality. Overall, AI-enhanced transaction routing helps financial institutions deliver more accurate, timely, and personalized customer service.

Challenges With Automation In Financial Services

Technical Complexities

The financial services sector is adopting automation to improve operational efficiency and streamline processes. However, integrating these new technologies with existing systems presents significant challenges. Key issues arise from the need to understand the complexities of legacy systems and modern automation tools. Differences in architectures, data formats, and communication protocols complicate integration.

Legacy systems, crucial to the financial services industry, often lack the interfaces for seamless integration and may use outdated protocols. This situation requires careful planning to avoid disruptions to operations while ensuring data integrity and security.

Despite these challenges, effective integration of automation solutions is essential for the industry to remain competitive. Achieving communication between legacy and new systems requires a thorough understanding, extensive testing, and possibly customized solutions. Successfully adopting automation tools can improve operational efficiency, accuracy, and speed.

Organizational Resistance To Change

The financial services industry is transforming due to automation and artificial intelligence (AI) advancements. This shift enhances efficiency but raises job security concerns among employees, as automation may replace some roles traditionally held by humans. Therefore, organizations need effective change management strategies. Transparent communication is crucial to explain the reasons for these technological changes and how they will benefit the organization and its workforce.

Additionally, implementing upskilling programs is vital in reducing resistance to change. These initiatives provide employees with the skills necessary to adapt to new technologies and processes. Investing in workforce skill development helps facilitate a smooth transition, reduces resistance, and supports employee morale while creating new career opportunities within the organization.

According to the McKinsey Global Institute, digitization and automation may require up to 375 million workers worldwide to change occupational categories by 2030, emphasizing the need for retraining efforts, especially for mid-career, older employees. By focusing on these strategies, financial services firms can effectively address the automation challenges and prepare their workforce for the evolving work landscape.

Data Accuracy And Security

In financial services, data accuracy is essential for the effective deployment of automation technologies. Accurate data is vital for automated systems to perform tasks efficiently. Minor inaccuracies can lead to significant errors, such as flawed financial reports or incorrect risk assessments. Organizations must prioritize high data accuracy to ensure automated systems function correctly and minimize costly mistakes.

Data security is equally important due to the sensitive nature of financial information. Financial institutions are prime targets for cyber threats, necessitating strong security measures. Implementing advanced encryption, secure data storage, and strict access controls is critical for protecting against data breaches. Prioritizing data security helps financial institutions safeguard their data, maintain customer trust, and comply with regulations.

Both data accuracy and security are crucial in the financial services sector, supporting effective automation while addressing vulnerabilities from cyber threats. Focusing on these areas enables financial institutions to leverage automation for growth and innovation.

Regulatory Compliance

Financial institutions operate within a regulated framework, facing challenges in integrating automation while adhering to compliance. An article in the ABA Banking Journal discusses AI regulation in the financial sector, noting that while existing regulations continue to evolve, necessitating constant vigilance from financial institutions.

The article highlights a significant executive order from President Biden in October 2023, which set new standards for AI safety and security, including safety testing measures, best practices for AI content authentication, and new cybersecurity programs to address software vulnerabilities.

Additionally, ongoing legislative efforts in the U.S. Congress aim to protect consumer data, focusing on the Algorithmic Accountability Act of 2023. This act regulates generative AI systems, providing protection for individuals in critical areas such as housing, credit, and education, emphasizing the need for ethical AI use while safeguarding consumer rights and privacy.

Integration Issues

In the financial services sector, coordinating automation across various departments presents integration challenges due to the distinct tasks each department handles. The automation requirements of a customer service department differ from those of a risk management department, leading to compatibility issues when unifying automated systems.

Seamless integration is essential for successful automation implementation. Without it, data silos can form, leading to inefficiencies and inaccuracies in decision-making. For instance, a lack of integration between sales and accounting departments can cause discrepancies in financial data, resulting in inaccurate financial reporting. To address these challenges, financial institutions often use middleware solutions or APIs (application programming interfaces) to facilitate communication between different automated systems. These solutions enable data exchange and operations without manual intervention, allowing financial institutions to leverage the benefits of automation and enhance efficiency and accuracy.

Balancing Human And Machine Workflows

In the financial services sector, integrating automated processes with human intervention is essential for operational efficiency. Automation enhances productivity and accuracy across tasks such as data analysis, risk assessment, and transaction processing. However, reliance on automation alone can lead to a lack of human oversight, crucial for areas requiring judgment and complex decision-making. For instance, while an automated system can process standard loan applications, exceptional cases often need a human loan officer's understanding and flexibility.

Effective handoffs between automation and human workers are critical at points where machine capabilities are surpassed by human input. A common scenario occurs in customer service, where an automated system handles initial inquiries, and human agents step in for more complex issues. Ensuring these transitions are smooth is vital for customer satisfaction and process efficiency.

The financial sector must navigate the challenges of balancing automation and human oversight. This involves understanding both technological and human resources while adapting to ongoing technological advancements. When managed well, the collaboration between human skills and automated processes can improve operational efficiency and customer satisfaction.

Maintaining data accuracy and security is also crucial for successfully adopting automation technologies. The sector faces challenges like integrating new automation solutions with legacy systems and overcoming resistance to change within established organizational cultures. As the financial services industry continues to adopt automation and artificial intelligence, addressing these challenges strategically will be essential for optimizing workflows and maintaining a competitive edge.

Financial Services Use Cases

Digital Onboarding

Integrating automation and digital onboarding in the financial services sector improves the gathering and validation of customer information, enhancing operational efficiency and customer experience. AI chatbots and virtual assistants effectively collect crucial data through structured inquiries and can understand natural language. These systems reduce the time needed for data acquisition by asking precise questions and validating responses in real-time, minimizing errors in the data collection process.

A key feature is the seamless transition from automated responses to human interaction for more complex issues. When automated responses are insufficient, live agents can step in, equipped with the customer's previous interaction history, allowing for personalized solutions. This transition enhances customer satisfaction by providing tailored support and improving the overall experience while enabling the AI system to learn and improve continuously.

Developers can refine and improve the system by identifying situations requiring human intervention, leading to more advanced AI capabilities.

Digital onboarding is crucial to modern customer account creation and identity verification. It uses artificial intelligence to streamline interactions, guiding customers through necessary steps and collecting personal data without physical paperwork. Security is maintained through data encryption, secure authentication, and compliance with data protection laws to reduce cyber threats.

In the financial services sector, digital onboarding offers several advantages. Automation and AI lower operational costs, allowing institutions to expand their customer base. A more convenient onboarding experience improves customer satisfaction and loyalty, providing financial institutions a competitive edge in the industry.

An example initial dialog segment between a chatbot and a new banking customer might go like this:

Bot: Hi, thank you for considering Baroda Bank as your financial services partner. I can help you with your account setup and identity verification.

Customer: OK, I'd like to apply for a new loan.

Bot: What type of loan?

Customer: A home improvement loan.

Bot: OK, please enter the age of the main borrower...

Automating onboarding using bots will change how financial institutions grow their customer base. This approach streamlines the onboarding process, enhancing customer satisfaction and loyalty. It provides financial institutions with a competitive edge in the market.

Figure 8: Chatbot onboarding Baroda Bank retail loan example

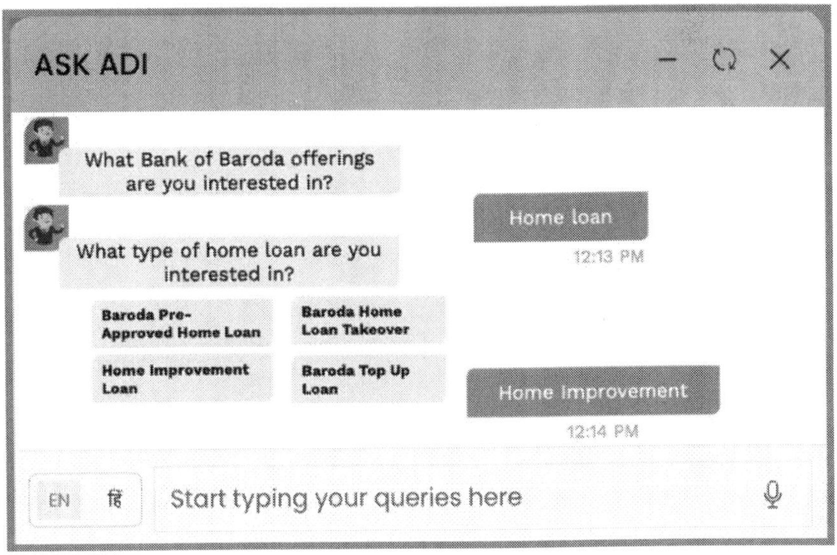

Table 8: Benefits of digital onboarding use cases

Digital onboarding capability	Chief benefits
Automated onboarding with bots	Enables institutions to quickly expand their customer base; more seamless onboarding boosts customer satisfaction and loyalty and establishes a competitive advantage for financial institutions
Consistent data gathering	Significantly reduced time for data acquisition; minimized errors and omissions in data collection; enhanced operational efficiency
Escalation to humans	Empathetic support tailored to specific needs prevents potential frustration and ensures a positive overall experience; refinement and enhancement of the system based on identified needs for human intervention, fostering the development of more advanced AI functionalities
Secure interactions	Integrity of digital onboarding maintained; protection of sensitive information against cyber threats reduces risks and enhances client trust; compliance with data protection laws reduces the chance of lawsuits and fines

Automated systems improve data-gathering efficiency, reducing time and errors and enhancing operational efficiency. This results in a better customer experience and more reliable financial services.

It is important to note that human intervention, when necessary, can be seamlessly integrated into situations requiring empathetic support, refining the system with more advanced AI functionalities. Additionally, ensuring secure interactions and compliance with data protection laws minimizes the risk of cyber threats and legal repercussions, further solidifying the trustworthiness and integrity of the financial institution's digital onboarding processes.

Omnichannel Loan Origination

In the financial services sector, particularly in omnichannel loan origination, various stakeholders play essential roles, each with distinct motivations, intents, tasks, and challenges. Borrowers primarily focus on understanding current mortgage rates and obtaining lower interest rates for their existing loans. Their goal is to achieve pre-approval for refinancing and to close on a new loan by the end of the month.

To accomplish this, they need to quickly and accurately complete pre-approval forms and can seek live assistance when necessary. However, they encounter challenges such as difficulties in credit approval and the limitations of automated systems when transactions involve complex situations or emotions.

Brokers are motivated to originate new loans for bonuses and ensure customer satisfaction. They build trust with mortgagors and promote additional services. Key tasks include verifying automated information and easing the approval process. Challenges involve negotiating higher rates for low credit scores and coordinating escrow and appraisals, especially near month-end deadlines.

Supervisors assist brokers by aiming to facilitate deal closures during the first call, working towards achieving year-end bonuses through effective transaction assistance. Their role involves guiding brokers around potential obstacles and streamlining the approval process. They monitor broker performance in real-time and offer to coach when necessary. However, they face their own challenges, including lengthy handoffs that may lead borrowers to seek competitors and the cumbersome nature of manual credit check processes.

A critical issue is the reliance on voice-only access to brokers, which can result in wait times that may cause potential clients to look for alternatives. Additionally, the absence of after-hours support for customers who are unable to make calls during business hours could hinder service. The first-come, first-serve approach for leads generated through referral sites further emphasizes the need for prompt responses in this environment.

To address these issues, integrating AI chatbots and virtual assistants can be highly effective. These tools can gather accurate customer information through structured queries and natural language

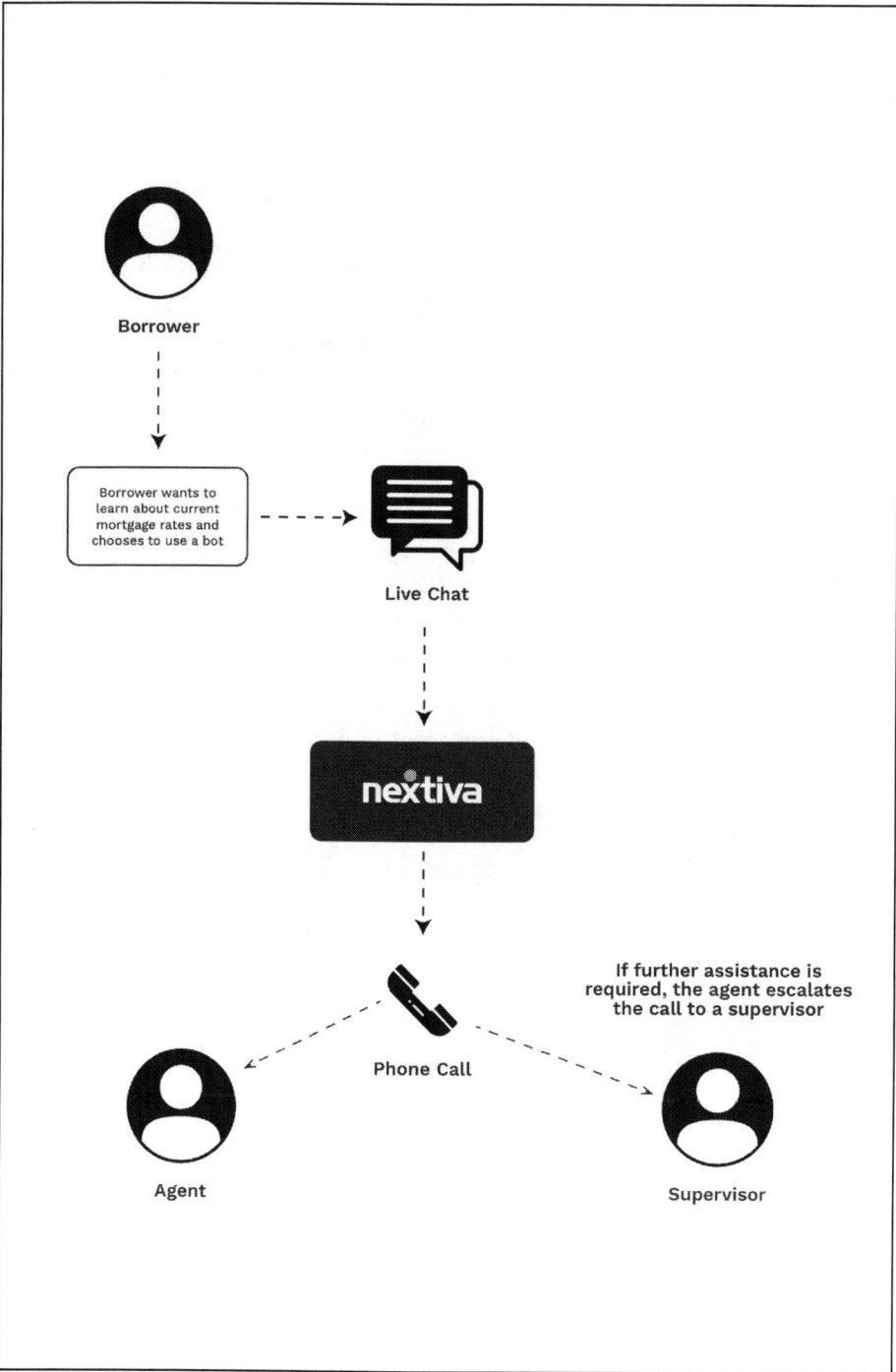
Figure 9: Omnichannel loan origination

processing. They facilitate smooth transitions to live agents with all necessary context, minimizing the need for customers to repeat information. Furthermore, AI technology can lessen the data entry burden for live agents and enable intelligent routing, connecting customers to the most appropriate licensed broker.

The implementation of this solution offers several benefits. Providing customers with multiple channels for communication and access to after-hours support can enhance engagement and improve closing rates. Intelligent routing decreases the likelihood that a customer on hold will abandon their call, reducing the risk of losing potential business to competitors. Utilizing customer-facing digital forms can also mitigate data entry errors by agents.

Overall, this solution streamlines the loan origination process by leveraging an omnichannel platform with workforce management capabilities. Mortgagors can initiate conversations with bots through live chat and seamlessly transition to phone conversations with customer service agents as needed. If additional assistance is required, agents can engage supervisors. This illustrates how an omnichannel approach can enhance communication across various channels, ultimately supporting effective customer service in loan origination.

Integrating AI tools with traditional support systems can enhance the loan origination process and improve customer experience in financial services. AI chatbots and virtual assistants efficiently gather accurate customer information through structured queries and natural language understanding, reducing the need for customers to repeat themselves. This process also minimizes manual data entry for live agents, reducing errors and improving efficiency.

Providing multiple communication channels, including after-hours support, can increase customer engagement and improve loan closing ratios. Proactive notifications keep customers informed about their application status, which helps reduce inquiries and boost satisfaction. By effectively combining AI with human agents, financial institutions can create a more responsive customer service experience, ultimately improving overall efficiency.

Table 9: Benefits of omnichannel loan origination

Omnichannel loan origination capability	Chief benefits
AI chatbots and virtual assistants	Collect accurate customer information through structured data queries and natural language comprehension
Bot dialog transferred to live assistants with full context	Customers do not have to repeat themselves, improving the experience
Data entry is reduced with the use of bots	Lessens the workload on live agents, reducing errors and increasing efficiency
Intelligent routing to the best available licensed broker	Ensures customers are connected to the right agent quickly, reducing the chance of abandonment
Customer choice of channel and after-hours support	Increases customer engagement and closing ratios
Proactive notifications	Keeps customers informed, reducing the number of inquiries and increasing satisfaction

Credit Card Disputes And Fraud Claims

In financial services, managing credit card disputes is essential for maintaining customer trust and loyalty. Clients often need to investigate suspicious credit card activity and determine if their card information has been compromised. To resolve these disputes, they must provide details related to notifications received and past credit card activity. However, many clients struggle with an overload of information and find it challenging to understand the necessary steps in the dispute process.

Support agents aim to assist clients facing issues and handle a high volume of calls. Their priority is to establish trust and reassure clients that their concerns will be addressed promptly. Key tasks include confirming suspicious activity on credit cards and transferring clients

Figure 10: Credit card dispute solution

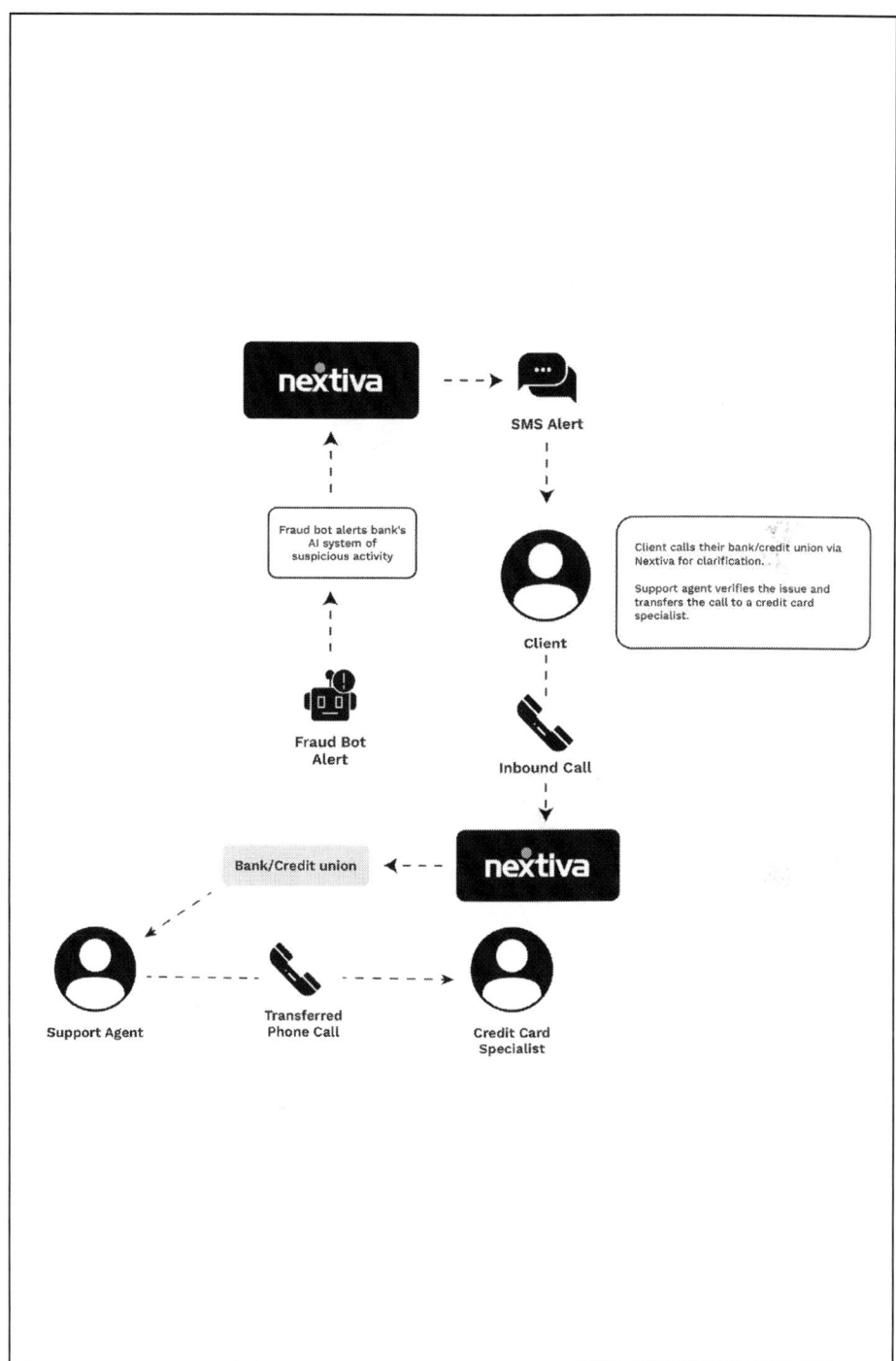

to credit card specialists when necessary. Nonetheless, support agents often face hurdles such as managing long queues and assisting clients who may abandon calls due to extended wait times.

Credit card specialists focus on providing expert guidance, retaining clients post-dispute, and assuring clients about the security of their cards. They support clients through new credit card applications when needed and offer detailed explanations regarding the nature of disputes. Their challenges involve addressing the concerns of distressed clients while explaining the dispute resolution process clearly and effectively.

The primary issues in this scenario include lengthy investigative processes that allow for the potential escalation of suspicious activity, clients' inability to act promptly, and the risk of losing clients to competitors with more efficient technological solutions. A potential solution is the integration of real-time monitoring and alerts within contact center operations. Real-time monitoring can immediately detect

Table 10: Benefits of disputes and fraud claims use cases

Disputes and fraud claims capability	Chief benefits
Real-time monitoring and alarms	Enables immediate detection of suspicious activity before escalation
Integration with contact center	Allows for better financial management and faster resolution of issues
AI-driven fraud detection system	Helps enhance security by continuously monitoring accounts in real-time
Proactive client communication	Gives banks and credit unions a competitive edge by improving customer service and satisfaction
SMS alerts and efficient call routing	Speeds up investigative processes and allows clients to take immediate action upon receiving alerts

suspicious activity, improving security and financial management by continuously overseeing accounts.

The advantages of an AI-based fraud alert and advanced contact center solution include the acceleration of investigative processes through the automatic detection of suspicious transactions. This enables financial institutions to respond swiftly when alerted. This method not only enhances the protection of clients' financial information but also provides financial institutions a competitive advantage by ensuring timely responses and effective management of credit card disputes.

Advanced technologies enable banks and credit unions to improve the credit card dispute process and enhance customer satisfaction. Real-time monitoring detects suspicious activity quickly, helping to prevent unauthorized transactions. Integration with contact center operations allows clients to receive timely alerts and take action through SMS notifications or direct support calls.

A smooth transition from support agents to credit card specialists ensures clients receive tailored solutions. By leveraging AI-driven fraud detection systems, financial institutions strengthen security measures while demonstrating their commitment to client safety. This efficient handling of disputes fosters trust and builds stronger relationships with clients, ultimately supporting long-term growth and success.

Account Balance And Transaction Inquiries

In financial services, managing personal finances relies on timely access to account balances and transaction inquiries. These functionalities provide customers with real-time account information for effective monitoring of their financial status. This exploration will examine the impact of advancements in AI and automation on these aspects.

AI improves the speed, accuracy, and convenience of services such as balance verifications and transaction records. It grants customers immediate access to financial data, enhancing transparency and efficiency in banking. This journey will clarify the significant effects of AI on account balance and transaction inquiries in the financial services sector.

AI chatbots and voice assistants provide a convenient way for customers to access real-time account information. Users can inquire about account balances, review recent transactions, and explore account history through voice commands or text queries. For example, a customer might ask, "What's my checking account balance?" The chatbot or voice assistant responds promptly and accurately, offering immediate information without traditional communication methods.

AI systems monitor account activity in real-time, notifying customers of events like large withdrawals, direct deposits, or suspicious transactions. Alerts are sent via SMS, email, or push notifications, allowing customers to verify unusual activity. For example, if a large transaction occurs, an instant alert is sent for verification.

In a practical application, when a customer asks their banking app, "What's my current account balance?" the AI chatbot provides the exact balance, such as "Your checking account balance is $2,338.17." Additionally, if a paycheck is deposited, the system sends a notification like, "Your direct deposit of $1,650 has been credited to your account."

Transaction inquiries often involve checking the clearance status of a check. Financial providers offer this function to enhance customer experience. This allows customers to verify the processing status of their deposited or issued checks in real-time, providing immediate visibility into their accounts. The primary benefits include transparency and financial planning. This feature enables customers to track transactions, reducing uncertainties and disputes. It also provides insights into their available balance, allowing informed decisions about future expenditures and investments.

Automation plays a crucial role in streamlining processes for clients. One notable application is the provision of loan payment breakdowns. For instance, when clients record a mortgage payment in an accounting application like QuickBooks, they need to allocate the payment into components such as principal, interest, insurance, and taxes. While an amortization schedule can help, it often does not provide a comprehensive breakdown. Financial institutions can use technology, like interactive voice response systems or bots, to deliver this breakdown via phone or mobile application, eliminating the need for clients to wait for a representative. This approach simplifies the process for clients and improves their overall experience.

Real-time access to account balances and transaction histories is essential for managing personal finances. AI and automation technologies improve this accessibility by providing instant insights into financial data. Features such as balance checks and transaction overviews, enabled by AI tools like chatbots and voice assistants, make managing financial information easier.

AI systems also enhance security by monitoring account activities and sending alerts for significant events, such as large withdrawals or unusual transactions, prompting immediate action. Automation simplifies routine tasks like checking transaction clearances and detailing loan payments for better financial management. These advancements are transforming the financial services landscape to be more efficient and user-friendly.

Table 11: Benefits of automated balance and transaction inquiries

Automated balance and transaction inquiries capability	Chief benefits
Instant balance checks and transaction inquiries	Enhances speed, accuracy, and convenience for the customer
Real-time account activity monitoring	Enables immediate customer notifications of specific events
Automated alert delivery through various channels	Allows customers to promptly verify unusual activity or take necessary action
Instant alert on large transactions	Provides quick verification process for customers
Proactive notification of significant account events	Improves the customer experience through timely and pertinent updates
Checking the clearance status of a check or debit charge	Enhances customer experience and financial oversight

Billing And Payment Support

AI and automation enhance billing and payment support in the financial services industry by sending timely reminders about upcoming bills and payment obligations. AI systems can detect billing cycles and send notifications via email, SMS, or app alerts. This is particularly useful for utility providers and subscription services, as they can notify users before payments are due. Customized alerts improve relevance and payment compliance.

In payment processing, AI-driven chatbots handle inquiries about payment statuses and facilitate transactions. These bots provide real-time information and assist with common queries. The integration of AI with automated payment gateways enables secure online transactions. Additionally, AI plays a role in fraud detection, analyzing payment data to identify anomalies and potentially fraudulent activities. This approach streamlines the payment process and enhances security.

Automation can send messages from a bank to a customer via SMS. For example: "Hi Albert! Your car loan payment of $440 is due on July 9th. Click here to make an online payment." The AI system generates reminders based on billing cycles and personalized details. Preference management, including communication channels and opt-in choices, is essential. Modern CX systems can store this information in CRM records to align with customer preferences.

In financial services, a "Promise to Pay" is a commitment by a customer to settle a financial obligation within a specified period. This is often used when customers cannot immediately pay their loans or credit cards when due. It offers customers flexibility, helps avoid late payment charges, and protects their credit rating. For financial institutions, it provides certainty regarding funds recovery, aiding risk management and cash flow. Thus, "Promise to Pay" benefits both customers and financial entities.

Agreements can sometimes cause discomfort among customers. Automating the process can alleviate this apprehension and improve operational efficiency. For example, an interactive voice response (IVR) system can be effective in determining a customer's promise-to-pay date, along with opt-in reminders. Customers may approve SMS

Figure 11: Consumer portal offers "no shame" self-service

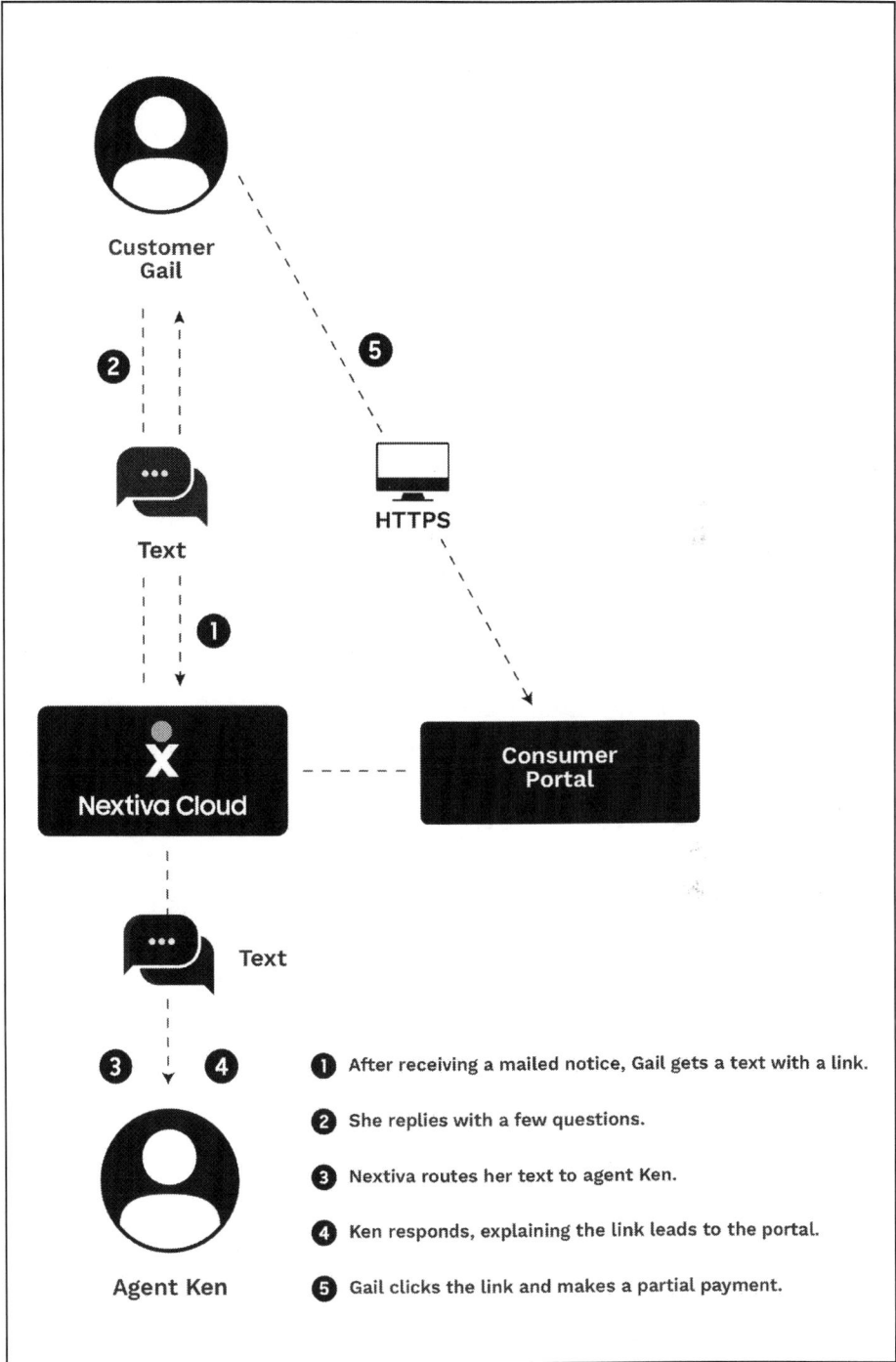

1. After receiving a mailed notice, Gail gets a text with a link.
2. She replies with a few questions.
3. Nextiva routes her text to agent Ken.
4. Ken responds, explaining the link leads to the portal.
5. Gail clicks the link and makes a partial payment.

notifications on the day of their paycheck as a reminder to fulfill their payment obligation.

In asset recovery, automating debt verification documentation is essential. This process validates the existence and specifics of a debt for the consumer, facilitating recovery for creditors.

Typically, this documentation is provided to the debtor by the debt collector at initial contact or within five days. It includes the name and address of the collector, the creditor's name, and the debt amount. This ensures transparency, accuracy, and fairness in the debt recovery process while protecting the debtor's rights and enabling efficient asset recovery for creditors.

Automating debt documentation streamlines the retrieval process by allowing access to verification documents through a customer portal. This reduces the need for direct interaction with debt collection agents, lowering potential embarrassment for debtors. Debtors can validate their debts independently and initiate payment on the same platform. This approach improves the efficiency and transparency of the debt recovery process while maintaining user dignity and privacy.

Cedar Financial has developed an approach to asset recovery that uses automation to improve consumer debt management. The company's customer service portal allows consumers to automate transactions, which helps reduce discomfort during these interactions. The portal enables tasks such as "QuickPay" payments, setting reminders, making payment promises, and accessing validation documents. These features aim to make financial transactions more convenient for consumers.

Cedar facilitates document verification within the portal, allowing bank clients to submit validation documents. Collaboration with Nextiva enabled the integration of data dips into the system. Cedar also developed a payment gateway function linked to the portal, providing clients with a platform for managing documents and payments.

The advantages of this system include faster consumer engagement and more efficient interaction. The availability of validation documents fosters trust by enabling verification of transaction authenticity. Additionally, self-serve capabilities help consumers avoid awkward debt-related discussions, improving user experience and payment

Table 12: Benefits of billing and payments use cases

Billing and payment capability	Chief benefits
Automated transactions	Improved efficiency, engagement, and trust among consumers; increased convenience and enhanced consumer experience
Document verification	Simplifies document and payment management, ensuring transaction authenticity and enhancing trust
Payment gateway	Improved efficiency and consumer satisfaction; PCI compliance improves consumer trust
Automated Promise-to-Pay	Enhances customer flexibility in managing financial commitments; helps avoid late payment fees and negative impacts on credit scores; offers financial institutions better risk management and cash flow; builds an environment of trust and fiscal stability between customers and financial bodies; alleviates customer discomfort and streamlines operational efficiency
AI-driven bots handle inquiries and facilitate transactions in payment processing	Enhances customer service by providing real-time information and efficient query resolution
Advanced algorithms in AI systems for fraud detection during transactions	Increases transaction security by identifying and preventing fraudulent activities
Personalized reminders via SMS	Improves communication efficiency and ensures customers are timely informed about due payments
Storage of customer preference information in modern CX systems	Ensures that communication and payment processes respect customer preferences and privacy

outcomes. This system provides a solution tailored to consumer needs while enhancing trust and engagement.

Justin Franklin, director of communication and engagement at Cedar Financial, notes that integrating automation has improved debt recoupment, resulting in higher liquidation rates and increased engagement within 30 days of the initial notice.

AI and automation improve billing and payment processes by enhancing efficiency, reducing errors, and ensuring timely customer communication. They simplify billing and payment support by sending reminders and streamlining transactions. These technologies also apply to operational processes like "Promise to Pay" agreements and debt verification, improving efficiency and customer experience in complex transactions.

Two-Tiered Intelligent Voice Routing

In the financial services sector, an intelligent voice routing system is implemented to improve the management of mortgage leads through automation and effective contact handling. Mortgage seekers often seek to understand various mortgage options and navigate the home-buying process, prompting them to seek expert assistance. Their primary activities include completing forms to request contact from mortgage brokers and asking for clarification on specific issues. However, they often encounter challenges such as an overwhelming amount of information online and difficulty grasping the complexities of the mortgage process.

First-tier outreach agents aim to generate qualified leads and increase awareness of brokerage services. Their goal is to establish trust with mortgage seekers and facilitate a smooth transition to licensed brokers. To achieve this, they verify the information provided by mortgagors and reassure them about the mortgage process. Nevertheless, these agents face challenges, including increasing competition for leads and the necessity for quick contact with potential customers. On the other hand, second-tier licensed brokers focus on converting these qualified leads into customers, often motivated by performance incentives such as bonuses.

Figure 12: Two-tiered intelligent voice routing

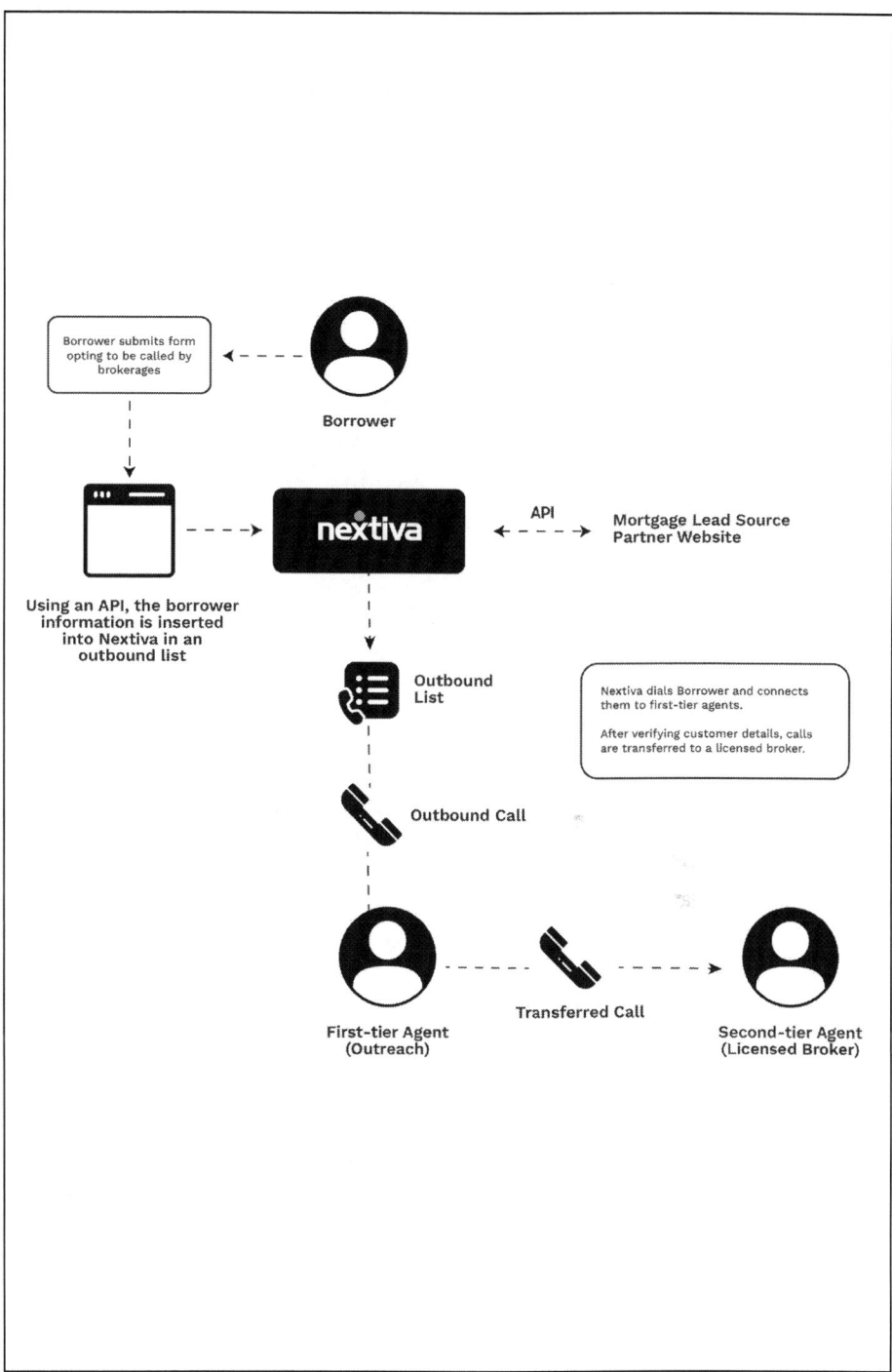

Their responsibilities include guiding mortgagors through the mortgage process, helping them find suitable mortgage options, and positioning themselves as experts in the field. They, too, encounter obstacles, such as lengthy turnaround times and the extensive details involved in explaining mortgage products.

A significant issue in this landscape is the difficulty in identifying and reaching qualified leads, exacerbated by competition and inefficiencies in manual outreach efforts. A viable solution is the integration of APIs and automated outbound dialing, which enables access to contact information for leads who have expressed interest in being contacted. This automation facilitates trust-building and allows agents and brokers to engage with leads more efficiently, ensuring that brokerage firms can compete effectively by reaching multiple leads simultaneously. Benefits of this approach include compliance with regulations by contacting only opted-in leads, utilizing dynamic scripts for intelligent call routing, and minimizing the time agents spend on dialing.

Ultimately, this intelligent voice routing system optimizes the mortgage lead management process through automated third-party

Table 13: Benefits of two-tiered intelligent voice routing

Billing and payment capability	Chief benefits
API integrations and outbound dialing	Provides contact information of qualified leads who have already opted in to be contacted
API integrations and outbound dialing	Helps agents and brokers establish trust and credibility faster with the submitted information
API integrations and outbound dialing	Saves time and helps brokerage remain competitive by dialing all leads on a list simultaneously
Dynamic scripting	Allows agents to use intelligent routing for faster handoff times

API integrations. When prospective borrowers express interest by submitting a form, their information is incorporated into an outbound call list. The system then automatically initiates calls, directing them to first-tier agents who verify the information provided. Once verification is complete, the call is transferred to a licensed broker in the second tier. This structured workflow ensures prompt contact with potential customers while accurately verifying their details, improving operational efficiency and the overall customer experience.

This structured approach to mortgage lead management creates an efficient process that benefits time savings, compliance, and customer satisfaction. Financial institutions can quickly connect with interested customers by automating initial contacts through API integrations and outbound dialing, reducing manual efforts and minimizing the risk of losing leads to competitors.

Dynamic scripting further enhances efficiency by allowing agents to route calls intelligently and provide quicker handoffs, improving the customer experience. Ensuring compliance by contacting only opted-in leads protects the brokerage from legal issues, while automation enables agents to focus on meaningful interactions instead of repetitive tasks.

This system streamlines operations and builds customer trust, helping financial institutions remain competitive and promote sustainable growth.

Mortgage And Home Loan Queries

In financial services, particularly with mortgages and home loans, there are opportunities for automation and artificial intelligence in customer service. Addressing inquiries about mortgage terms, payment schedules, and interest rates is a critical application area. Customers often have complex questions regarding their mortgages that can be challenging for human agents to manage.

By incorporating AI, these inquiries can be handled promptly and accurately, improving the customer service experience. AI systems can be programmed to understand and respond to mortgage-related questions, providing instant and precise answers. This efficiency enhances customer satisfaction and allows human agents to focus on more complex issues, optimizing operational effectiveness in financial services.

Virtual mortgage assistants offer tailored assistance for borrowers by answering inquiries about mortgage conditions, interest rates, and eligibility requirements. They elucidate the distinctions between fixed-rate and adjustable-rate mortgages, clarify the qualification criteria for various loan programs, and provide detailed information on down payments, closing costs, and prepayment penalties. Furthermore, they assist borrowers throughout the application process.

Financial hardship assistance is a major focus for many financial institutions, especially for customers facing late payments or foreclosure. AI-powered customer service platforms can deliver immediate guidance to individuals in these situations. They can provide information on loan modification, repayment plans, or forbearance options and help customers navigate these processes with step-by-step instructions.

AI can provide information about the foreclosure process, customer rights, and actions to prevent foreclosure. This includes connecting customers with resources for legal aid, housing counseling, or financial planning.

AI can also reach customers at risk of late payments or foreclosure using predictive analytics. This proactive communication can help address issues early and potentially prevent worsening situations.

The use of AI can improve the management of late payment issues and foreclosure, benefiting both financial institutions and customers.

AI and automation improve mortgage services by providing accurate information and efficient calculations. They handle inquiries about mortgage terms, payment schedules, and interest rates, delivering instant and customized responses. This enhancement boosts customer satisfaction and allows human agents to focus on more complex inquiries. Virtual mortgage assistants can guide borrowers through the application process and offer details about various mortgage aspects.

Financial hardship assistance is another key area for financial institutions. AI customer service platforms can guide those facing challenges like late payments or foreclosure, offering information on options such as loan modification and repayment plans. AI can also engage proactively with at-risk customers, facilitating early intervention.

Overall, the application of AI and automation in managing issues related to late payments or foreclosure can render the process less daunting and more manageable for customers whilst simultaneously decreasing the workload for customer service representatives.

Table 14: Benefits of loan query use cases

Loan query capability	Chief benefits
Virtual mortgage assistants	Offers clarity on mortgage options, helping borrowers make informed decisions
Automated eligibility criteria	Assists borrowers in understanding what's needed to qualify for specific loan programs, saving time and confusion
AI-assisted application process	Simplifies the mortgage application process, making it less daunting for borrowers
Loan calculators	Makes tedious math problems simple for customers, increasing their overall satisfaction
Late payment guidance	Enhances customer experience by offering personalized support and clearly defined paths to resolve payment issues
Foreclosure status	Empowers customers with knowledge and resources to navigate foreclosure situations more effectively, potentially avoiding them altogether
Proactive customer outreach	Prevents escalation of financial hardships through timely support, improving customer loyalty and financial stability
Customer service representative load reduction	Enhances operational efficiency within financial institutions and allows customer service representatives to focus on complex issues, improving overall service quality; reduces attrition from agent burn-out

Figure 13: AI-assisted retirement planning

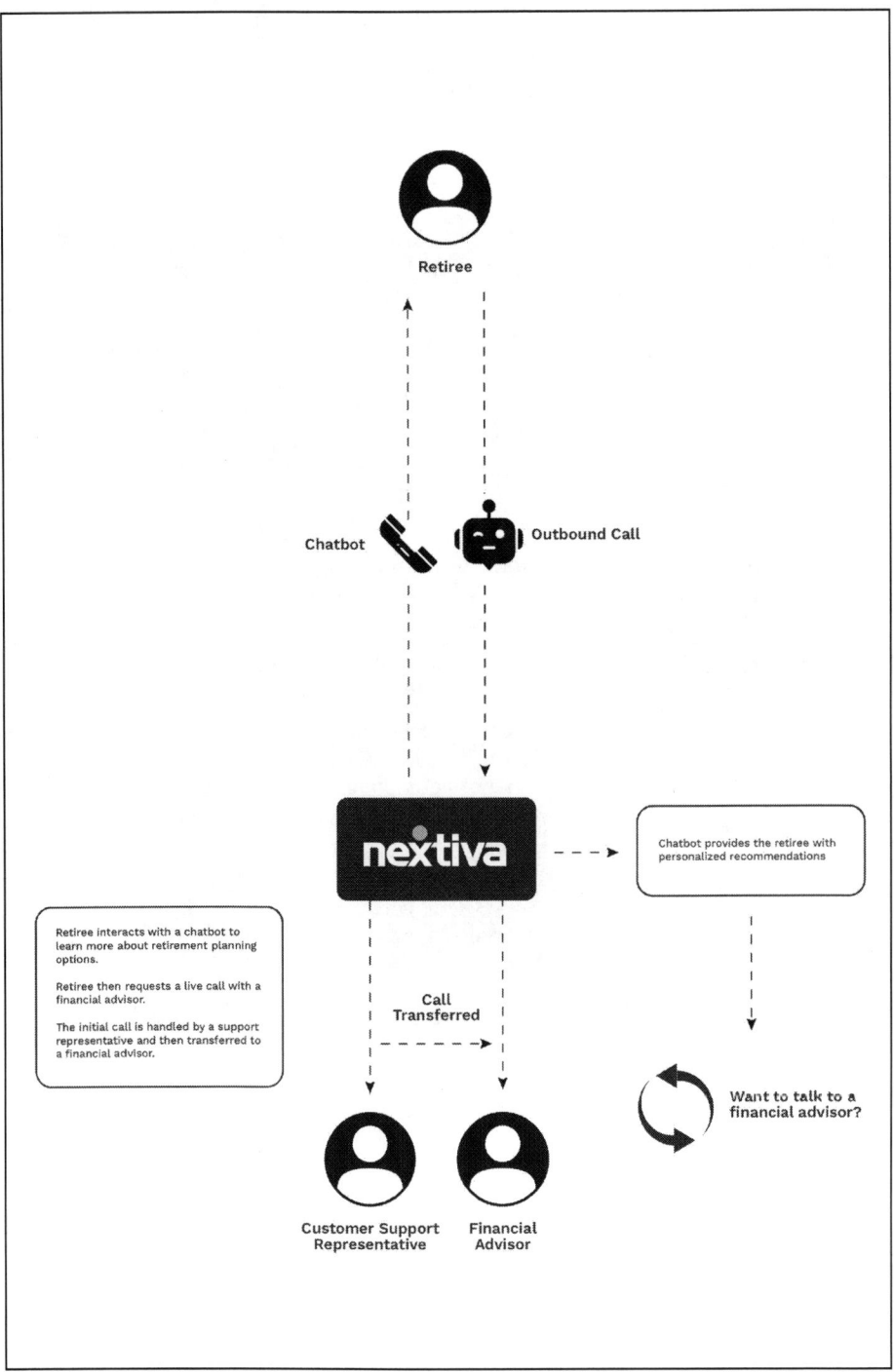

AI-Assisted Retirement Planning

A central issue in retirement planning is the time-consuming gathering of all necessary information to provide personalized assistance. This can lead to errors in data collection and a lack of continuous support for clients outside regular business hours. To address these challenges, implementing an automated retirement calculator, such as a chatbot, presents a viable solution. This chatbot can guide potential clients by collecting relevant personal information and providing personalized recommendations with the data collected. By utilizing this technology, clients can better understand how to align their savings with their retirement objectives, thus streamlining the planning process and enhancing overall satisfaction.

In retirement planning and education, a structured approach significantly improves the experience for retirees. As individuals approach retirement, they are primarily motivated by the desire to secure a comprehensive plan that ensures their financial stability during their later years.

This includes a strong need to understand their various retirement options, enabling informed decisions on how best to preserve their capital. Retirees often seek reliable financial information to support their choices regarding retirement planning. However, they frequently face challenges such as changes in spending needs and market fluctuations that complicate their planning efforts.

Customer service representatives play a vital role in this process. Their main objective is to assist retirees efficiently and improve the company's service level agreements (SLAs). To achieve this, they strive to connect retirees with the most suitable financial advisors, ensuring their inquiries are promptly addressed. This requires a thorough understanding of retirees' needs, which can be challenging due to the sometimes-vague nature of those needs and the lack of personalized service. Despite their best efforts, representatives often encounter obstacles in providing customized assistance, leaving retirees uncertain about their options.

On the other hand, financial advisors are motivated by helping retirees make informed choices about their economic future while expanding their client base. They work to establish their expertise in the field and guide retirees through the array of available options. Their responsibilities include facilitating the sign-up process for various retirement plans and enrolling clients for ongoing updates and support. However, financial advisors also face significant challenges, such as managing retirees' expectations and maintaining long-term client relationships.

An automated retirement calculator supports a practical use case for retirement planning assistance that utilizes a contact center platform integrating a chatbot and a workflow engine. Retirees can interact with the chatbot to examine various retirement planning options, with the chatbot offering personalized recommendations based on their specific needs. For those who require more detailed guidance, we highlighted the option to request a live call with a financial advisor, prompting the chatbot to initiate an outbound call.

The initial conversation is handled by a customer support representative, who gathers essential information and addresses any immediate concerns. Following this exchange, the call is transferred to a financial advisor who provides tailored advice based on the retiree's circumstances. This approach effectively demonstrates how the combination of automation and personalized service can enhance the retirement planning experience, ensuring that retirees receive structured and relevant support.

The implementation of an automated retirement calculator, such as a chatbot, addresses key challenges in retirement planning by streamlining the data collection process and providing personalized assistance. This technology enables retirees to gather essential information, understand various retirement options, and receive tailored recommendations based on their unique circumstances. While customer service representatives facilitate initial interactions and financial advisors offer detailed guidance, the integration of automation with personalized support enhances the overall experience for retirees, ensuring they receive timely and relevant assistance in achieving their financial stability during retirement.

Table 15: Benefits of AI-assisted retirement planning

AI-assisted retirement planning capability	Chief benefits
Automated retirement calculator chatbot	Automates tasks, allowing financial advisors to focus on client relationships
Capable of 24/7 service	Available for clients whenever they want, offering around-the-clock service
Personalized recommendations based on input data	Makes financial literacy education less daunting
Alignment of savings with retirement objectives	Helps deliver financial literacy education faster and more efficiently

Credit Line Approval Virtual Assistant

Credit line approvals can be a complicated and time-consuming process for banks and their clients. Utilizing a virtual assistant can help streamline this process and improve the overall customer experience. Many clients seek to increase their credit lines to enhance their credit scores, which may enable them to make significant purchases or to qualify for loans, such as a new car or home. To initiate a credit line increase, clients typically need to provide relevant information for approval and articulate their reasons for seeking the increase. However, they may encounter challenges along the way, including concerns about the possibility of denial and the need to demonstrate their financial capability to support the requested increase.

Support agents seek to secure credit for the credit card issuer while addressing client inquiries. Their primary goal is to establish trust and initiate the credit line increase approval process. They gather necessary information from clients and aim to understand the reasons behind their requests. However, they often face challenges such as explaining denials and managing client rejections. Similarly, bank account managers strive to inform clients about the implications of increasing their credit lines and maintaining existing relationships.

Their responsibilities include setting up new transaction or account management procedures and providing assistance to clients. They also encounter obstacles, including the time needed to implement new procedures and remaining neutral while advising clients.

The current credit line approval process is problematic due to its labor-intensive nature, which requires clients to repeatedly restate their information and often results in lengthy approval times. To address these issues, implementing a credit line approval virtual assistant could be beneficial. This virtual assistant would use natural language processing to assess a client's eligibility, operate across multiple channels, and streamline the approval process to provide faster feedback.

To enhance and streamline the credit line increase process, a balanced solution that combines a virtual assistant with human support can be deployed. This approach includes an intelligent routing and customer experience platform, allowing various interactions among a bank client, a chatbot, contact center representatives, dedicated support agents, and bank account managers.

The process begins when a bank client contacts the institution through a chat interface, engaging with a chatbot designed to guide them through completing the credit line approval form. The chatbot will ask relevant questions and collect the necessary details in an accessible manner. Once the client submits the information, the system conducts a credit check to evaluate the client's creditworthiness based on the provided data.

After the credit check, the client receives immediate feedback regarding their approval status. If approved for an increase, they may request a personalized callback to discuss the next steps. Nextiva, the automated call platform, will initiate a phone call to the client, ensuring timely communication according to their preferences. The call is then routed to a support agent trained to handle credit line inquiries, minimizing delays in connecting clients with the appropriate resources.

The support agent will verify the client's details and, if necessary, transfer the call to a bank account manager with specialized knowledge to finalize the credit line increase process. This structured approach demonstrates how automation and intelligent routing can work together to improve the efficiency and responsiveness of credit

FINANCIAL SERVICES

Figure 14: Credit line approval virtual assistant

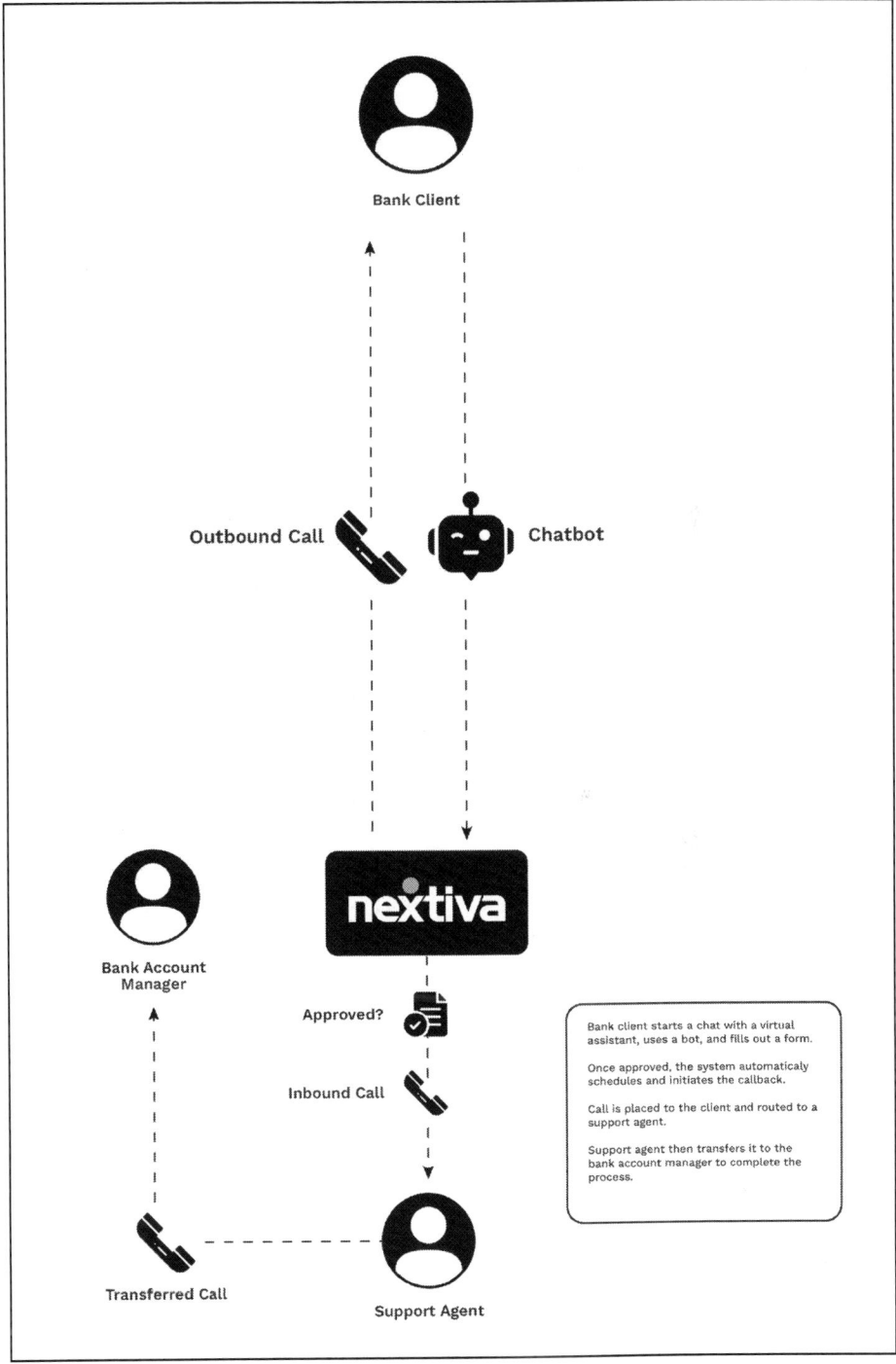

line increase requests. By streamlining client interactions and expediting approvals, the system aims to enhance the overall customer experience for bank clients.

A virtual assistant can simplify the credit line approval process for both banks and clients. Utilizing natural language processing and an omnichannel approach minimizes the need for clients to repeatedly provide their information, resulting in faster approvals for major purchases, such as new apartments. This allows support agents to concentrate on more complex issues, ultimately enhancing customer satisfaction.

Integrating a virtual assistant enhances efficiency by automating credit checks and providing immediate updates on approval status. Intelligent routing ensures clients are connected to the appropriate resources, reducing delays. This organized approach ensures effective management of the credit line and strengthens client relationships.

Table 16: Benefits of credit line approval virtual assistant

Credit line virtual assistant capability	Chief benefits
Credit line approval virtual assistant	Allows employees to focus on more complex issues, improving operational efficiency
Natural language processing	Evaluates client's eligibility accurately without human intervention
Omnichannel virtual assistant	Meets clients on their preferred channels, enhancing convenience
Streamlined process	Provides prompt feedback to clients, reducing wait times
Automated credit check	Reduces the need for clients to repeat themselves, improving customer satisfaction and loyalty

Customer Complaint Resolution

Managing customer complaints is key to effective customer service in financial services. This involves resolving grievances quickly to ensure customer satisfaction. Artificial intelligence (AI) and automation can enhance complaint resolution processes by speeding up complaint categorization and routing to the appropriate departments, reducing response times. AI also helps analyze complaints to identify recurring issues and implement improvements.

Furthermore, AI can tailor responses to complaints, which improves customer satisfaction. This approach helps maintain customer loyalty and can attract new customers. Integrating AI and automation in complaint resolution can improve efficiency and customer service in the financial industry.

Effective complaint management is essential for customer trust and regulatory compliance. AI technology enhances this by automatically collecting customer complaints from emails, chatbots, and social media, ensuring that all complaints are addressed efficiently. Automating this process reduces manual labor and minimizes the risk of missing important feedback.

It's important to distinguish between general inquiries and actual grievances. AI algorithms can accurately identify complaints, allowing institutions to focus on resolving genuine issues and improving customer satisfaction.

Once complaints are identified, categorizing them is crucial for resolution and analysis. AI uses natural language processing (NLP) to classify complaints into categories, such as product issues or billing errors. This structured approach enables financial institutions to route complaints to the appropriate departments for quicker resolution and better customer service.

Understanding the severity of complaints is essential for prioritizing responses and mitigating risks. AI assesses the impact of each complaint, identifying cases that may cause significant harm. This prioritization allows institutions to focus on high-risk complaints and proactively address issues that could lead to regulatory penalties or reputational damage.

AI continuously analyzes complaint data to identify patterns and trends that indicate underlying problems. Real-time alerts help institutions address issues before they escalate, improving complaint management.

Table 17: Benefits of complaint resolution use cases

Complaint resolution capability	Chief benefits
Complaint capture	Prioritization of customer trust helps to simplify the complaint collection process, thus ensuring quicker resolution of issues; reducing the need for manual labor minimizes the chance of missing any feedback
Complaint identification	Accurate complaint identification optimizes resource allocation, which in turn increases customer satisfaction and improves adherence to compliance requirements
NLP-based categorization	More accurate concern classification, rapid routing of complaints, faster resolution times, improved customer service, ensuring client queries are addressed promptly and efficiently
Consumer harm qualification	Minimizes risks effectively by tackling the most critical issues first; customer impacts a top priority, engendering a spirit of customer loyalty; steps to mitigate harm protect clients; avoidance of regulatory penalties, ensuring compliance with laws and regulations; protection of brand reputation, which is vital for maintaining trust and credibility
Automated trend alerts and monitoring	Unnecessary escalation avoidance promotes a responsive management approach—this ensures that potential challenges are addressed swiftly, allowing for more effective and efficient management practices
Simplified and automated reports for training and regulatory reporting	Efficient allocation of resources, leading to the prompt resolution of any concerns raised

Additionally, AI-driven escalation management helps identify and address complex or sensitive complaints. Algorithms analyze the content and sentiment to determine complexity and severity, enabling effective resource allocation and timely resolution.

Integrating AI and automation technologies into the financial services sector enhances customer complaint management. These tools facilitate categorizing and routing complaints, accurately identifying genuine grievances, and prioritizing and resolving issues efficiently.

AI helps analyze complaint trends, increasing efficiency and compliance while maintaining customer trust and satisfaction. Leveraging AI in complaint resolution allows financial institutions to better understand and address customer needs, promoting loyalty and attracting new clients.

ATM And Card Issues

Integrating artificial intelligence (AI) and process automation enhances the resolution of ATM and card-related issues in the financial services sector. For example, when a card is reported lost, an AI system can instantly block the card and initiate the replacement process without human intervention. This reduces the resolution timeframe and the risk of fraudulent transactions.

If a customer faces issues at an ATM, such as the machine retaining their card or not dispensing cash, an AI-equipped system can register the incident, alert the relevant department, and provide the customer with confirmation and an estimated resolution timeline.

AI also helps monitor ATM transactions to identify potential issues before they affect customers. For instance, if an ATM often runs low on cash or a specific card type has higher failure rates, AI can notify the bank for prompt action. Adopting AI and automation is crucial for improving customer service in the financial services industry.

AI systems streamline the replacement process when customers report their card as lost or stolen. The AI verifies the customer's identity and initiates an order for card replacement, informing the customer about the status and estimated delivery time.

AI-powered chatbots assist users in locating nearby ATMs based on location, offering real-time information on ATM availability, operating hours, and services. When a user asks about the nearest ATM, the chatbot lists nearby ATMs with addresses and directions.

The application of AI in predicting when ATMs require maintenance aims to reduce downtime. By analyzing historical data, potential issues can be identified for proactive maintenance. For example, an ATM manufacturer uses predictive maintenance to schedule service or order parts autonomously when sensors detect anomalies like excessive vibration.

AI-enhanced cameras at ATMs monitor for security and operational efficiency. Machine vision technology can detect tampering, skimming devices, or unauthorized access attempts. For instance, an AI-equipped ATM camera can identify someone installing a card skimmer and alert security.

Automated fraud detection through AI analyzes transaction patterns to identify potentially fraudulent ATM withdrawals or card misuse. Unusual behavior, such as multiple large withdrawals in a short time, triggers alerts for further investigation, enhancing security measures.

AI-powered kiosks at ATMs assist users with common issues like card jams, PIN resets, and cash dispensing errors. They provide step-by-step instructions, enabling users to resolve these concerns. For instance, if a user experiences a card jam, the AI system offers detailed guidance for retrieving the card and continuing the transaction.

The integration of artificial intelligence (AI) and process automation streamlines the resolution of ATM and card-related issues in the financial sector, enhancing customer service and operational efficiency. AI systems expedite processes like blocking and replacing lost cards, managing ATM malfunctions, reducing fraud risks, and improving incident resolution times. Proactive monitoring capabilities of AI help anticipate and rectify potential ATM service disruptions, facilitating swift corrective actions.

AI-powered tools like chatbots and self-service kiosks improve customer interactions by providing real-time assistance and troubleshooting guidance. Predictive maintenance through AI analysis minimizes ATM downtime, and AI-enhanced security features, including surveillance cameras and transaction pattern analysis, contribute to fraud prevention and transaction safety. Adopting AI-driven

Table 18: Benefits of ATM and card issue use cases

ATM and card issue capability	Chief benefits
Self-service ATM troubleshooting	Provides AI-powered guidance for users facing common ATM issues; offers step-by-step instructions reducing friction for customers
Automated fraud detection	Helps prevent fraudulent ATM withdrawals or card misuse
AI-enabled ATM cameras	Automatically detects suspicious activities like tampering and skimming attempts; real-time alerts help prevent fraudulent activities
Predictive maintenance for ATMs	Reduces ATM downtime through proactive maintenance scheduling
ATM locator chatbots	Makes the delivery of cash much quicker for customers, removing frustration
Card replacement automation	Streamlines the replacement process for lost or stolen cards; customer service implication is increased loyalty and sense of security for customer

innovations improves reliability, security, and customer satisfaction in ATM services, making it vital for financial institutions focused on service delivery.

Loan Repayment Assistance

With the advancement of digital transformation, customer service in loan repayment assistance has improved through automation and AI technologies. These innovations enable customized repayment strategies tailored to each borrower's financial profile. AI algorithms analyze income, expenditure, and financial behavior to recommend optimal repayment terms. Automation streamlines the application process for assistance, enhancing efficiency. AI chatbots handle routine inquiries, allowing customer service representatives to focus on more complex concerns. This combination of human expertise and AI support improves the borrower experience throughout the loan repayment journey.

AI-powered chatbots respond immediately to borrower inquiries, such as loan balances, at any time. They can access real-time data to help borrowers understand interest accumulation and redirect human representatives to more nuanced issues.

When borrowers consider making additional payments, AI systems analyze their financial data to offer tailored advice. This enables informed decisions aligned with their financial goals.

In default risk analysis, AI can forecast potential defaults by analyzing borrowers' financial data. Changes in employment status may flag higher risk, allowing financial institutions to proactively engage with borrowers to offer loan modifications or forbearance to prevent defaults.

AI chatbots guide borrowers through repayment options, explaining the implications of different strategies, such as fixed versus variable interest rates. Providing a comparative analysis empowers borrowers to choose the most suitable repayment plan.

Automated payment reminders via email or SMS keep borrowers informed of payment due dates and amounts, reducing the chances of missed payments. These reminders simplify financial management and help avoid late fees and adverse credit impacts.

In summary, AI and automation significantly enhance loan repayment assistance in the financial services industry, improving borrower experience and operational efficiency.

Imagine a scenario where a borrower has a question about their loan balance at midnight. With AI-powered chatbots, borrowers can receive immediate responses at any hour. These chatbots can fetch the current balance and explain how interest accumulates using real-time data. This 24/7 support enhances the borrower experience and allows human customer service representatives to focus on more complex inquiries.

For borrowers considering additional payments on their loans, AI can analyze their financial data—like income and expenses—to provide tailored advice, helping them make informed decisions that align with their financial goals.

In default risk analysis, AI can forecast potential defaults by analyzing borrowers' financial data. For example, a change in employment status may indicate a higher risk of default, allowing institutions to engage proactively with the borrower to offer options like loan modification or forbearance.

Additionally, AI bots can assist borrowers in understanding repayment options and comparing strategies like fixed versus variable interest rates. This helps borrowers choose the repayment strategy that best suits their financial situation.

Automated payment reminders play a crucial role in the loan repayment process. Timely reminders via email or SMS containing payment due dates, amounts, and methods help borrowers stay informed and reduce the likelihood of missed payments. Including online payment links simplifies the management of financial obligations and helps borrowers avoid late fees and negative credit effects.

Table 19: Benefits of loan repayment use cases

Loan repayment capability	Chief benefits
Automated customer support	Improves customer service by providing immediate responses and freeing up human customer service representatives for more complex inquiries
Personalized financial advice	Empowers borrowers to make informed decisions that align with their financial goals
Default risk analysis	Helps prevent defaults and maintain a healthy loan portfolio
Automated payment reminders	Ensures that borrowers don't miss their loan repayments, which helps them avoid late fees and negative impacts on their credit score
Bot-assisted repayment options guidance	Enables borrowers to make informed decisions that best suit their financial situation; personalized guidance helps borrowers choose the most beneficial repayment strategy

AI and automation significantly impact improving loan repayment assistance in the financial services industry. As these technologies evolve, they promise to enhance the borrower experience and the operational efficiency of financial service providers.

Health Savings Account (HSA) Support

Health savings account (HSA) support provides assistance to clients regarding their HSA inquiries, including eligibility prerequisites, contribution limits, tax implications, and the use of HSA funds. The goal of HSA support is to ensure that clients understand how HSAs work to optimize their benefits.

In finance, integrating AI and process automation can improve HSA support. AI chatbots can provide immediate answers to common questions, reducing wait times and allowing human agents to focus on more complex issues. Process automation can streamline account management, contributions, and spending tracking for clients. Additionally, AI can analyze customer behavior to offer personalized recommendations for better HSA utilization.

AI chatbots can help assess a customer's eligibility for an HSA by evaluating their health insurance plan details, including deductible thresholds and coverage. This improves customer understanding and operational efficiency while reducing the workload for service agents.

AI also assists customers in understanding contribution limits and tax benefits associated with HSAs. Bots can explain annual contribution limits and the tax benefits of pre-tax contributions and tax-free withdrawals for qualified medical expenses, enhancing financial literacy and confidence in managing HSAs.

In automated expense tracking and reimbursement, AI can improve traditional methods. An AI system can scan and interpret medical invoices and receipts, identify eligible expenses, and initiate reimbursements from HSAs. This automation saves time and reduces the risk of human error, leading to accurate tracking of expenses and reimbursements.

AI can also manage health savings account (HSA) balances by providing alerts for low balances or opportunities for investment. If the system detects a balance above a certain minimum, it can suggest investing extra funds in HSA-eligible options. This helps customers avoid penalties linked to low balances and maximize returns through investments.

Additionally, AI can analyze healthcare spending patterns to offer tailored recommendations for optimizing HSA usage. This personalized engagement encourages informed decision-making around healthcare expenditures and enhances the utility of HSAs.

Table 20: Benefits of HSA support use cases

HSA support capability	Chief benefits
HSA eligibility assessment with bots	Reduces wait times for eligibility checks, enhancing customer satisfaction; automates complex processes, improving operational efficiency; frees up customer service agents to focus on more complex inquiries
Automation of HSA contribution and tax benefit navigation	Empowers customers with knowledge about tax advantages, encouraging optimal HSA contributions; promotes financial literacy, leading to better financial planning and decision-making; increases confidence among users in managing their HSAs effectively
Automation of expense tracking and reimbursement	Provides accurate tracking of medical expenses, ensuring eligibility for reimbursements; saves time for customers by automating the reimbursement process; minimizes errors in expense tracking and reimbursement, improving reliability
Proactive HSA balance management	Alerts customers about low balances, preventing potential penalties; identifies opportunities for tax-advantaged investment, maximizing returns; prepares customers for future healthcare expenses through efficient fund management
Personalized education for optimizing HSA use	Offers personalized recommendations, encouraging informed healthcare spending; increases engagement by delivering tailored advice based on spending patterns; inspires a proactive approach to HSA management, maximizing account benefits

Integrating AI and process automation in financial services can enhance support for health savings accounts (HSA). AI-powered chatbots provide immediate responses to HSA-related inquiries, reducing wait times and allowing human agents to focus on more complex questions. Process automation streamlines HSA management, including account openings, contribution tracking, and expense monitoring.

AI can assess customer eligibility for HSAs based on health insurance details and clarify contribution limits and tax benefits. In automated expense tracking, AI scans medical invoices and receipts to identify eligible expenses and facilitate reimbursements. AI also manages HSA balances, providing notifications for low balances and tax-advantaged investment opportunities. Additionally, AI-driven education helps individuals make informed choices regarding their HSAs

Financial Literacy And Education

In the realm of financial services, particularly regarding financial literacy and education, a structured, platform-based approach can significantly enhance the effectiveness of these initiatives. Credit union members are increasingly motivated to improve their financial literacy and actively seek information about the educational resources offered by their credit unions. Their top priorities include providing accurate contact information, specifying preferred learning styles, and opting in to receive regular updates that align with their interests. However, they often face challenges such as feeling overwhelmed by the sheer volume of credit union news and finding suitable resources that cater to their specific learning preferences.

Support agents play a crucial role in this educational process. They are driven by the desire to assist as many customers as possible while simultaneously improving the overall member experience. Their tasks involve verifying member information, establishing trust, and directing members to the appropriate resources that can aid in their financial literacy journey. However, support agents encounter significant challenges, such as managing doubtful customers who may be skeptical about the resources being offered and the risk of call abandonment

FINANCIAL SERVICES

Figure 15: Financial literacy platform

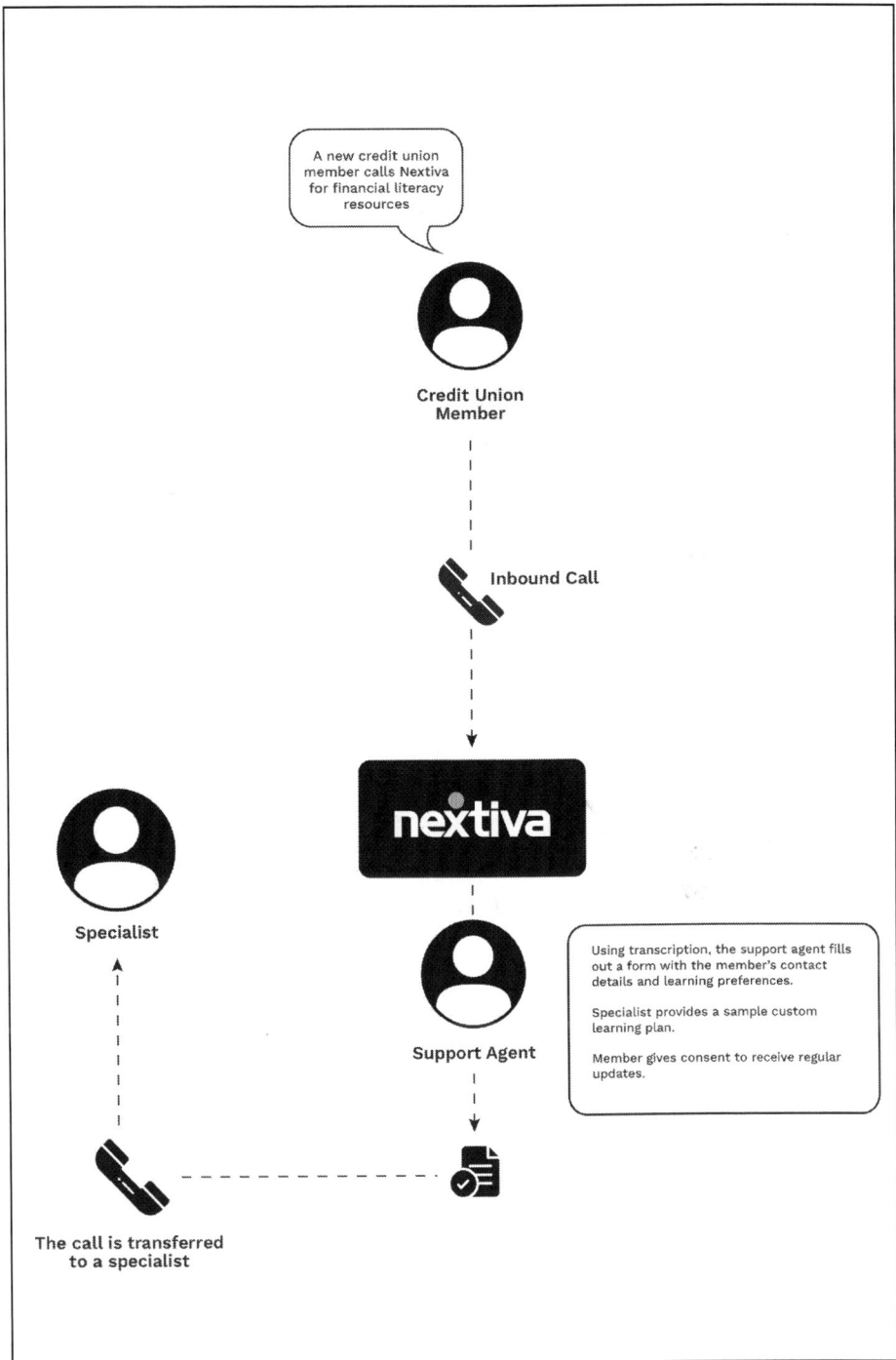

when members feel their concerns are not being addressed promptly or adequately.

Specialists address more intricate member inquiries, working toward enhancing satisfaction ratings and ensuring that individual needs are met. Their responsibilities include obtaining customer consent for updates and providing tailored examples of custom learning plans catering to the various educational backgrounds and preferences of members. Nevertheless, they face hurdles in persuading customers to commit to receiving updates and ensuring a high opt-in rate for automated communications, which are vital for ongoing engagement and support.

The primary difficulties in delivering effective financial literacy education stem from the labor-intensive nature of face-to-face or phone interactions, the overwhelming amount of information members need to absorb, and the lack of customizable learning paths tailored to individual needs and styles. The solution involves offering flexible, customizable learning paths that allow members to engage with content that resonates with them. Additionally, leveraging AI for transcription can minimize the repetitive nature of sharing information, thereby enhancing communication efficiency between members and support staff. Automation of certain aspects of the educational process can save time and resources, allowing for a deeper focus on personalized member interactions.

A typical scenario might involve a new credit union member calling a contact center equipped with advanced AI technology for transcription and summarization. The member seeks valuable resources to improve their financial literacy and is promptly routed to a support agent who can assist them. During this interaction, the agent collects the member's contact information and learning preferences, using AI-based transcription to summarize the member's needs for specialists and supervisors efficiently. This streamlined process helps ensure no critical details are lost and the member feels heard.

If the member wishes to speak with a specialist, the call can be seamlessly transferred without requiring the member to repeat their information, maintaining a smooth customer experience. The specialist then presents a clear example of a custom learning plan tailored to the member's specific interests and goals while obtaining their consent to receive regular updates. This innovative process reflects a modern approach to personalizing financial education, enabling members to enhance their financial literacy at their own pace, thus empowering them to make informed financial decisions and ultimately achieve greater economic well-being.

Enhancing financial literacy among bank and credit union patrons can be achieved through a structured, platform-based approach that offers customizable learning paths tailored to individual member needs. By utilizing AI for transcription and summarization, credit unions can streamline communication, ensuring effective interactions between members and support staff. This also makes it easier to transition members to specialists when targeted guidance is needed.

Automating educational processes saves time and allows for more personalized engagement with members. By securing consent for updates and showcasing customized learning plans, credit unions can foster a proactive educational environment that encourages members to utilize available resources. This approach not only improves the overall member experience but also empowers individuals to enhance their financial literacy at their own pace, leading to better decision-making and greater satisfaction.

Table 21: Benefits of the financial literacy platform

Financial literacy platform capability	Chief benefits
Customizable learning paths	Makes financial literacy education less daunting
AI-based transcription	Eliminates the need for members to repeat themselves, saving time
Automating education processes	Saves time and money by streamlining the delivery of financial literacy education
Automated member updates	Helps deliver financial literacy education faster and more efficiently
Personalized support and resources	Enhances financial planning for members by providing tailored assistance

Healthcare

IN THE HEALTHCARE industry, adopting advanced technologies such as automation, AI, and enhanced contact center solutions is revolutionizing patient care. These innovations streamline administrative processes, improve patient interactions, and enable more personalized and efficient service delivery.

AI-powered systems assist in diagnosing conditions, predicting patient needs, and providing real-time support. At the same time, automated processes manage routine tasks like appointment scheduling and follow-up reminders, ensuring that healthcare professionals can focus more on direct patient care. Contact centers equipped with omnichannel platforms ensure seamless communication across various channels, allowing patients to access support and information conveniently.

Integrating advanced technologies enhances patient experience and optimizes efficiency in healthcare organizations. These automation and contact center solutions are among the top implementations, but healthcare continues to explore many other innovative technologies and strategies for better patient care and operational efficiency.

Top Automation Targets In Healthcare

There are several major automations that practitioners plan for in the healthcare industry. These targets include contact center agent assistance and transaction automation, interaction with electronic medical records (EMRs), and interaction with customer relationship management (CRM) systems.

A brief explanation of these key areas below highlights how they collectively aim to enhance operational efficiency, reduce administrative burdens, and elevate the quality of patient care. Each target addresses distinct aspects of healthcare operations and is vital in improving overall service delivery.

Contact Center Agent Assistance And Transaction Automation

Within the realm of customer experience (CX) and contact centers, AI-based agent assistance and transaction automation can streamline operations and elevate patient care. This automation is focused on aiding agents in the more efficient and effective handling of customer interactions. Just one example of this is in the realm of behavioral health and contact centers. Here, AI can be leveraged to detect suicidal ideation/homicidal ideation (SIHI) during live patient interactions, ensuring the potential escalation of the conversation to a specialist.

Furthermore, transcription and summarization tools serve to transcribe spoken language into written text and condense the salient points from a discourse. This empowers agents to allocate their focus more toward the interaction itself as opposed to note-taking, consequently bolstering customer engagement.

Additionally, AI-based agent assist technologies offer real-time guidance to agents grounded on the context of the conversation. For instance, these technologies may propose the optimal next course of action or furnish the agent with pertinent information gleaned from the patient's history. This engenders more personalized and effective communication, thereby augmenting the overall customer experience. Consequently, automation within the contact center bears the potential to notably heighten operational efficiency, agent productivity, and customer contentment within the healthcare sector.

Interaction With Electronic Medical Records (EMRs)

Electronic medical record (EMR) systems serve as digital repositories for storing comprehensive patient health information, encompassing medical history, diagnoses, medications, lab results, and treatment plans. This centralized data repository presents a prime target for automation, given its critical role as the central hub for patient information accessed by numerous healthcare practitioners. To streamline patient support, front-office workers can leverage customer experience (CX) applications and systems to access EMR systems, thereby reducing operational friction.

The automation of billing and coding processes within healthcare facilities streamlines code assignment and claim submission, leading to substantial reductions in administrative burdens. Likewise, automating data entry and retrieval processes facilitates the seamless integration of information from diverse sources, such as lab reports and physician notes, directly into the EMR system.

For example, the availability of new lab results can trigger automatic updates to a patient's record, ensuring timely and accurate information accessibility. Automated appointment reminders, delivered through SMS, email, or voice calls, play a vital role in minimizing no-show rates, optimizing clinic schedules, and enhancing patient engagement. Moreover, automated medication alerts provide an additional layer of safety by identifying potential drug interactions or allergies based on the patient's recorded data.

A tangible instance of automation is evident when a patient visits a clinic, where the automated system retrieves their EMR, alerting the physician to relevant information such as allergies or chronic conditions during the consultation. This comprehensive approach to automation not only enhances operational efficiencies but also significantly uplifts the quality of patient care.

Interaction With Customer Relationship Management

Electronic health record (EHR) systems, as well as customer relationship management (CRM) systems, are crucial for managing patient interactions across multiple communication channels, including phone, email, chat, and social media. Within CRM systems, automation plays a pivotal role in enhancing efficiency and patient satisfaction. Notably, the utilization of omnichannel routing allows for the automatic directing of inquiries to the appropriate agent based on specific variables such as skillset, language, or urgency.

The integration of AI-powered chatbots and virtual assistants further optimizes the process by efficiently handling routine inquiries, appointment scheduling, and management of frequently asked questions. Furthermore, automating follow-up communications, encompassing post-appointment follow-ups, surveys, and feedback requests, ensures consistent and ongoing patient engagement.

Additionally, real-time guidance offered to agents during calls significantly enhances their efficiency and the accuracy of the information provided. This may involve the integration of a knowledge base that provides up-to-date information on procedures, insurance coverage, and commonly asked questions.

Automated decision trees can also assist agents in navigating troubleshooting steps or escalation paths, while contextual pop-ups offer pertinent information, such as recent lab results during a call. For instance, in the scenario of a call concerning a prescription refill, real-time guidance ensures that the agent verifies the patient's identity, checks the prescription's status, and relays accurate instructions.

The introduction of automated coaching tools can substantially improve agent performance by ensuring adherence to best practices. Quality monitoring of call recordings facilitates the analysis of agent performance, pinpointing areas for improvement and enabling targeted coaching sessions. Ensuring script adherence contributes to maintaining consistency and reliability in patient communications.

In addition, providing automated feedback on soft skills, such as communication, empathy, and active listening, enhances the overall patient experience. For example, after a call, an automated system could evaluate an agent's tone, resolution time, and compliance adherence, subsequently offering personalized coaching tips to refine their approach. The comprehensive utilization of automation in CRM systems promotes a more efficient, accurate, and patient-centered approach to healthcare communication.

By implementing these automation strategies, healthcare contact centers can improve patient experiences, reduce operational costs, and ensure the delivery of accurate, timely support.

Challenges In Healthcare

The healthcare industry faces big challenges, especially with staff shortages and burnout, which have worsened because of the COVID-19 pandemic. The Association of American Medical Colleges (AAMC) predicts that there will be a shortage of over 50,000 healthcare workers within the next decade. This means that current healthcare professionals are struggling to meet patient needs, which affects the quality of care.

Rising healthcare costs are another major issue. These high costs are due to administrative expenses by insurance providers, payment models that focus on the number of services rather than their quality, and the high prices of pharmaceuticals and medical devices. New healthcare technologies, an aging population, and more chronic conditions also add to the problem. High costs make people avoid seeking necessary medical care, leading to undiagnosed or untreated conditions.

Despite spending a lot on healthcare, the United States often doesn't achieve better health outcomes. This highlights the need for strategies to lower costs and improve the efficiency of healthcare delivery. Ensuring data privacy and security is crucial for healthcare organizations, requiring strong measures to protect patient information while benefiting from automation tools.

Staff Shortages And Burnout

As mentioned briefly above, the healthcare industry faces a shortage of doctors and registered nurses (RNs). GlobalData Plc's 2023 report for the AAMC, "The Complexities of Physician Supply and

Demand: Projections From 2021 to 2036," analyzes supply and demand scenarios using current data on healthcare trends and physician habits. The report highlights that overburdened healthcare professionals are struggling to meet service demands, which affects patient care.

Rising Healthcare Costs

The rising healthcare costs are a pressing concern, attributed to several complex factors that intertwine and exacerbate the situation. One of the primary drivers behind these escalating costs is the significant role that insurance providers play, encompassing substantial administrative expenses. This scenario is further exacerbated by the prevailing payment models for medical providers, which tend to prioritize the quantity of services over the quality, often leading to unnecessary and costly medical procedures or tests.

Additionally, the escalating costs of pharmaceuticals and medical devices contribute significantly to the broader issue. The advent of new healthcare technologies, while advancing treatment possibilities, also comes with higher price tags, particularly in the U.S., where prices for these innovations are notably higher compared to other countries. This issue is further compounded by demographic shifts, including an aging population that naturally increases the demand for healthcare services, thereby driving up costs.

Moreover, the prevalence of chronic conditions, which require long-term care and management, places additional strain on healthcare expenditure. This situation results in a detrimental cycle where high healthcare costs deter individuals, especially those in worse health, from seeking the necessary medical care. This avoidance can lead to further health deterioration as conditions remain undiagnosed or untreated. Alarmingly, despite the substantial healthcare spending, the U.S. does not consistently see superior health outcomes, as evidenced by poor performance in various indicators of quality, such as life expectancy.

Given these challenges, it is imperative to address the issue of escalating healthcare costs through comprehensive strategies. By considering policy reforms, enhancing the efficiency of healthcare delivery, and promoting preventive care, it is possible to alleviate the financial burden on individuals while simultaneously improving health outcomes and the overall efficacy of the healthcare system.

Platform Implementation Costs

The integration of automation in healthcare systems is associated with both significant costs and challenges. These financial expenditures extend beyond the initial technology acquisition to include maintenance, upgrades, and staff training. For facilities operating with constrained resources, such costs can become prohibitive, delaying the realization of automation's benefits like efficiency enhancements and error reduction. This situation is particularly acute for smaller or rural healthcare entities that often lack the capital to invest in cutting-edge technological solutions. The expectation of a delayed return on investment adds another layer of complexity as the tangible benefits of automation unfold over time, posing a challenge in justifying the initial financial outlay.

Additionally, the deployment of automation technologies is fraught with the potential for system errors arising from various sources, such as software flaws, hardware malfunctions, or data integration problems. Such errors can disrupt healthcare operations, impede patient care, and, in severe cases, endanger patient safety. For instance, inaccuracies in automated medication dispensing systems could lead to serious medication errors.

The costs associated with identifying and rectifying these errors further strain limited budgets and, in extreme cases, may necessitate returning to manual procedures. This disruption not only impedes patient care but also erodes staff confidence in automated systems, complicating future technology adoptions. It underscores the necessity for meticulous planning, comprehensive testing, and ongoing vigilance to mitigate these challenges and facilitate a successful transition to automated healthcare processes.

Resistance To Change

Resistance to the introduction of new technologies presents a formidable challenge. Healthcare practitioners often adhere to established routines and practices, making them hesitant to embrace technological advancements that appear complex or cumbersome, fearing it could lead to job redundancy or lessen their significance in patient care. The apprehension toward change is not only due to the technical complexities associated with new systems but also stems from concerns over job security and the potential implications on their professional roles. As such, addressing both the tangible and psychological barriers to change is essential for fostering a conducive environment for technology adoption.

To navigate these challenges, a multifaceted approach emphasizing inclusion and education is pivotal. Engaging healthcare professionals in the technology selection process empowers them, ensuring that new systems align with their needs and are user-friendly.

Concurrently, a comprehensive training program is indispensable, equipping staff with the necessary skills and confidence to utilize new technologies effectively. Beyond practical considerations, it is crucial to address healthcare professionals' emotional and psychological reservations, offering reassurance regarding job security and articulating the benefits of technological advancements for personal and professional growth. Through these efforts, healthcare facilities can cultivate a supportive culture that embraces change, laying the groundwork for successful automation implementation.

Legacy Systems

Legacy systems in healthcare organizations, characterized by outdated information technology infrastructures, present significant challenges to operational efficiency and the integration of modern automation tools. These systems, while operational, lack the advanced features and flexibility of contemporary technologies, leading to compatibility issues and delays in data processing. For instance, an outdated electronic health record system may not be compatible with new automated appointment scheduling tools, hindering access to essential patient information. The need to transition from these legacy systems to cutting-edge technologies is evident to ensure seamless integration and enhance operational capabilities.

Transitioning to modern IT infrastructures requires meticulous planning and execution to minimize disruptions to healthcare operations. This involves conducting a thorough evaluation of existing systems, identifying the specific needs of the new system, and developing a detailed plan for the transition.

Key steps in this plan include data migration, system testing, and comprehensive staff training to ensure a smooth changeover while maintaining operational continuity. Despite the significant financial investment and the logistical challenges involved, upgrading to modern technologies is indispensable for healthcare organizations. It improves operational efficiency and patient care and contributes to establishing a more sustainable healthcare system by leveraging digital transformation and automation advancements.

Data Privacy And Security

Data privacy and security hold paramount importance in the healthcare system, with healthcare organizations bearing the critical responsibility of safeguarding patient data against breaches. This data encompasses sensitive details such as medical histories and personal identifiers, safeguarded under laws like the Health Insurance Portability and Accountability Act (HIPAA) in the United States. Ensuring adherence to these regulations is essential not only to comply with legal requirements but also to maintain patients' trust. However, adopting automation tools presents a dual challenge for these organizations: they must harness the efficiency and accuracy benefits these tools offer while protecting sensitive patient information from potential cyber threats.

To effectively balance the boon of automation with the imperative of data security, healthcare organizations are tasked with deploying robust security measures like encryption and access controls. This approach requires meticulous strategic planning to assess data security needs, select suitable automation tools, and devise a foolproof plan for their secure implementation. Engaging stakeholders—including healthcare professionals, patients, and technology vendors—in the planning process ensures that the automation solutions meet the multifaceted needs of all parties involved and uphold stringent data protection standards. Ultimately, a steadfast commitment to improving patient care through secure, well-implemented automation initiatives allows healthcare organizations to advance healthcare delivery without compromising on the essential pillars of data privacy and security.

Numerous challenges are associated with healthcare in general, emphasizing the need for thoughtful implementation of automation and AI. The healthcare industry is grappling with staff shortages, particularly among doctors and registered nurses, leading to widespread burnout. At the same time, healthcare costs are on the rise due to complex factors, while cybersecurity threats loom larger with the shift toward digital health records and telemedicine. Additionally, integrating automation into healthcare systems incurs substantial costs and hurdles, encompassing initial technology acquisition, maintenance, upgrades, and staff training.

Moreover, healthcare practitioners' reluctance to adopt new technologies due to their complexity and potential impact on job security poses a significant barrier. This resistance is further complicated by the presence of legacy systems, which hinder operational efficiency and the integration of modern tools. Amidst these challenges, maintaining data privacy and security remains a critical responsibility for healthcare organizations, underscoring the importance of protecting patient data against breaches.

Top Automation Use Cases In Healthcare

There are numerous opportunities to use AI and other forms of automation in healthcare scenarios. Let's look at the most popular use cases that address some challenges.

Billing And Claims Queries

In the context of assisting patients with billing inquiries, insurance claims, and payment-related issues, various personas play crucial roles. Patients often seek to understand billing details and insurance coverage or resolve billing issues and insurance claims. Their primary intent is to inquire about billing statements and insurance claims and request prior authorization for procedures or medications. However, they face challenges navigating complex billing systems and insurance processes while managing multiple bills and payment deadlines.

Healthcare specialists aim to ensure patients receive prompt help and provide excellent service. Their primary tasks involve verifying the reason for calls and transferring them to the appropriate person or department. However, they face challenges managing a high volume of calls and balancing administrative tasks like taking notes and caller information while on the phone.

Billing specialists focus on verifying claim denials and improving reimbursement rates while providing excellent service to patients. Their tasks include processing and verifying insurance claim submissions and assisting patients with all billing-related questions. They often face challenges managing a high volume of insurance claims and billing inquiries and ensuring accuracy in medical coding and billing processes.

To address these challenges, technology, specifically AI, can play a significant role. AI-powered prior authorization systems are designed to streamline the process by analyzing a wealth of data, including patient's medical history and treatment plans. These systems predict the likelihood of authorization approval based on historical data and clinical guidelines, improving efficiency and accuracy in the authorization process.

Healthcare institutions are increasingly implementing natural language processing (NLP) for automated medical coding. AI models extract pertinent information from unstructured data sources such as clinical notes and physician documentation, automating the assignment of billing codes for procedures, diagnoses, and treatments. This ensures accurate billing codes, such as CPT for procedures and ICD-10 for diseases, are assigned efficiently.

Robotic process automation (RPA) for claims management uses bots to execute routine tasks like validating patient information, verifying coverage, and processing claims quickly. Bots can also identify discrepancies or errors in claims submissions, flagging them for review to reduce claim denials and facilitate faster reimbursement.

AI-driven virtual assistants can revolutionize how patient queries about bills, copayments, and payment plans are handled by delivering

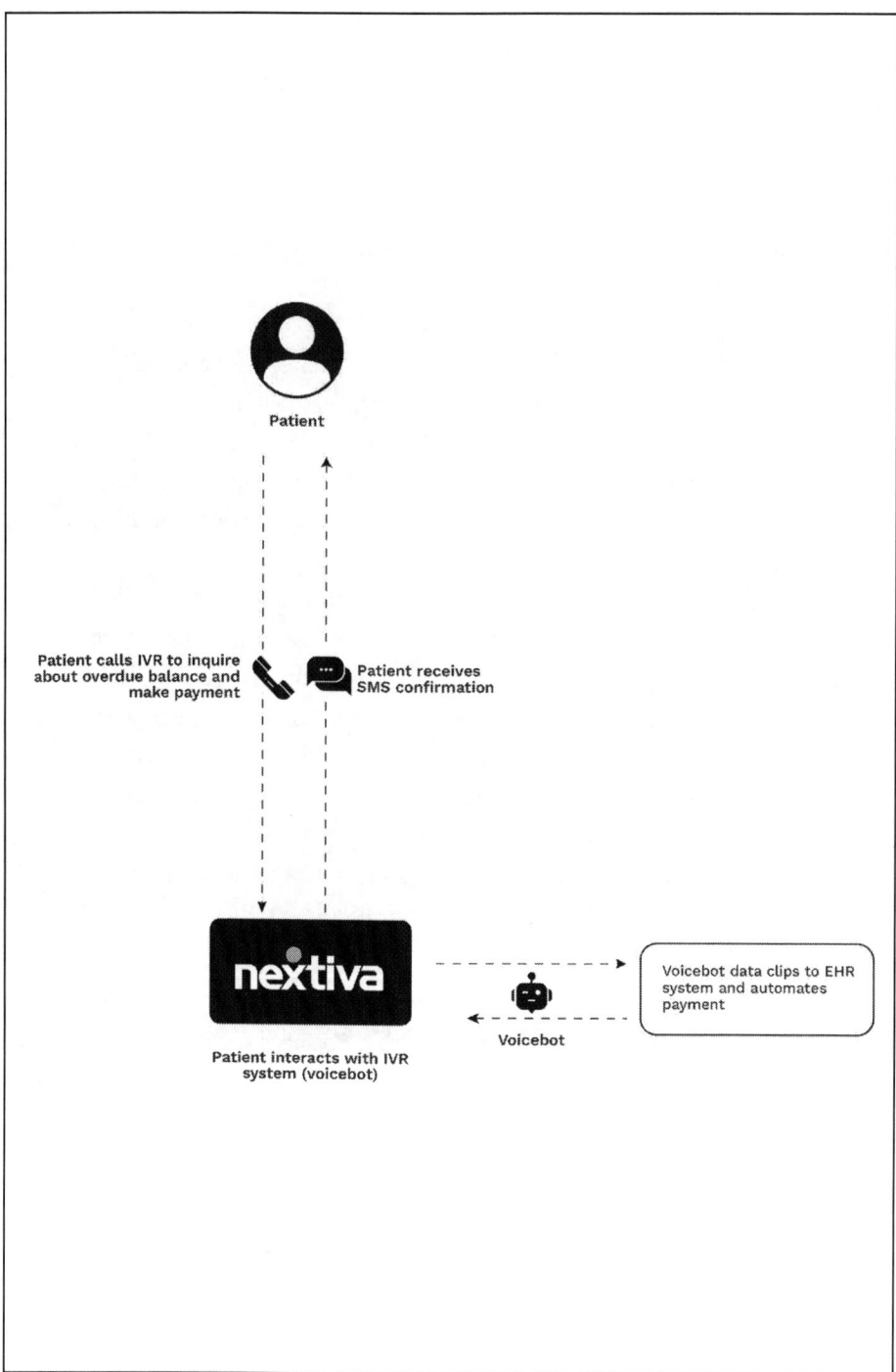

Figure 16: Billing and claims query using voicebot

accurate information and guiding patients through payment procedures. These systems can also send personalized reminders to patients with outstanding balances via SMS, email, or phone calls, improving payment compliance and reducing accounts receivable.

In fraud detection and prevention, AI-based anomaly detection models analyze billing data to detect unusual patterns that might indicate fraud or billing errors. Predictive analytics, powered by AI algorithms, identify high-risk claims early, allowing insurers to prevent improper payments and enhance billing process security.

Finally, AI can generate short, clear summaries for explanation of benefits (EOB), replacing long, traditional documents. These summaries explain services provided, insurance coverage, and patient financial responsibility, improving understanding and reducing confusion.

Overall, integrating AI and automation into healthcare systems enhances efficiency and accuracy, reduces administrative burdens, ensures accurate billing, facilitates faster reimbursements, and ultimately improves the overall patient experience.

As an example of how AI and automation can be used in such a billing or claims query scenario, the illustration here depicts how a patient initiates a query by calling an interactive voice response (IVR) system to pay an overdue balance. The IVR system (aka voicebot) interacts with the caller to gather information and route the call accordingly. Once the patient makes the payment, an SMS confirmation is sent to them, confirming that the payment has been processed successfully.

The IVR system is integrated with a unified customer experience management platform, such as what is available from Nextiva. The IVR handles the interaction between the patient and the healthcare system, utilizing a chatbot to facilitate the process. This chatbot interacts with the patient, aiding and ensuring that the payment process is smooth and efficient.

Subsequently, the data from the voicebot is automatically integrated into the electronic health records (EHR) system. This automation ensures that the patient's payment is accurately recorded and updated in their health records, streamlining the billing process and reducing the need for manual intervention.

This process highlights the efficiency and effectiveness of integrating technology in healthcare settings to handle billing and insurance queries, thereby improving operational efficiency and enhancing the overall patient experience.

In summary, artificial intelligence (AI) can be put to work to significantly enhance patient support regarding billing inquiries, insurance claims, and payment-related issues through various applications. Automated prior authorization, facilitated by AI, optimizes the evaluation of a patient's medical history and treatment plans to verify

Table 22: Benefits of automated billing and claim queries

Automated billing and claim queries capabilities	Chief benefits
AI-powered prior authorization	Improves efficiency and accuracy of the prior authorization process; enhances patient care by predicting the likelihood of an authorization being approved
Automated medical coding	Ensures accurate assignment of billing codes for procedures, diagnoses, and treatments; facilitates efficient conversion of physician's narrative into standardized codes
Claims management process automation	Enhances efficiency by surpassing manual methods in claim processing; reduces errors by identifying discrepancies in claims submissions
Patient billing chatbots	Provides accurate information and navigates patients through payment procedures; enhances payment compliance by dispatching personalized reminders to patients
Automation for explanation of benefits	Improves patient understanding by offering clear and concise explanations; reduces confusion about the services provided, insurance coverage, and financial responsibility

insurance coverage for designated procedures or medications. This AI capability notably augments the probability of authorization approval, thereby enhancing both efficiency and accuracy. Moreover, healthcare institutions are adopting natural language processing (NLP) technologies for automated medical coding. By extracting essential information from unstructured data, AI models support the automation of medical coding, promoting the accurate assignment of billing codes.

Additionally, robotic process automation (RPA) can be leveraged to help claims management perform routine tasks more efficiently than traditional manual approaches. Furthermore, AI-enabled bots can be used to identify inaccuracies or errors in claims submissions, contributing to a reduction in claim denials and accelerating the reimbursement process. Overall, the deployment of AI-powered applications can vastly improve the management of patient inquiries concerning bills, copayments, and payment plans. AI can also offer precise information and even issue personalized reminders to patients with pending balances.

Appointment Scheduling

Contact center practitioners in healthcare can utilize AI-powered chatbots and robotic process automation (RPA) to handle repetitive customer service tasks. These advanced solutions can be programmed to converse with patients regarding their health concerns. Furthermore, chatbots can assist patients in navigating through different systems to find suitable doctors and available appointment times and facilitate the scheduling process with much less friction than manual methods. This allows patients to easily set, reschedule, or cancel their appointments through the chatbot interface. These advancements boost employee productivity by freeing them from mundane tasks and significantly reduce no-shows through timely reminders and follow-ups. Additionally, patients can enjoy a seamless customer service experience available 24/7, making healthcare access more efficient and user-friendly.

Here are several use cases using automated routines, agent-assisted routines, and hybrids.

In a scenario where live agents assist with appointment scheduling, they play a crucial role during the post-transaction wrap-up process by helping patients set up future appointments. This becomes particularly relevant after a patient has undergone a consultation or procedure. By utilizing the data collected from surveys designed for agent viewing, these agents can gain insights into the patient's forthcoming healthcare requirements. Subsequently, leveraging this understanding, they can schedule follow-up appointments that align with the patient's documented preferences. This approach not only guarantees a seamless continuation of the patient's healthcare journey but also significantly enhances their experience by offering care that is tailored to their specific needs.

Another approach to appointment setting is a hybrid system that combines the efficiency of AI with the personal touch of a live agent. Following an interaction with a patient, the live agent inputs the necessary information into the system. The AI then uses this data to automatically arrange an appointment based on the patient's preferences and sends out an electronic "appointment card." The system also sends reminders to the patient via their preferred communication channel. If the patient wishes to reschedule or has any queries, they can directly contact the live agent. This system ensures that the scheduling process is efficient while still providing the patient with the option to interact with a human if needed.

These use cases demonstrate how the integration of live agents into the appointment scheduling process can provide a more personalized and efficient service to patients. They also highlight the potential of combining AI and human intervention to enhance the overall patient experience. By implementing such systems, healthcare providers can ensure that their services are efficient, effective, and patient-centric.

In addition, an AI-driven system can be designed to send personalized appointment reminders to patients efficiently. By monitoring upcoming appointments, it ensures that reminders are sent out through SMS, email, or any other channel preferred by the patient. This not only substantially reduces the number of no-shows but also optimizes clinic schedules and significantly improves patients' adherence to their appointment schedules.

Figure 17: Automation in appointment scheduling

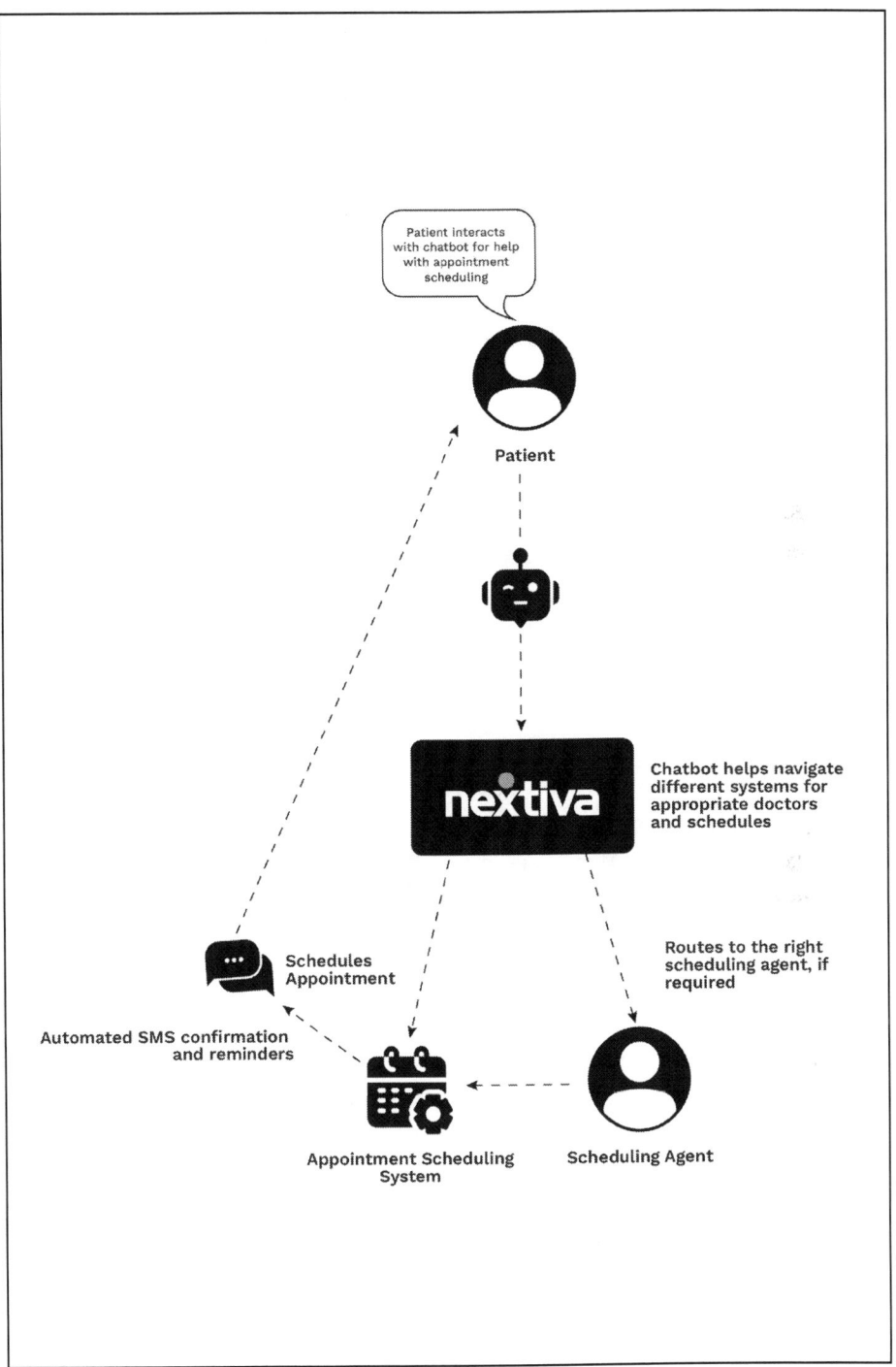

Artificial intelligence systems may also be employed to manage waitlists for appointments efficiently. Imagine the capability to monitor cancellations in real time and swiftly reschedule patients from the waitlist into newly available slots. Furthermore, AI can be used to assess and prioritize patients based on the urgency of their medical conditions. This ensures that those in critical need receive care promptly. The implementation of such technology not only enhances the utilization of healthcare resources but also significantly reduces the waiting period for patients. Additionally, by ensuring that patients with urgent healthcare needs are prioritized, the overall quality of care provided is substantially improved.

An appointment scheduling application can be further enhanced with AI to enable predictive scheduling. Machine learning algorithms can be programmed to predict the likelihood of no-shows or cancellations. By analyzing historical data, including a patient's past appointment history and other relevant factors, these predictions can be made. The system can then intelligently overbook appointments, ensuring that the healthcare provider's time is utilized efficiently, even in cases of no-shows or cancellations. This capability promises to improve the productivity of healthcare providers and reduce idle time. Additionally, it ensures that more patients can receive care within the same timeframe, thereby improving patient satisfaction.

In summary, the integration of live agents and AI into the appointment scheduling process significantly enhances the efficiency and personalization of patient care. Live agents utilize patient data and feedback to schedule follow-up appointments that cater to individual healthcare needs, ensuring a seamless healthcare journey. Moreover, combining AI's efficiency with the human touch of live agents offers a hybrid system where artificial intelligence handles appointment scheduling, sends electronic reminders, and enables patients to interact with live agents for a personalized experience. This method ensures effectiveness and patient satisfaction by blending swift scheduling with personal attention.

Furthermore, AI-driven systems extend their utility by sending personalized reminders, managing waitlists efficiently, and employing predictive scheduling to improve healthcare resource utilization. They monitor real-time cancellations to offer timely appointments to waitlisted patients and utilize machine learning to anticipate no-shows or cancellations, allowing for intelligent overbooking.

This technology-driven approach reduces patient waiting times and no-show rates and prioritizes urgent medical needs, enhancing the overall quality of care and patient satisfaction. These advancements promise a more patient-centric service, optimizing healthcare providers' productivity and elevating the patient experience through timely and personalized care.

Table 23: Benefits of automation in appointment scheduling

Appointment scheduling capability	Chief benefits
Live agent-assisted scheduling with downstream process automation	Ensures continuity in the patient's healthcare journey; enhances the patient's experience by providing personalized care; improves patient satisfaction and adherence to their appointment schedules
Hybrid appointment scheduling	Provides a more efficient scheduling process; offers the patient the option to interact with a human if needed; enhances the overall patient experience by combining AI efficiency with human touch; ensures that the healthcare provider's services are patient-centric
AI-driven personalized appointment reminders	Substantially reduces the number of no-shows; optimizes facility schedules; improves patients' adherence to their appointment schedules
AI-powered waitlist management	Enhances the utilization of healthcare resources; significantly reduces the waiting period for patients; ensures that patients with urgent healthcare needs are prioritized, improving the overall quality of care
Predictive scheduling with AI	Improves the productivity of healthcare providers and reduces idle time by intelligently overbooking appointments; ensures that more patients can receive care within the same timeframe, thereby improving patient satisfaction

Figure 18: Automation of medication refills

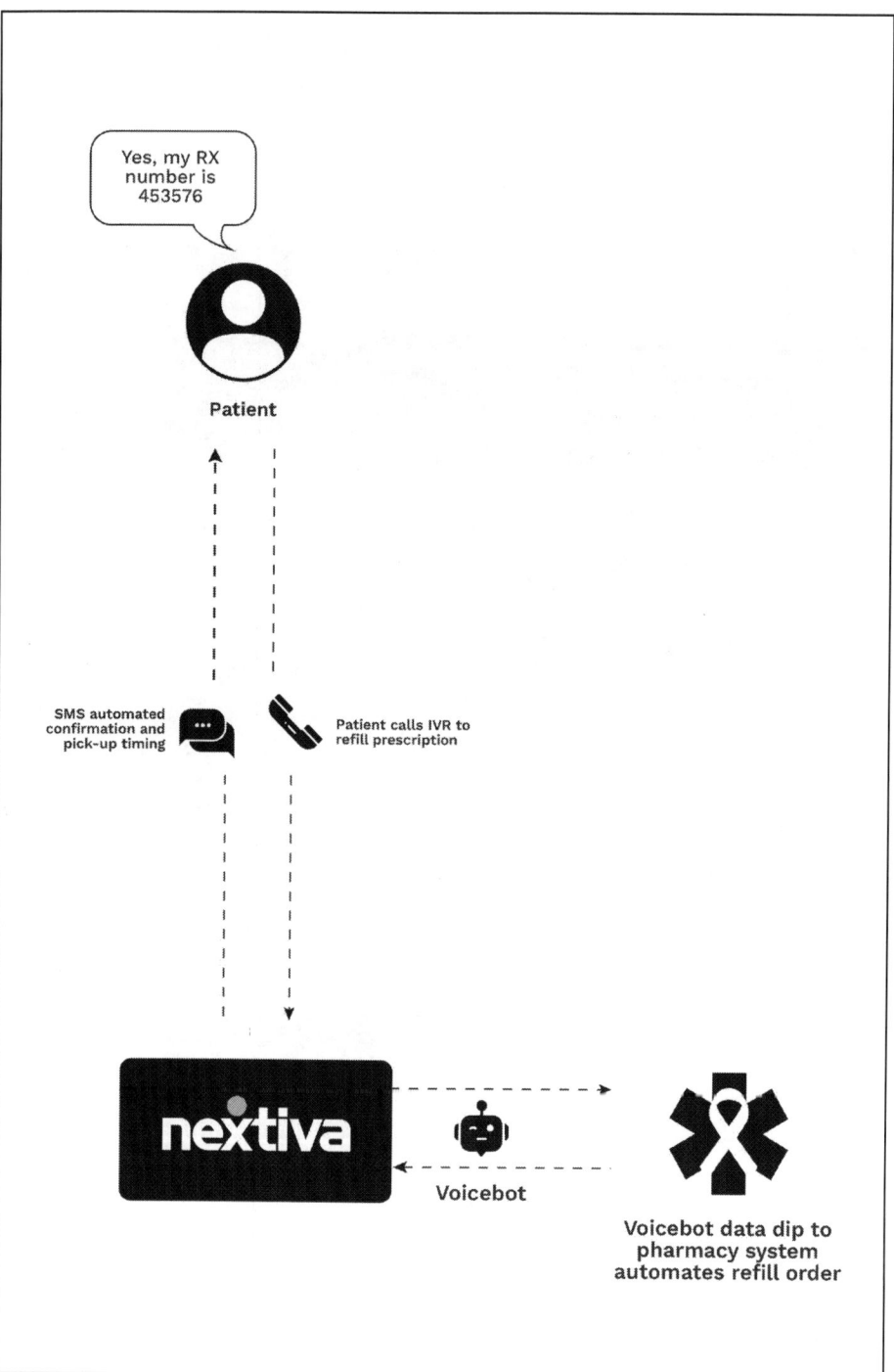

Medication Refills

In the ever-evolving healthcare landscape, automation and artificial intelligence (AI) are fundamentally reshaping conventional practices, particularly within prescription refill services. Sophisticated systems, such as telephonic prescription refill mechanisms integrating interactive voice response (IVR) and natural language processing (NLP), are revolutionizing patients' medication management processes.

These systems, complemented by live customer service support, virtual assistants, and integrated medication management services, are meticulously crafted to streamline refill procedures, alleviate the burden on healthcare providers, and enrich the patient's experience.

The fusion of technology and human intervention exemplifies AI's potential in delivering efficient, impactful, and patient-centric healthcare services. From automating refill requests to optimizing inventory management, AI is at the vanguard of fostering operational efficiency and enhancing health outcomes.

The development of an over-the-phone prescription refill system that incorporates IVR and NLP offers a modern solution to traditional pharmacy practices. This innovative system is adept at understanding and processing refill requests made verbally by patients. Upon receiving a call for a refill, the system, powered by NLP, swiftly kicks into action, interpreting the patient's spoken requests. It then validates these requests against the patient's medical records before proceeding with the refill.

Designed to cater to patients who either prefer or require telephonic communication for such tasks, this system significantly reduces the workload of healthcare providers by handling a large volume of refill requests autonomously. Additionally, its capability to operate 24/7 ensures that patients can request prescription refills at their convenience, offering unprecedented flexibility in managing their medications.

Providing live customer service assistance for prescription refills involves a unique approach where a live agent assists patients directly.

When patients call for help with their prescription refills, the customer service agent can immediately access their records and medication history through an electronic health record (EHR) system. Using an "agent-facing shopping cart," the agent is then able to facilitate the refill process for the patient. This method offers a high level of personalized support, particularly beneficial for those who are unable or prefer not to use automated systems. By ensuring the refill process is both accurate and efficient, the likelihood of errors is significantly reduced. Additionally, the agent's ability to answer any questions enhances the overall patient experience and satisfaction with the service.

These use cases illustrate the potential of combining technology and human intervention in the healthcare industry. By implementing systems like these, healthcare providers can offer services that are efficient, effective, and centered around the patient's needs and preferences. They also highlight the potential of using AI and human intervention together to enhance the overall patient experience. By implementing such systems, healthcare providers can ensure that their services are not only efficient and effective but also patient-centric. This approach can lead to improved patient satisfaction, better adherence to medication schedules, and, ultimately, better health outcomes.

Apart from IVR and agent-assisted refills, virtual assistants can also be utilized to automate prescription refills. The use of AI technology enables the automation of prescription refills, offering a way to enhance efficiency in healthcare settings. Many healthcare providers are beginning to adopt cloud-based AI applications that seamlessly integrate with electronic health records (EHRs). These systems simplify the refill process by receiving and processing requests, consolidating patient data, and using an evidence-based rules engine to validate each request. Consequently, healthcare providers can reduce the clerical workload, with the majority of requests being managed without the need for provider review, thereby saving time for clinical staff. In addition to pharmacy operations, chatbots can also play a crucial role in automating medication refills by facilitating approvals, communicating with pharmacies, and alerting patients.

Another scenario where refills are important is in integrated medication management services. These services involve keeping track of a patient's medication history and prescription costs and using automated messaging to send reminders and educational messages to patients. Reminders are helpful in keeping patients on schedule with their medications, ensuring their overall health is not negatively affected due to running out of medications. Furthermore, proactive wellness care improves patient awareness and overall health. Additionally, generative AI can be employed to improve stock management and accuracy in filling prescriptions. Amazon already uses AI for this purpose. AI helps optimize medication stock levels and speeds up the prescription fulfillment process. Utilizing AI in healthcare institutions strategically boosts operational efficiency and enhances patient care simultaneously.

In summary, automated or semi-automated prescription refills offer providers an excellent way to enhance the experience of patients who rely on a dependable method to receive their medications accurately and on time. From interactive voice response (IVR) and natural language processing (NLP) systems for over-the-phone requests to live customer service support and integrated medication management services, the potential is truly exciting. These innovative solutions can quickly understand and process verbal refill requests, provide instant

Table 24: Benefits of automated medication refills

Medication refill capability	Chief benefits
Over-the-phone prescription refill systems	Reduces healthcare providers' workload by handling large volume of refill requests autonomously; operates 24/7, allowing patients to request prescription refills at their convenience
Live customer service with automation assistance for prescription refills	Offers personalized support; reduces the likelihood of errors; enhances the patient experience and satisfaction with the service
Virtual assistants for automating prescription refills	Reduces clerical workload, saves time for clinical staff, enhances efficiency in healthcare settings
AI-based medication management services	Keeps patients on schedule with their medications, improves patient awareness and overall health, optimizes medication stock levels, speeds up the prescription fulfillment process, boosts operational efficiency, and enhances patient care

access to patient records, automate prescription refills, and monitor medication history.

The benefits are numerous: reduced workload for healthcare providers, around-the-clock availability, personalized assistance, and increased efficiency. Moreover, the incorporation of AI in these systems not only ensures precision and convenience but also enhances overall health outcomes. This harmonious integration of technology and human touch is streamlining healthcare services and fostering a more patient-focused approach, nurturing optimism and a brighter future for healthcare.

Health Information Access

Automated and AI-driven systems for prescription refills and health information access are revolutionizing healthcare operations. Over-the-phone systems, virtual assistants, and AI-based medication management services streamline prescription refills by handling large volumes of requests, reducing healthcare providers' clerical workload, and improving patient convenience and satisfaction.

Implementing advanced health information access systems helps healthcare entities avoid non-compliance penalties and enhances data security. AI-powered routines monitor patient portals for HIPAA compliance, automatically document actions, and deploy machine learning to identify potential threats, providing a robust security layer compared to human monitors.

In healthcare contact centers, agent assist technology can enhance patient safety by providing accurate information about medications, reducing the time agents spend on information retrieval, and supporting nurse practitioners in delivering timely and well-informed guidance. This approach helps prevent medication errors and improves patient satisfaction by ensuring they receive accurate and comprehensive information.

AI-driven medication management services, using chatbots or IVR systems, aid in medication adherence by delivering reminders and educational content and responding to patient queries. These systems ensure patient data privacy and security while improving engagement and health outcomes through automated support and proactive monitoring.

In summary, automated health information access is increasingly common, providing personalized data and aiding compliance with regulations like HIPAA. Automation can also benefit contact center–based systems, reducing information retrieval time and improving overall efficiency. AI-driven medication management services can also be implemented using chatbots or IVR systems to manage patient medication adherence through automated messages. We've only scratched the surface of the number of viable use cases for health information access that can leverage automation.

Table 25: Benefits of health information access use cases

Health information access capability	Chief benefits
Automated access to health information with automated detection of non-compliance to HIPAA	Avoidance of non-compliance penalties: Automated compliance helps healthcare entities uphold stringent compliance with healthcare regulations, thereby avoiding penalties associated with non-compliance. Enhanced security: AI-powered routines can swiftly detect and address threats, providing an additional layer of security for patient data compared to human monitors.
Knowledge base (KB) form of agent assistance for care coaches	By ensuring that patients receive accurate and comprehensive information about their medications, KB technology can play a crucial role in enhancing patient safety and satisfaction. It can help prevent medication errors and adverse drug events, which are significant issues in healthcare.
AI-based summarization of healthcare calls	AI can also analyze the data from the interactions between the agents and patients. These insights can be used to identify common issues or concerns among patients, allowing healthcare providers to address them proactively.
AI-driven medication management services (bot or IVR)	Improve patient engagement and medication best practices adherence, which equate to improved health outcomes.

Telehealth Support

Automated health information access is becoming more common, helping healthcare entities comply with regulations such as HIPAA and enhancing security with AI-powered routines. AI systems can monitor and address threats more efficiently than human monitors, preventing non-compliance penalties. AI-based summarization tools analyze healthcare calls, providing insights into common concerns and improving proactive care.

Telehealth support involves using digital technologies for remote healthcare services. AI-powered chatbots facilitate personalized consultations, though human intervention remains essential for complex cases to ensure optimal patient care. This balance between AI and human expertise enhances the telehealth experience.

Remote patient monitoring (RPM) systems utilize wearable devices to collect health data and enable early detection of health issues and timely intervention. AI algorithms analyze this data, triggering alerts for healthcare providers about potential concerns. RPM systems help reduce hospital readmissions and improve patient outcomes by continually monitoring patients' health.

Clinical decision support systems (CDSS) offer evidence-based recommendations for patient care. AI-based CDSS enhances healthcare delivery by managing patient dialogues and providing relevant medical guidelines. These systems use a comprehensive medical knowledge base, allowing healthcare providers to make informed decisions, resulting in improved patient outcomes and satisfaction.

Telehealth solutions combine AI and human expertise to enhance healthcare delivery. Chatbots with human support and RPM systems facilitate early detection of health issues, enabling timely medical intervention and reducing hospital readmissions. These systems ensure that healthcare providers are alerted to potential health concerns, improving patient outcomes.

AI-powered tools like CDSS improve care quality by offering personalized patient care and freeing clinicians' time for direct patient interaction by automating routine tasks. This integration extends quality healthcare to remote areas, ensures swift responses to health anomalies, and achieves cost savings by detecting issues early and efficiently allocating resources.

Table 26: Benefits of telehealth automation

Telehealth automation capability	Chief benefits
Telehealth chatbots with human intervention	Achieving a balance between AI and human expertise is crucial for providing an effective and empathetic telehealth experience
Remote patient monitoring data collection and anomaly detection	RPM systems facilitate early detection of health issues, enabling timely intervention and treatment, thus reducing the likelihood of more severe health complications. Also, by continually monitoring patients' health and signaling potential concerns to healthcare providers, RPM systems can help reduce hospital readmissions, leading to improved patient outcomes and optimized utilization of healthcare resources.
AI-based clinical decision support systems for clinical recommendations	Continuous learning can lead to progressively better patient care. Another benefit is that AI can help provide personalized care by considering the patient's unique medical history and current health status when making recommendations.
CDSS note-taking with AI	Automation routines can quickly process and analyze large amounts of data, reducing the time clinicians spend on data analysis and increasing the time they can spend interacting with patients. In addition, AI can help reduce errors in diagnosis and treatment by providing evidence-based recommendations, leading to more accurate and reliable patient care. By improving efficiency and reducing errors, AI can lead to significant cost savings in the healthcare sector.
CDSS remote accessibility	AI-powered telehealth can provide access to high-quality healthcare in remote areas or for patients who cannot visit a healthcare facility.
Remote patient monitoring with contact center linkage	RPM allows for real-time monitoring of patient's health data, enabling immediate response to any detected anomalies. Contact centers can quickly respond to emergencies based on alerts from the RPM system, potentially saving lives by dispatching ambulances or contacting relevant healthcare providers.
Automation of remote patient monitoring with interactive voice response and bots	IVR systems may be used to automate initial patient outreach, saving time and resources while ensuring patients are promptly contacted when an anomaly is detected. In addition, AI bots continuously analyze incoming data to spot trends and provide immediate feedback or advice to patients based on their health indicators.
Remote patient monitoring data collection with AI	By reducing unnecessary hospital visits and enabling healthcare providers to focus on patients who need immediate attention, RPM fosters a more efficient allocation of healthcare resources. Timely and appropriate care enabled by RPM leads to enhanced patient outcomes. By reducing hospital admissions and enabling early detection of health issues, RPM can lead to significant cost savings in the healthcare sector.

Healthcare Process Navigation

Navigating the complex processes of healthcare can be overwhelming for patients. This journey can be significantly streamlined by integrating automation, artificial intelligence (AI), contact center technology, and human expertise.

Automation can handle repetitive tasks, improving efficiency. With its ability to analyze vast amounts of data, AI can provide valuable insights and guide patients through their healthcare journey. Contact center technology ensures timely and accurate responses to inquiries, while human beings bring a level of empathy and understanding that is crucial in healthcare, especially for complex or sensitive issues.

Together, these elements work in harmony to help patients understand and navigate complex healthcare processes, ultimately enhancing patient experience and outcomes. For instance, AI-powered chatbots can handle routine customer service tasks, freeing human agents to focus on more complex issues. This integration allows patients to schedule their appointments and manage their health more effectively.

AI-enabled RPA bots can automate tasks like prior authorization and claims processing, making these processes more efficient and understandable for patients. While AI and automation improve accuracy and reduce manual effort, live agents remain crucial for dealing with complex or emotionally charged tasks. This balanced approach ensures patients feel supported and informed throughout their healthcare journey.

In summary, navigating the intricate healthcare landscape presents considerable challenges for patients. The amalgamation of automation, artificial intelligence, contact center technology, and human expertise markedly enhances the efficiency and clarity of this process. Automation streamlines operations by managing routine tasks, whereas AI offers deep insights, guiding patients comprehensively through their healthcare journey. Contact center technology ensures prompt and precise responses to queries, acting as an essential conduit between patients and healthcare providers. Importantly, the human element adds a layer of empathy and understanding that is vital in healthcare, particularly when addressing complex or sensitive matters.

These components synchronize to demystify the healthcare navigation process for patients, thereby improving their experience and overall outcomes. For example, deploying AI-powered chatbots in conjunction with robotic process automation (RPA) bots alleviates the burden on human agents by taking on standard customer service tasks, allowing them to concentrate on more intricate issues. This

Table 27: Table: Benefits of automated healthcare process navigation

Automated healthcare process navigation capability	Chief benefits
AI-powered chatbots integrated with robotic process automation	This integration enables handling routine customer service tasks, freeing human agents to focus on more complex issues; it also empowers patients with the ability to schedule their appointments, thereby streamlining the process and offering flexibility
AI-enhanced appointment scheduling	Makes the scheduling process flexible and patient-centered, reducing the likelihood of missed appointments
Live agent assistance in conjunction with AI and automation	Live agents provide a personal touch, stepping in when necessary for complex health issues or specific scheduling requirements
RPA bots automating prior authorization	This not only speeds up the process but also helps patients understand why certain services or medications are approved or denied
Automation of claims processing	The automation of this process leads to quicker responses to claims, which not only expedites the process but also aids patients in understanding how their claims are processed and evaluated
Interactive voice response (IVR) for claims inquiries	These systems provide automated responses at any time, offering convenience to patients who may ask about claims when no live agents are available

optimization not only makes the process more efficient but also aids patients in understanding the rationale behind the approval or denial of services or medications.

Moreover, AI systems are instrumental in managing patient appointments and issuing reminders to mitigate missed appointments. Should a patient need to reschedule or cancel, the AI system can promptly adapt, demonstrating the system's flexibility and patient-centric approach. Despite the advantages of automation, the compassionate interaction provided by live agents remains indispensable, especially for emotionally sensitive tasks such as claims processing.

Discharge Planning

Discharge planning, a critical part of transitioning patients from hospital to home care, benefits significantly from automation, artificial intelligence (AI), and contact center technology. AI can provide tailored post-discharge instructions that align with each patient's medical condition and home environment. This not only saves time for healthcare providers but also enhances the patient's experience by offering clear, personalized guidance.

Automated alerts throughout the patient's journey, including reminders for wound care and medication adherence, help minimize complications and improve care plan adherence. These alerts, sent through preferred communication channels, offer convenience and underscore the preventive aspect of healthcare. AI systems can also efficiently schedule follow-up appointments, considering patient and provider availability, and integrate with patient portals for seamless access and control over scheduling.

Medication management post-discharge is another area where AI and automation shine. AI can analyze patient records to identify potential medication interactions and discrepancies, with automated systems alerting contact centers to initiate timely communication with patients. This integration with electronic health records (EHRs) ensures that updated medication lists are readily available for personalized advice during patient interactions.

Contact centers equipped with AI tools provide continuous support for patients with questions about their medication regimen.

Automated reminders for medication refills or intakes boost adherence, while the contact center's proactive engagement ensures comprehensive care. The continuous learning capability of AI systems further enhances their effectiveness, providing insights to contact center agents for better patient support.

In summary, the strategic integration of journey orchestration, automation, and AI in contact centers improves personalized

Table 28: Benefits of AI-enabled discharge planning

AI-enabled discharge planning capability	Chief benefits
AI-aided post-discharge instructions	Enhances efficiency and saves valuable time for healthcare providers and patients alike
Automated alerts for the patient journey	Enhances adherence to care plans to minimize the risk of complications; underscores the preventive aspect of healthcare management
Automatic scheduling of follow-up calls	Delivery of consistent and accurate instructions; ensures adherence to prescribed care instructions; allows agents to concentrate efforts on handling more nuanced and complex patient interactions
Automatic scheduling of follow-up appointments in tandem with portals	Empowers patients by giving them control over their care schedule and enhances accessibility with 24/7 availability
AI-based medication review	Can initiate immediate communication to address any concerns, thereby reducing the risk of adverse drug events
Contact center linkage with AI and electronic health records (EHRs)	Enhances the accuracy of sharing medication lists with patients and their primary care providers; provides agents with data to offer personalized advice and respond to patient inquiries with greater accuracy
Proactive patient engagement	Aids in boosting medication adherence and enhances overall patient outcomes

post-discharge instructions for patients. By tailoring instructions to individual needs, these technologies enhance relevance and efficiency while saving time for providers and patients. Automated alerts for wound care, medication adherence, and symptom monitoring improve adherence to care plans. AI systems handling routine tasks allow live agents to focus on complex interactions, optimizing resource allocation. Despite the benefits of AI and automation, human intervention remains crucial for addressing complex issues and ensuring a blend of technology and human touch that optimizes post-discharge care and patient engagement.

Compassionate Communication

Effective communication filled with compassion is a cornerstone in healthcare, setting the stage for a trusting relationship, reducing patient worry, and elevating the overall care experience. Recognized standards exist that specify what good compassionate communication looks like in practice.

Take, for instance, the Motivational Interviewing Treatment Integrity (MITI) standard. This tool measures how well healthcare professionals use motivational interviewing methods—a type of counseling that helps people find the motivation to make positive decisions and stick to them. Behavioral health groups often turn to the MITI standard to fine-tune their team's ability to listen in a way that reflects what the patient is saying.

This kind of listening, known as reflective listening, actively shows understanding and thoughtful consideration of the patient's words. Reflective listening involves accurately capturing and reflecting back on patients' thoughts and feelings, validating their experiences. This technique not only aids in rapport-building but also motivates patients to discuss their concerns and motivations more openly, resulting in richer, more productive dialogue.

Beyond evaluation, the MITI framework is a tool for constructive feedback aimed at refining how care is given outside of research settings. It helps to ensure a consistent level of skill and ethical practice in these interactions. In essence, embedding MITI-informed agent-assist

Table 29: Benefits of compassionate communication assistance

Compassionate communication assistance capability	Chief benefits
Emotion recognition	AI analyzes facial expressions and voice tone to enhance empathy and active listening in telehealth
Language translation	AI overcomes language barriers, allowing for communication in preferred languages and promoting mutual understanding
Agent assists in compassionate communication	AI aids in helping agents stay engaged using reflective listening and compassionate orientation, putting patients at ease
Chatbot engagement	Offers personalized information and empathetic support, improving patient engagement and the organization's reputation

technology in healthcare customer service centers fosters a more supportive, patient-centric care atmosphere.

In conclusion, artificial intelligence and automation present substantial advantages in compassionate communication within the healthcare sector. These technologies can enhance empathetic exchanges and streamline patient care through applications such as emotion recognition in telehealth, mitigating language barriers, customized patient interaction via chatbots, and agent-assist technology to provide real-time coaching for agents to uphold compassionate communication ideals. Consequently, automation and AI can play a pivotal role in improving the healthcare experience and cultivating a favorable industry reputation.

Difficult Situation Handling

The integration of AI and automation in contact centers significantly enhances the delivery of personalized post-discharge instructions. By tailoring information to individual needs, these technologies not only improve the relevance and efficiency of communication but also save time for providers and patients. Automated alerts for wound care, medication adherence, and symptom monitoring help ensure compliance with care plans, while AI systems handling routine tasks allow live agents to focus on more complex interactions.

In the context of patient engagement, AI-driven emotion recognition and sentiment analysis technologies offer innovative means to assess a patient's emotional and mental state in real-time. This capability allows healthcare providers to deliver timely, personalized care, which can be instrumental in addressing critical mental health issues. Additionally, virtual health assistants (VHAs) provide immediate support, guide patients through coping strategies, and schedule urgent appointments as necessary, ensuring continuous and consistent care.

Predictive analytics, combined with thorough data analysis, represent a significant advancement in crisis intervention within healthcare settings. By collecting and examining historical patient information, AI systems can identify emerging patterns and predict potential crises, enabling proactive interventions. This approach fosters seamless collaboration between contact center agents and clinicians, ensuring that serious cases are promptly escalated and managed effectively, ultimately contributing to improved patient outcomes.

The illustration here depicts a scenario involving a patient with depression and anxiety. Here, the effectiveness of integrating predictive analytics and AI with contact center operations becomes clear. In essence, the AI system can detect expressions of self-harm that could be easily missed by a care coach. Chat or SMS discussions can be easily monitored using category predictions in which SIHI (suicidal ideation/homicidal ideation) can be detected. This model not only facilitates timely interventions but also ensures that care is continuously tailored to the evolving needs of patients.

The incorporation of emotion recognition and sentiment analysis technologies in healthcare offers a significant approach to patient care.

Figure 19: Use of AI in SIHI escalations

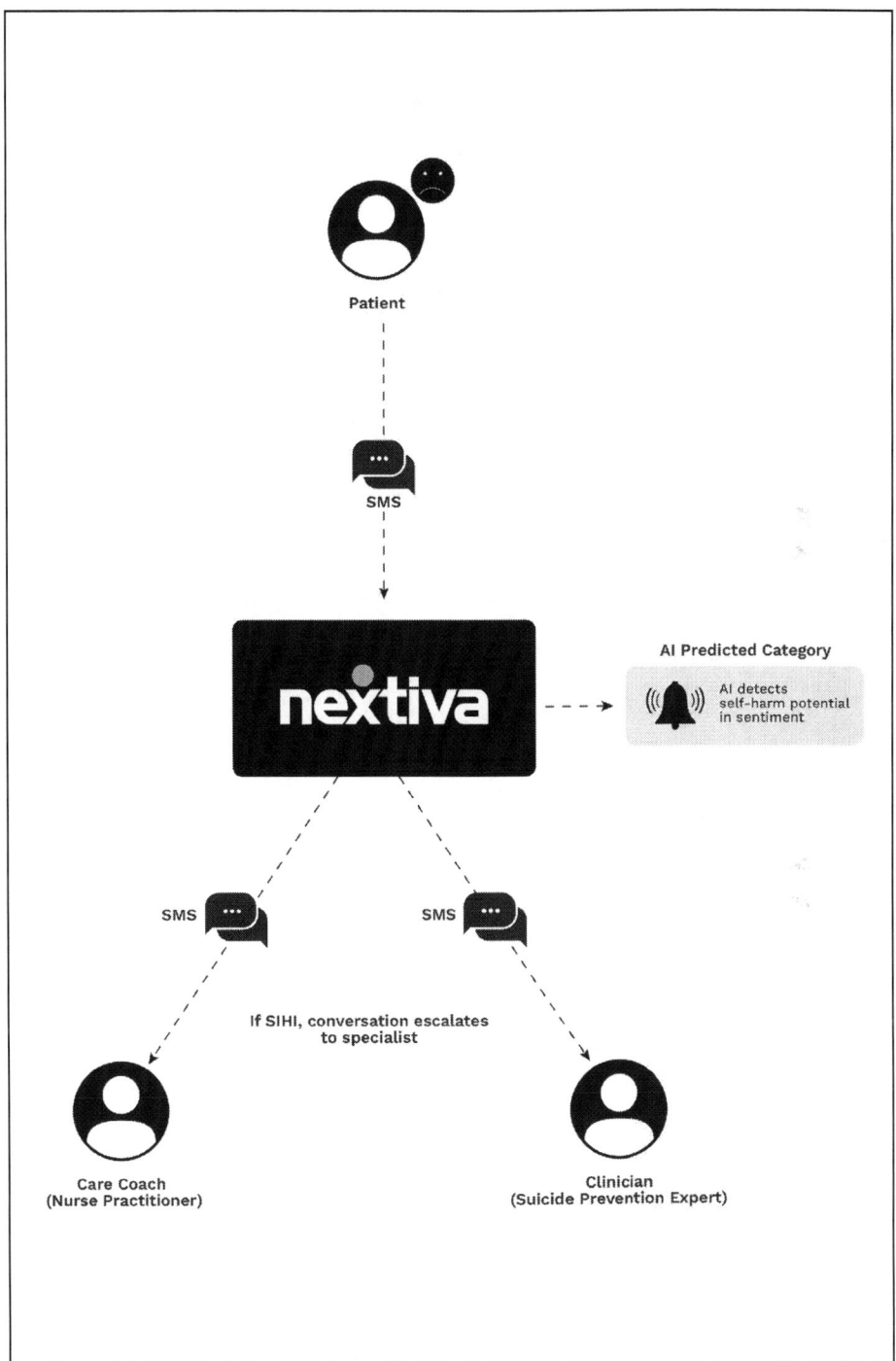

Table 30: Benefits of AI classification for difficult situations

Difficult situation handling capability	Chief benefits
Chat dialog monitoring for SIHI (suicidal ideation/ homicidal ideation) using AI	Detects self- or other person harm intentions consistently, providing the ability to catch harmful behavior before it happens
Independent virtual health assistants (VHAs)	VHAs are available around the clock, ensuring that patients have access to support at any time, even outside of regular clinic hours
VHAs, alongside clinician assistance	VHAs manage initial patient interactions, identify needs, and escalate complex cases to human clinicians, allowing them to focus on patients needing more detailed care
Predictive analytics for crisis intervention using AI models and data analysis	AI can identify patterns and predict potential crises, such as emotional distress or self-harm
Proactive patient engagement in a contact center environment	Contact center agents can proactively reach out to at-risk patients through calls, texts, or emails, offering support and resources; based on the AI's analysis, agents can provide personalized advice and connect patients with appropriate healthcare services

By enabling real-time, accurate assessment of a patient's emotional and mental state, AI-driven platforms empower healthcare providers to deliver timely, personalized care. This enhances the quality of healthcare and opens new avenues for effectively addressing critical mental health issues, ultimately contributing to the overall well-being of the patient community.

Integrating virtual health assistants (VHAs), both independently and alongside human clinicians, can augment healthcare delivery by offering efficient and immediate support. VHAs, available 24/7, can manage initial patient interactions and triage needs, ensuring human clinicians focus on more complex cases. Predictive analytics and data analysis allow AI systems to identify potential crises, facilitating proactive interventions. This collaborative model ensures timely interventions and continuous patient support, improving healthcare outcomes and patient satisfaction.

In these use cases, the synergy between AI technologies and contact center operations heralds a new era in healthcare. Now, proactive crisis intervention can significantly improve patient outcomes. By offering timely, personalized care and fostering a collaborative care environment, healthcare providers can effectively address crises before they escalate, ultimately enhancing patient well-being and overall healthcare efficiency.

Insurance Services

THE INSURANCE SECTOR plays a crucial economic role by collecting premiums, investing, and managing risks. For example, automobile insurance covers driving-related risks, including liability for injuries or damage to others and protection for the policyholder's vehicle. This ensures that drivers are financially protected in case of accidents or other incidents on the road.

Similar protections benefit homeowners insurance, which protects against losses and damages to a residence and its contents. Of course, life insurance pays a death benefit to beneficiaries upon the policyholder's death, providing financial security in exchange for premiums.

Given the complexity of these insurance varieties, transactions between potential policyholders, existing customers, and insurance companies necessitate patience, diligence, and meticulous attention to detail. This complexity underlines why the insurance services industry is primed for enhancements through automation and the integration of artificial intelligence.

Top Automation Targets For Insurance Services

In the insurance industry, automation is driving significant changes. Insurance companies are adopting innovative technologies to improve efficiency, accuracy, and customer satisfaction. Automation, particularly through advancements in artificial intelligence (AI) and machine learning, is reshaping how insurance providers interact with customers, manage risks, and drive sales. It streamlines processes such as customer service, claims processing, and policy management, offering numerous opportunities for improvement. This discussion will highlight the key areas where automation is implemented to enhance the insurance sector. What follows here are the top automation targets practitioners are investing in.

Customer Service

The realm of customer service experiences a significant transformation with the integration of chatbots and virtual assistants. These digital tools provide round-the-clock support, adeptly addressing common queries, assisting with policy details, and guiding customers through the claims process seamlessly. Automated email responses further augment this by efficiently managing frequently asked questions and routine inquiries, ensuring that customers receive timely and accurate responses. The adoption of such technology in customer service roles underscores a commitment to enhancing customer satisfaction and operational efficiency.

Marketing And Sales

The marketing and sales domain significantly benefits from automation, particularly in lead generation and crafting personalized offers. By analyzing customer data, AI enables identifying and cultivating potential leads through targeted marketing strategies. Furthermore, personalized insurance offers and recommendations, driven by AI, enhance the customer experience, ultimately fostering increased sales opportunities. This strategic use of automation in marketing and sales initiatives highlights the potential for increased precision and personalization in customer outreach efforts.

Claims Processing

The field of claims processing stands to gain immensely from automation, with automated claims assessment and fraud detection utilizing artificial intelligence at the forefront of innovation. Through automated claims assessment, the necessity for manual review is substantially diminished, as claims are evaluated efficiently against predefined criteria. Furthermore, the incorporation of machine learning algorithms plays a pivotal role in identifying and flagging potential fraudulent claims. This not only boosts the accuracy of the claims process but also its overall efficiency, offering a more streamlined approach to claims handling.

Policy Management

The automation of policy management, through mechanisms such as automated renewal reminders and sophisticated document management systems, simplifies the intricacies involved in policy administration. Automated notifications ensure customers are promptly informed about policy renewals and upcoming payment obligations, thus maintaining policy activity. Similarly, document management systems effectively organize and manage policy documents, facilitating easy access and updates when necessary. This approach to policy management underscores the importance of efficiency and customer engagement in the digital age.

Regulatory Compliance

The enhancement of regulatory compliance through automated compliance monitoring and the establishment of audit trails signifies a major step forward in minimizing risks and errors. Automation technologies play a crucial role in monitoring and reporting on adherence to regulatory requirements. For example, in a contact center context, this includes using AI to scan speech for compliance phrases. This not only aids in simplifying the compliance process but also significantly reduces the likelihood of errors, thereby reinforcing the organization's commitment to regulatory adherence and accountability.

Challenges With Automation In Insurance Services

As the insurance industry seeks to harness the potential of automation, it faces a constellation of complex challenges that necessitate the careful integration of technology with its established practices. These hurdles include navigating the intricacies of claims processing, the precision needed in actuarial calculations and risk assessment, the customization of policies to meet individual needs, adhering to varied regulatory frameworks across different regions, and the safe handling of sensitive customer data. Each of these aspects highlights the need for sophisticated, adaptable solutions that can address the unique demands of the insurance sector while pushing the envelope of technological innovation and compliance.

The Complexity Of Claims Processing

Insurance claims management represents a multifaceted arena, encompassing intricate evaluations, engagement of multiple parties, and the need for comprehensive documentation. The integration of advanced artificial intelligence (AI) and machine learning (ML) technologies for automating such procedures stands as a critical advancement. These technologies are tasked with the meticulous evaluation of claims, the identification and mitigation of fraudulent activities, and the adept management of anomalies. Given the diverse nature and the inherent complexities associated with claims, creating solutions that can efficiently navigate these challenges remains a daunting task for the insurance industry, underscoring the sector's unique requirements.

Personalization Of Policies

The essence of insurance policies lies in their ability to be tailor-made to address the explicit needs of individual customers, a feature that requires a high degree of customization. Automating this aspect of policy formulation while ensuring adherence to regulatory standards and maintaining the accuracy of policy details represents a complex endeavor. This task of personalization, especially in the realm of insurance, is significantly more challenging when compared to other industries, accentuating the unique challenges faced by the insurance sector in delivering customized solutions to its clientele.

Regulatory Variability Across Regions

A distinguishing challenge the insurance industry faces is navigating the labyrinth of regulatory frameworks that vary extensively across different regions and countries. The quest to automate operational processes while ensuring unwavering compliance with an array of regulatory requirements demands a flexible and responsive automated system. Such systems must be capable of continual updates and adjustments to align with evolving legal standards, highlighting the unique regulatory challenges that are intrinsic to the global insurance landscape.

Handling Of Sensitive Customer Data

Insurance entities are custodians of highly sensitive personal and financial data, entrusting them with a significant responsibility to protect this information. The drive toward process automation, therefore, must be balanced with rigorous data security measures and strict adherence to privacy laws and regulations. Establishing automated systems that can efficiently process sensitive data while ensuring robust data protection and privacy safeguards stands as a particularly unique challenge for the insurance industry, emphasizing the imperative of achieving a delicate balance between innovation and the protection of customer privacy.

Top Automation Use Cases For Insurance Services

In the insurance sector, particularly within customer service and contact centers, the integration of automation and artificial intelligence

(AI) is transforming operations. In this chapter, we will explore key use cases for automation and AI, emphasizing the balance between AI-driven solutions and live assistance. It's essential to balance the efficiency of automation in handling routine tasks with the need for live assistance in addressing complex issues.

Automated proactive customer engagement through updates helps build loyalty, while human agents provide necessary empathetic support and sophisticated problem-solving. In addition, automated voice of the customer (VOC) feedback collection is crucial for understanding customer perspectives, but human analysis and response remain vital for making meaningful improvements. AI-based identity verification enhances security during customer onboarding, and AI-powered customer retention insights use predictive analytics to create strategies to reduce churn. Despite these advancements, human agents are fundamental in building and maintaining trust and long-term customer relationships.

Automated Claims Processing

AI-powered prior authorization and claims processing aim to provide efficient and accurate services to clients, enhancing the overall experience. Claims representatives are motivated by the need to deliver swift and high-quality service, believing that speed combined with quality equates to excellent client service. Their primary intent is to streamline the prior authorization process and ensure patients receive quick approvals. Their key tasks include reviewing patient medical histories, adhering to insurance guidelines, and predicting approval likelihood. However, they face challenges like managing a high volume of requests and ensuring compliance with privacy laws.

Agents seek to reduce their workload and improve client satisfaction by utilizing AI chatbots to handle common inquiries and provide timely updates. Their main tasks involve auditing data access, investigating unusual access attempts, and ensuring adherence to privacy regulations. These agents also grapple with keeping up with evolving privacy laws and managing large volumes of data. Compliance specialists focus on ensuring privacy compliance and protecting sensitive data. Their intent is to monitor data access patterns and flag

Figure 20: Automated claims processing

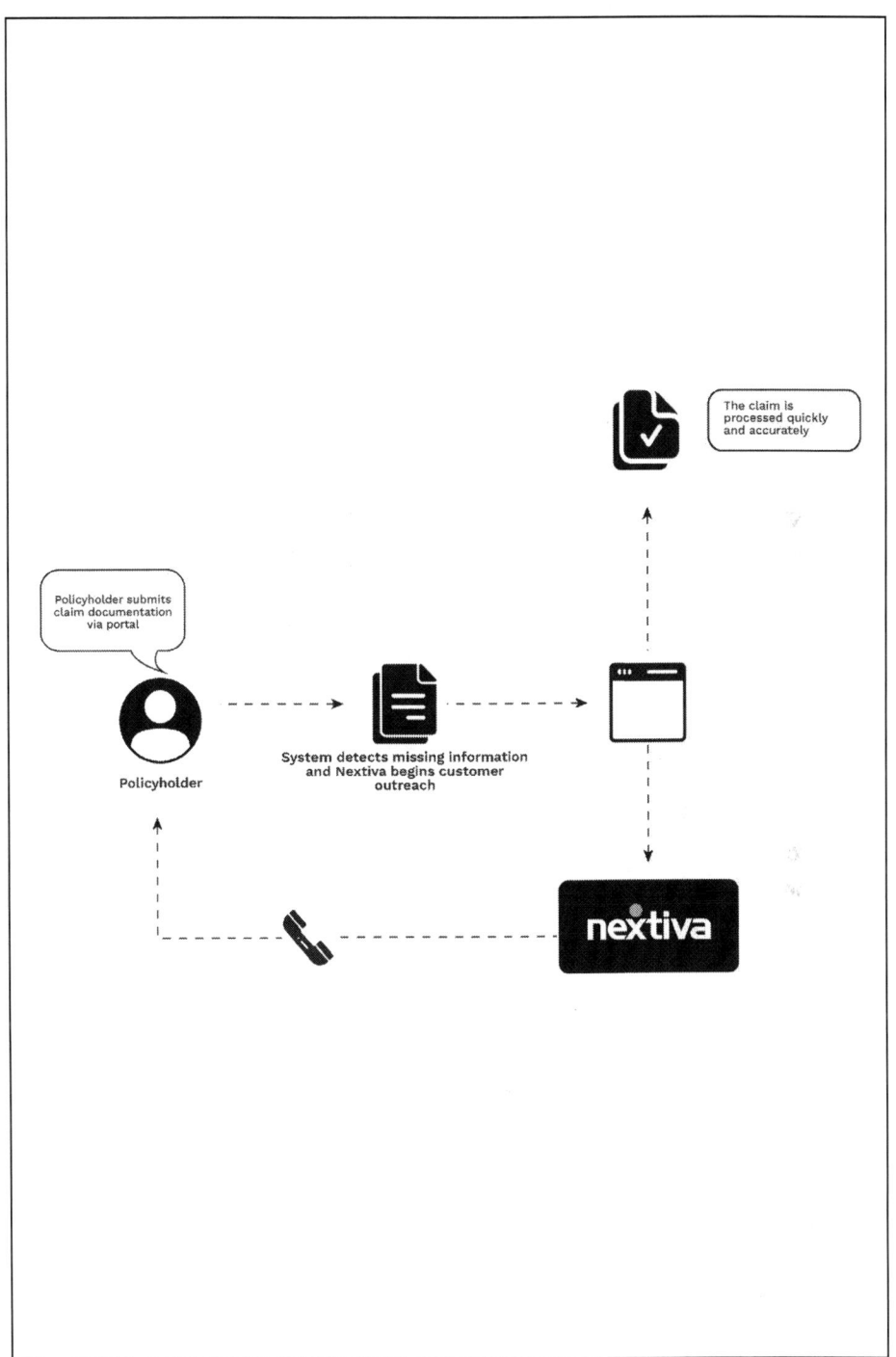

anomalies. They monitor claim data, detect anomalies, and investigate flagged claims, with challenges including identifying subtle fraud patterns and minimizing false positives.

The core problem with manual claims processing is that it is time-consuming and prone to errors. The solution lies in automation, where software handles tasks like data extraction and coverage verification, significantly reducing the need for manual input. The benefits include faster and more accurate claims processing, which shortens turnaround times and reduces errors. For instance, when an insurance policyholder submits a claim for a recent medical procedure, the automated system flags any incomplete claim forms and sends an

Table 31: Benefits of automated claims processing

Claims processing capability	Chief benefits
Automation for data extraction and coverage verification	Reduces the need for manual input, speeding up and improving the accuracy of claims processing
Chatbots for common inquiries	Reduces workload on agents and provides timely updates to clients
Semi-automated data collection	Reduces the need for manual input and speeds up the claims processing time, providing a more efficient and user-friendly experience for customers
Summarizing claims conversations and CRM integration	Ensures all relevant information is stored and easily accessible for future reference; additionally, the summary can be sent automatically to a claims adjuster for further action, which reduces risk of errors and improves the efficiency of the claims-handling process
Dispute resolution and escalation	Initial automation with human escalation ensures that straightforward disputes are resolved quickly while more complex cases receive the necessary human attention, improving overall efficiency and customer satisfaction

outbound call to notify the policyholder. After the policyholder provides the missing information, the automation software extracts the necessary data and verifies coverage, allowing for quick and accurate claim processing and minimizing delays.

This comprehensive approach to prior authorization and claims processing demonstrates the efficiency and accuracy gains achievable through automation. Insurance companies can significantly reduce the manual workload on their agents by implementing strategies such as automation software for data extraction and coverage verification, AI chatbots for handling common inquiries, and automated outbound calls for gathering missing information. This reduction in manual input not only speeds up the processing times but also enhances the accuracy of claims, thereby shortening turnaround times and minimizing errors. These improvements lead to a more streamlined operation, enabling companies to handle more claims with greater efficiency.

Furthermore, these automation strategies improve client satisfaction by providing timely updates and reducing the need for clients to repeat themselves, fostering a better client experience and loyalty. Ultimately, integrating AI and automation in prior authorization and claims processing optimizes operational efficiency and strengthens customer relationships by delivering faster and more reliable services.

Omnichannel Customer Engagement

Automation can play a significant role in enhancing customer engagement by delivering personalized communications such as reminders for policy renewals, payment deadlines, and significant alerts. This approach not only keeps customers well-informed but also fosters a sense of engagement by ensuring they are always up to date with the latest information. Such proactive engagement strategies are instrumental in maintaining customer loyalty. Automated systems can also respond to common customer inquiries, significantly reducing waiting times and ensuring prompt support.

Here's an example of a damage assessment use case where the initial entry point into an automated session is a smartphone application. Insurance companies process many claims, especially after a big storm. In these situations, and even in routine ones, customers can use a mobile app to upload photos of the damage. These photos are automatically transmitted and included as part of a claim, streamlining the process.

For instance, imagine a homeowner who experiences storm damage to their roof. They can use the insurance company's mobile app to upload photos of the damage. The automated system routes the images along with any notes from the policyholder to a claims adjuster, who quickly assesses the extent of the damage and estimates the repair costs. The system can then automatically send an SMS or in-app message to the client. This message could include an SMS bot interaction or a hyperlink directing the client to a website landing page for answering more questions about the claim or setting up an automatic callback to speak with the claims adjuster.

This streamlined process enhances efficiency and reduces the time required to process claims, ensuring that policyholders receive timely assistance in the event of damage.

An omnichannel customer engagement system can also be useful in implementing automated reminders about payment due dates. This is good for helping customers avoid late fees and ensuring their policies remain active and in good standing. By reaching out through various channels, such as SMS, email, or even push notifications from a mobile app, companies can cater to the diverse communication preferences of their clientele. Likewise, the integration of interactive voice response (IVR) systems can further personalize this assistance, offering the option to connect with a live agent for additional support.

There are other use cases that are worth exploring for insurance providers. For example, omnichannel outreach can be used to automate the sending of personalized offers for additional coverage tailored to meet unique customer needs. This proactive engagement can identify potential gaps in existing coverage and present suitable options, simplifying the customer's insurance portfolio and maintaining continuous protection. IVR systems can support this by connecting interested customers with live agents for more detailed information, ensuring comprehensive support and enhancing customer satisfaction.

In summary, automation can significantly enhance customer engagement by delivering personalized communications, such as reminders for policy renewals, payment deadlines, and important alerts.

INSURANCE SERVICES

Figure 21: Omnichannel customer engagement

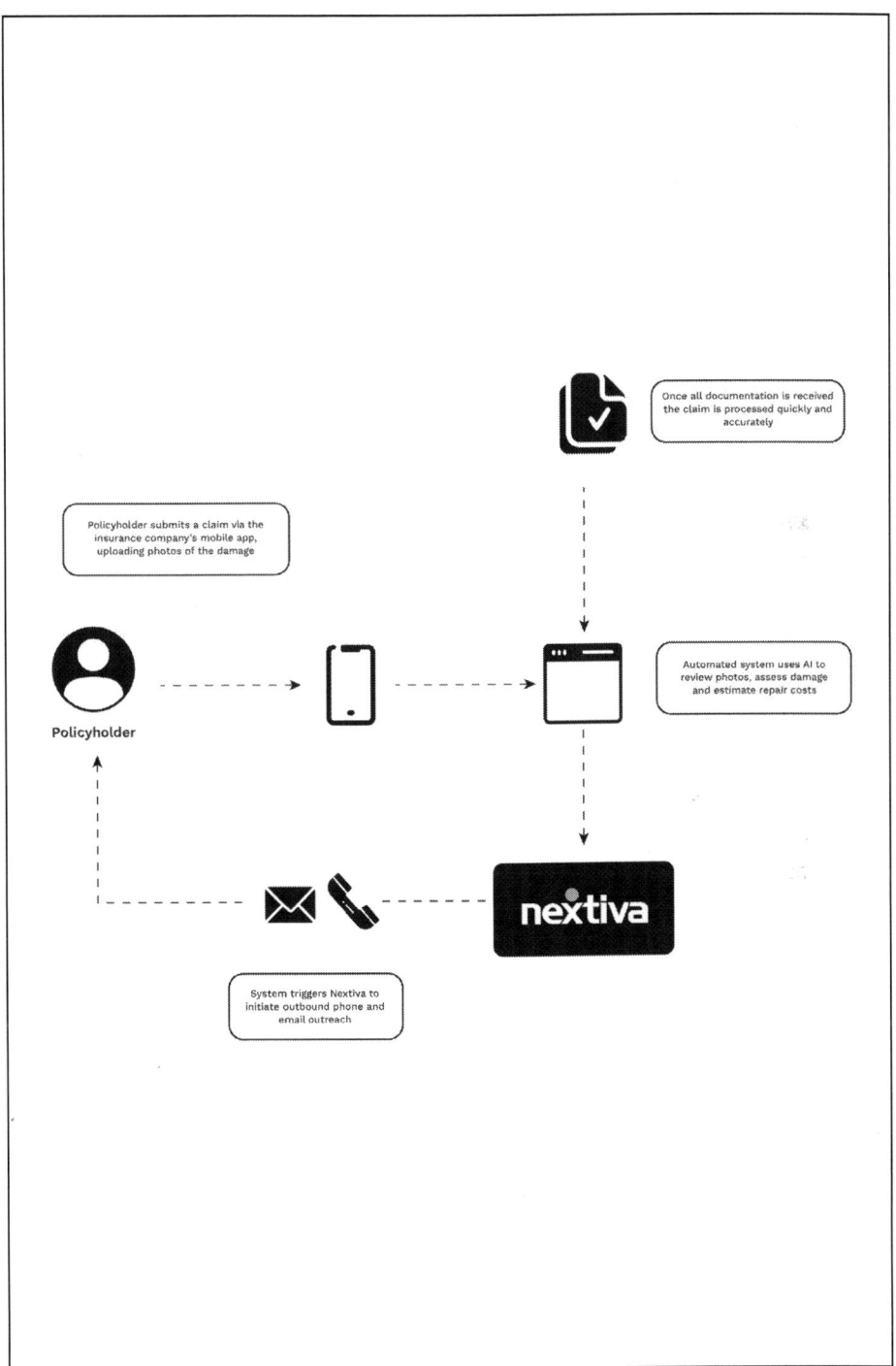

Table 32: Benefits of omnichannel customer engagement

Omnichannel customer engagement capability	Chief benefits
Automated reminders for policy renewals	Ensures continuous protection for customers and avoids any lapse in their coverage
Automated reminders for payment due dates	Helps customers avoid late fees and ensures their policies remain active and in good standing
Automated personalized offers for additional coverage	Provides tailored coverage options to meet unique customer needs, ensuring more holistic protection and enhancing customer satisfaction
Proactive engagement for upselling and cross-selling	Opens new avenues for upselling and cross-selling, significantly benefiting the insurer
Using automated systems as a bridge to compassion and practical assistance	Provides a humane touch to missed payments, offering solutions like payment extensions or new plans, fostering trust and loyalty
Automation for adding family members to existing policies	Streamlines the process, making it efficient and hassle-free, ensuring policyholders have the coverage they need
IVR systems to remind customers to update policy information	Offers a personal touch and extra assistance, solidifying customer satisfaction and ensuring timely updates to policies
Automated reminders for coverage age limits	Keeps parents informed and prompts them to take action, ensuring continuous protection for their children
Self-service portal link for reminder messages	Allows customers to effortlessly explore and purchase new policies suitable for their needs
Automated promoting for bundled insurance products	Provides customers with the convenience of managing multiple policies under a single account, simplifying their insurance portfolio and offering potential cost savings

This proactive approach keeps customers well-informed, fosters engagement, and helps maintain customer loyalty. Automated systems can also respond to common customer inquiries, significantly reducing waiting times and ensuring prompt support. For example, in damage assessment, customers can use a mobile app to upload photos of damage, which are automatically included in their claim, streamlining the process.

An omnichannel customer engagement system can implement automated reminders about payment due dates, helping customers avoid late fees and ensure their policies remain active. By reaching out through various channels like SMS, email, and mobile app notifications, companies cater to diverse communication preferences. Additionally, interactive voice response (IVR) systems can personalize assistance and offer connections to live agents for further support. Omnichannel outreach can also automate personalized offers for additional coverage, identifying gaps in existing policies and presenting suitable options. This ensures continuous protection and enhances customer satisfaction by providing comprehensive support and timely updates.

Intelligent Routing

AI technology can revolutionize how calls are routed in customer service settings, connecting customers with the most suitable agents to handle their inquiries. This process streamlines the customer service workflow and enhances the support provided. By employing intelligent algorithms, AI assesses a customer's needs and matches them with an agent whose expertise aligns with those requirements. This approach ensures customers can quickly connect to the right professional, improving resolution efficiency and effectiveness.

By implementing AI into call routing systems, real-time analysis of customer inquiries is possible. This allows the system to determine the nature of a call and route it to an agent best equipped to handle the situation. For example, a customer with questions about life insurance policies can be directed to a specialist in that area, bypassing generalist agents. This precision reduces wait times and minimizes the need for multiple transfers.

Figure 22: Intelligent routing of emails based on categories

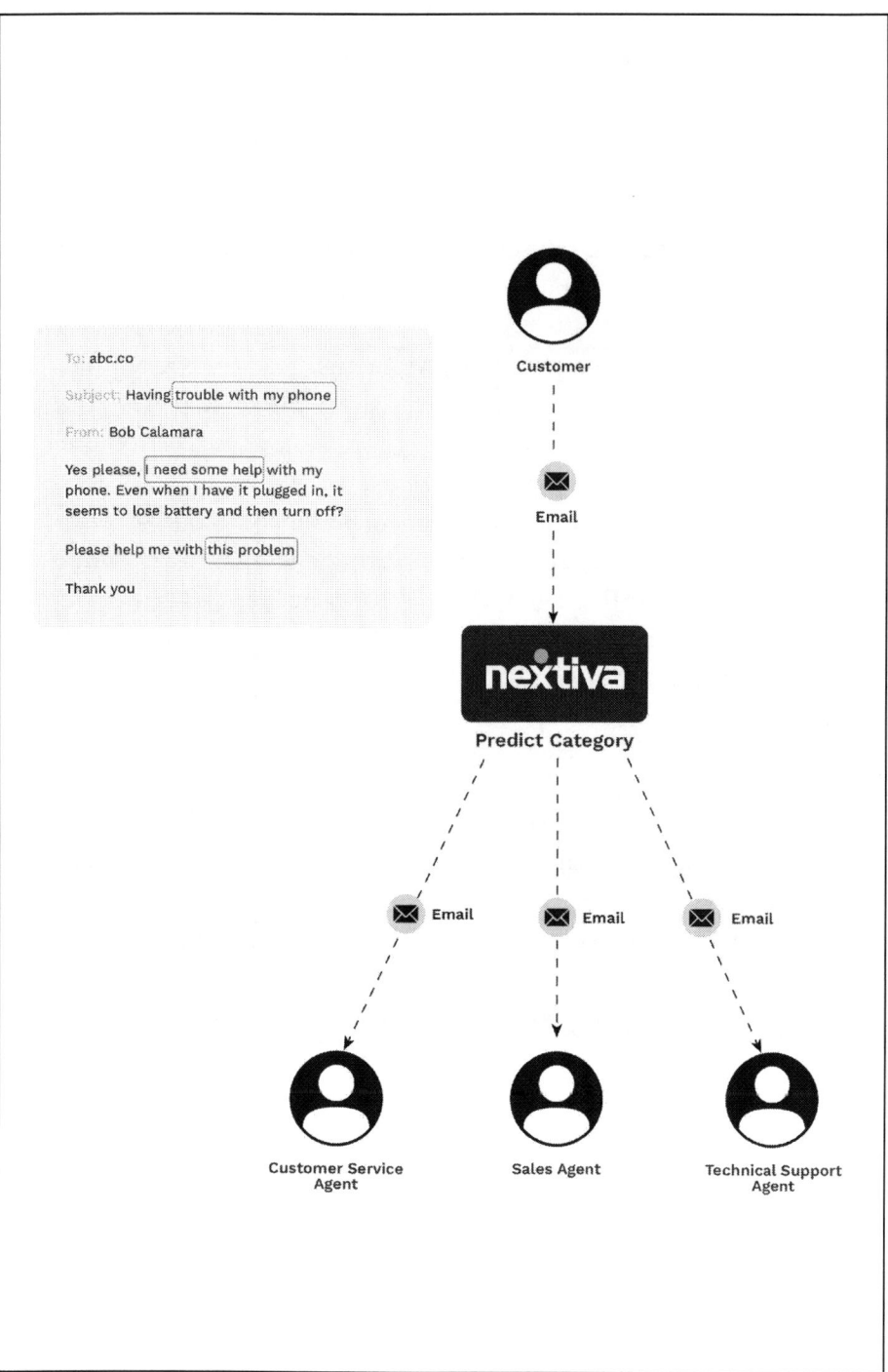

Skills-based routing relies on a database cataloging agent skills and proficiency levels, matching customer queries with agents with the necessary expertise. For instance, health insurance claims are directed to agents skilled in that field, while technical issues are assigned to agents with technical support backgrounds. This organized approach enhances the accuracy and efficiency of customer service, improving first-call resolution rates.

Intelligent routing also prioritizes calls based on factors such as urgency and customer value. High-priority customers or those with time-sensitive issues are connected to senior agents or specialized teams for premium service. This prioritization extends across various communication mediums, ensuring a high standard of service. This optimization reduces customer frustration and enhances satisfaction levels, improving the operational efficiency of the contact center.

AI's capabilities in the realm of customer service extend to linguistic adaptability, providing customers with support in their preferred languages. By automatically detecting the language a customer uses, AI ensures that the customer is promptly connected to an agent who is fluent in that language. This feature is especially beneficial in culturally diverse regions, offering non-native speakers the comfort of receiving assistance in their native language. Providing multilingual support goes a long way in improving accessibility and inclusiveness in customer service, contributing significantly to overall customer satisfaction.

Furthermore, AI's advanced sentiment analysis tools offer a nuanced understanding of a customer's emotional state based on their communication. This enables the system to identify and prioritize customers exhibiting signs of dissatisfaction or distress, ensuring they are quickly connected to agents or specialized teams adept at managing escalated situations. This proactive response can dramatically enhance the customer service experience, effectively addressing concerns before they amplify into larger issues. Employing such technology underscores a company's commitment to providing empathetic, customer-centric support, fostering stronger relationships and loyalty among its customer base.

Figure 23: Intelligent routing of emails based on language

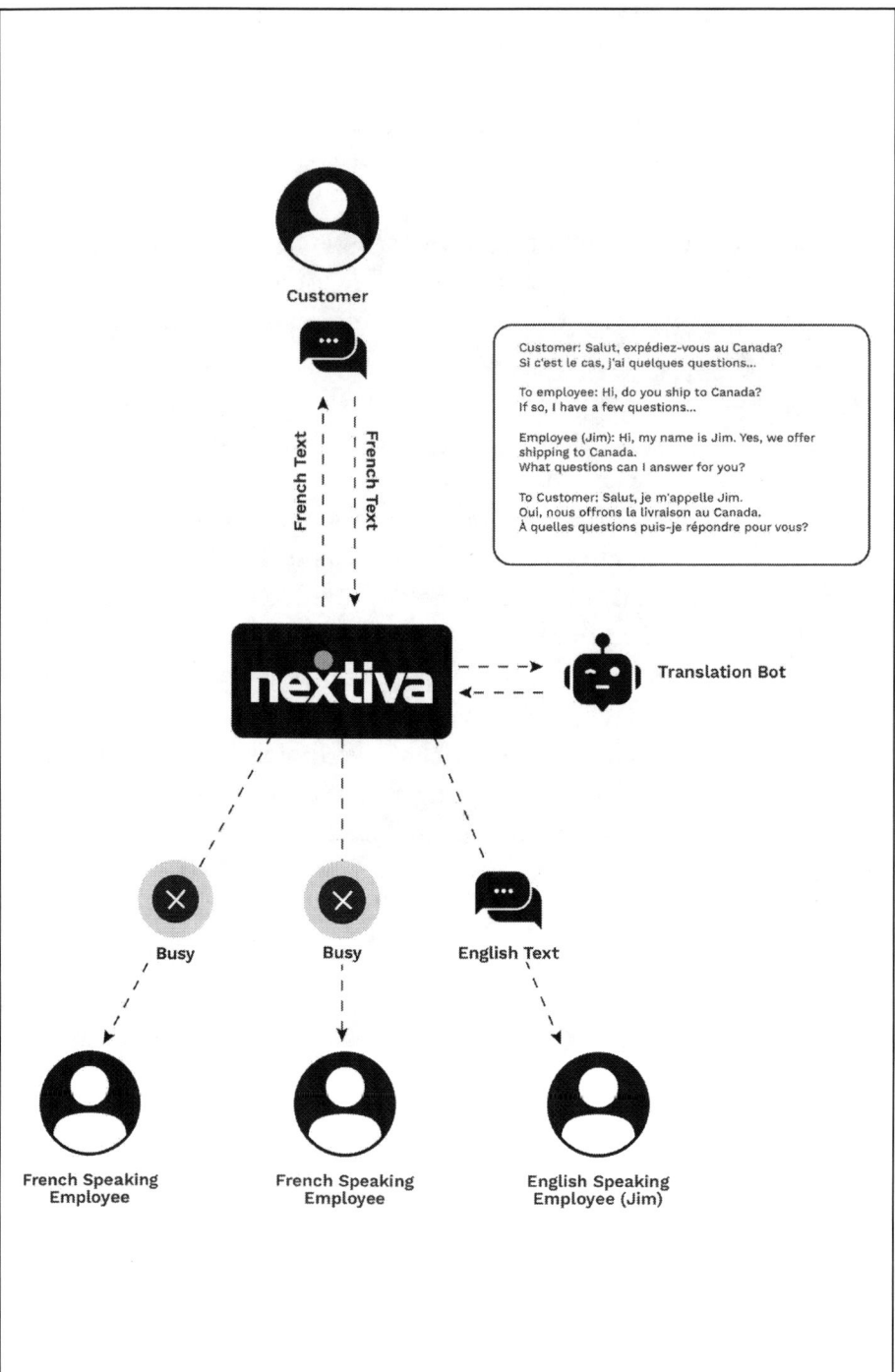

Table 33: Chief benefits of intelligent routing use cases

Intelligent routing capability	Chief benefits
Intelligent routing for a skills-based connection to suitable agents	This system matches customer queries with agents possessing the exact expertise needed, improving accuracy, efficiency, and first-call resolution rates, leading to higher customer satisfaction
Intelligent routing for prioritization of calls based on urgency and value	Prioritize calls by factors like urgency and customer value, ensuring high-priority customers or those with time-sensitive issues are quickly connected to specialized teams or senior agents for premium service
Intelligent routing for prediction categories	Categorizing content automatically drastically improves first-contact resolution and can process emails ten times faster than humans can re-direct them, contributing to quicker customer responsiveness
Intelligent routing for linguistic adaptability	AI's ability to automatically detect a customer's language and connect them to a fluent agent in that language improves accessibility and inclusiveness, contributing to overall satisfaction
Intelligent routing with advanced sentiment analysis	Through sentiment analysis tools, AI can gauge a customer's emotional state and prioritize those exhibiting signs of distress, ensuring they are quickly connected to skilled agents or teams, thus enhancing the customer service experience

Automated Appointment Scheduling

Automated appointment scheduling systems enhance the insurance industry by streamlining the coordination of meetings between customers and professionals. These systems enable customers to easily book, reschedule, or cancel appointments, providing immediate confirmations and reminders. This improves efficiency and user experience by reducing the need for ongoing communication and manual intervention.

Integrating these scheduling systems with existing customer relationship management (CRM) and policy management software ensures that agents are well-prepared for meetings. When an appointment is scheduled, relevant customer information and policy details are automatically retrieved, allowing agents to focus on addressing the customer's needs effectively. Additionally, real-time updates and notifications keep both customers and agents informed about any changes, reducing the likelihood of missed appointments.

During peak periods, such as natural disasters or policy renewal seasons, automated scheduling systems dynamically allocate appointment slots based on agent availability and the urgency of customer issues. This ensures that critical cases receive timely attention, optimizing operational efficiency. While automation manages routine tasks, human agents provide essential support for complex issues, maintaining a balance between efficiency and personalized service.

Automated scheduling systems also reduce the administrative burden on both customers and staff, allowing agents to concentrate on resolving customer problems. This shift not only enhances operational efficiency but also improves the quality of customer service. Ultimately, these systems transform the customer experience by making interactions more streamlined and efficient, fostering a more productive environment for both agents and customers.

Here's an example of a conversation between a customer and a call center agent. This is a typical scenario when a customer has trouble using a bot for assistance and needs human intervention. It is considered a best practice in this case for the dialog between the bot and the customer to have been put on the agent screen for context. Additionally, most modern contact center systems will use the credentials from the bot engagement to automatically pull up the customer record from the CRM system and automatically surface the claim in question.

Customer: "Hi, I'm having trouble scheduling an appointment with a technician via your online service. Can you help me?"

Agent: "Absolutely, I apologize for any inconvenience. Let me assist you with setting up the appointment. Could you please provide me with your account number and briefly describe the issue you're experiencing?"

Customer: "Of course, my account number is BKU-6654987. I'm having issues claiming benefits due to hail damage."

Agent: "Thank you for the information. It sounds like you need a specialist in property claims for hail damage. I'll check our specialists' schedules for you. Do you have a preferred date and time?"

Customer: "Tuesday and Thursday mornings work best for me."

Agent: "Great. We have a spot open with our property claims specialist on Tuesday at 10 a.m. Would you like me to book that for you?"

Customer: "Yes, that would be great."

Agent: "Done. Your appointment is confirmed for Tuesday at 10 a.m. You will receive a confirmation email shortly, and we'll send a

Table 34: Chief benefits of automated appointment scheduling

Automated scheduling capability	Chief benefits
Automated appointment scheduling	Reduces the need for back-and-forth communication and therefore makes it easier for customers to manage appointments; allows customers to select an available time slot that suits their schedule; provides confirmation and reminders for appointments, which builds trust and affinity with customers
Scheduling integration for real-time updates	Reduces the chances of missed appointments by ensuring timely communication and updates
Scheduling integration during emergencies	Ensures that critical cases are prioritized, providing timely support to customers in need; more cohesive and efficient scheduling process, ultimately improving customer satisfaction and operational efficiency
Efficient high-volume scheduling	Reduces wait times and ensures that customers receive timely support
Automated information retrieval	Ensures that agents are fully prepared for customer meetings; critical cases are prioritized and handled promptly

reminder the day before your appointment. Is there anything else I can do for you today?"

Customer: "No, that's everything. Thanks for sorting this out!"

Agent: "My pleasure! Have a great day, and we look forward to assisting you on Tuesday."

In summary, automated appointment scheduling significantly enhances customer service by allowing customers to schedule, adjust, or cancel appointments conveniently. This technology boosts user experience through increased flexibility and efficiency. Integrated scheduling systems enable agents to be well-prepared for meetings, improving interaction quality and productivity.

Combining automated scheduling with communication platforms provides real-time updates, reducing missed appointments and promoting seamless communication. During high-demand periods, such as natural disasters or policy renewals, automated systems manage appointments based on urgency and agent availability. This ensures that critical needs are prioritized, offering efficient and personalized services.

Insurance Call Transcription And Summarization

Automated transcription and summarization of customer calls address a significant problem faced by insurers: the frequent handling of customer calls related to claims, policy inquiries, and authorizations. By implementing AI to transcribe these calls in real-time, insurers can ensure accurate documentation of conversations, significantly improving record-keeping and providing a reliable reference for future interactions.

For instance, a customer calls the insurance company to inquire about a recent claim. The process begins with the customer calling the insurance company, which is managed with intelligent routing. Here, the caller can speak phrases that are analyzed and then used to route the caller to the properly skilled agent. The unified customer experience management (UCXM) platform facilitates the connection to a live agent who assists the customer while an AI system transcribes the call, ensuring every detail is accurately documented. This transcription is saved to the customer's record, ensuring a reliable reference

Figure 24: Insurance call transcription and summarization

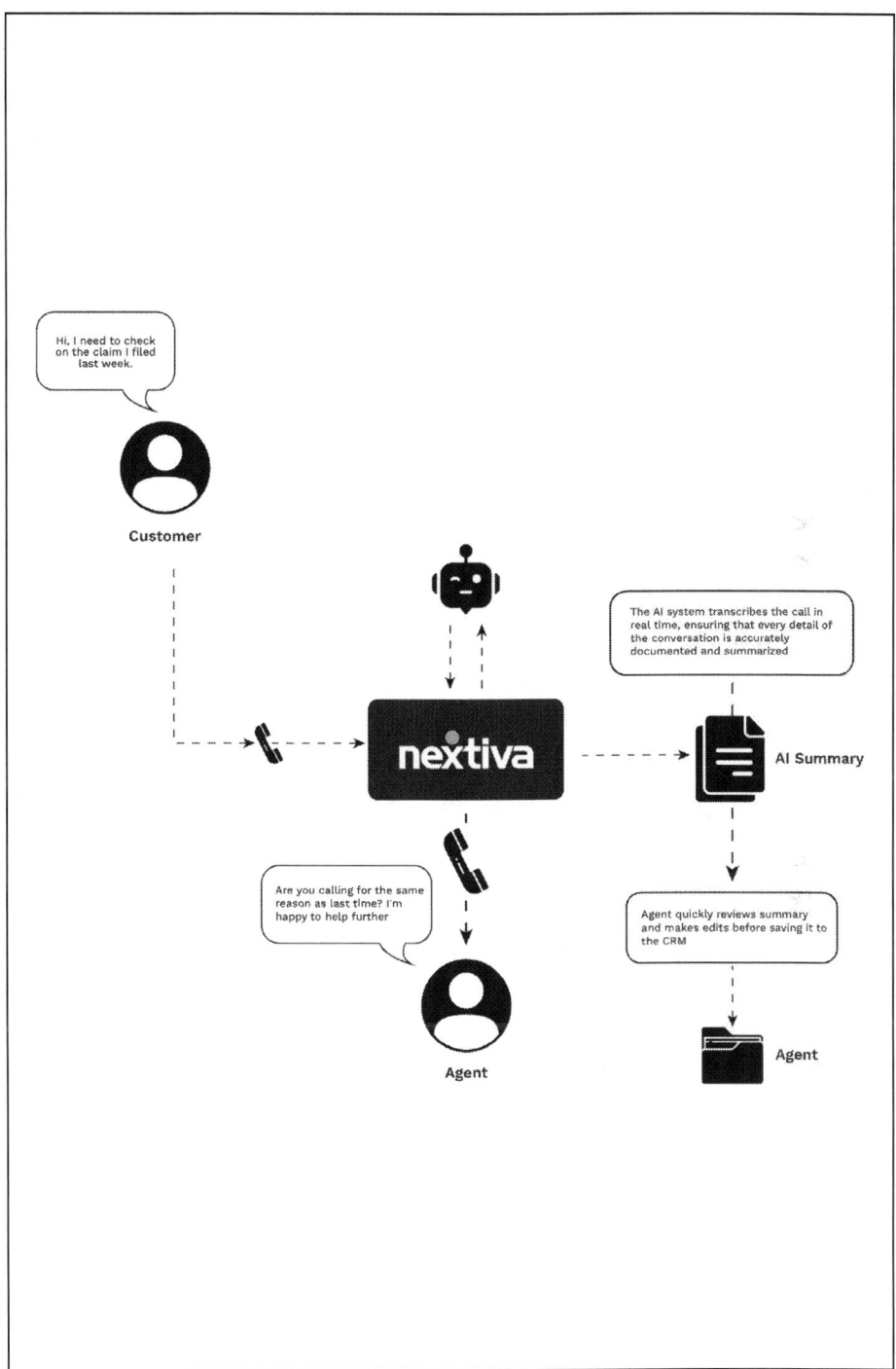

for future interactions and enhancing the overall quality of customer service.

The benefits of this technology are multiple. For the customer, it means their concerns and information are recorded accurately, reducing the need for repetition and minimizing misunderstandings. For the insurer, it streamlines the claims process by providing a precise record of each customer interaction, improving efficiency and enhancing the overall customer service experience. By incorporating AI transcription into their workflow, insurance companies can manage a high volume of claims more effectively, particularly during peak periods following significant events like storms or other natural disasters.

Other than the transcription itself, which helps to memorialize the transaction, AI can be used for other functions. For example, AI can be used to summarize the call, so the note-taking an agent must do in the post-call wrap-up period is significantly reduced. In addition, sentiment analysis can be performed so the feelings the customer is expressing can be noted. More importantly, an AI-based summary with sentiment built-in can show the arc of the conversation from a sentiment standpoint, highlighting moments of satisfaction or frustration, which can be crucial for quality assurance and training purposes.

This technology ensures that claims are processed swiftly and accurately, minimizing delays and significantly improving customer satisfaction. The seamless communication facilitated by real-time transcription between the customer and the live agent exemplifies how modern technology can optimize traditional processes in the insurance industry. Moreover, the data gathered from these interactions can be used to identify trends, improve service delivery, and tailor customer support strategies, further enhancing the efficiency and effectiveness of insurance operations.

In summary, automated transcription and summarization of customer calls solve the frequent issue of handling calls related to claims and inquiries, ensuring accurate documentation and improving record-keeping. This reduces the need for customers to repeat information, minimizes misunderstandings, and streamlines the claims process. By summarizing calls and performing sentiment analysis, the AI system reduces the agent workload and captures the emotional tone of conversations, enhancing overall customer satisfaction.

The insurer frequently receives inquiries about business hours, policy details, and claim status. Automation with a chatbot is the solution to this problem. AI chatbots handle these common inquiries, providing customers with quick and accurate answers. This results in faster response times and reduces the load on customer service staff. Additionally, chatbots offer 24/7 availability, ensuring assistance is available outside regular business hours. They provide consistency in answers, ensuring all customers receive the same accurate information, which supports customer loyalty and reduces confusion for both agents and clients. Moreover, chatbots free up human agents to handle more complex inquiries, thereby improving overall efficiency. They

Table 35: Benefits of call transcription and summarization

Transcription and summarization capability	Chief benefits
AI-powered real-time transcription	Enhances record-keeping accuracy and provides reliable references for future interactions
Real-time documentation of customer interactions	Reduces the need for customers to repeat information, minimizing misunderstandings
Streamlined claims processing	Improves efficiency and speed of claims handling, especially during high-volume periods
Integrated communication platforms	Enhances overall customer service experience by ensuring accurate and prompt support
AI summarization of calls	Reduces agent workload by minimizing post-call notetaking
Sentiment analysis	Captures customer emotions and provides insights into the conversation's sentiment arc

also facilitate data collection and analysis, allowing the company to identify common issues and improve services.

Imagine a customer who wants to know the business hours of their insurance company. They can use the company's chatbot to ask about the business hours, and the AI chatbot quickly responds with the information. Subsequently, they may ask about their policy details, and the chatbot provides the relevant information. Finally, they may inquire about the status of a recent claim, and the chatbot offers an update or escalates the inquiry to a human agent if needed. This quick and accurate response enhances the customer experience and reduces the load on customer service staff.

Chatbot For Answering Common Questions

Insurers frequently receive inquiries about business hours, policy details, and claim status. Automation with a chatbot can greatly reduce the workload associated with these queries. AI chatbots handle common inquiries with ease, providing customers with quick and accurate answers. This results in faster response times and reduces the load on customer service staff. Additionally, chatbots offer 24/7 availability, ensuring assistance is available outside regular business hours. They provide consistency in answers, ensuring all customers receive the same accurate information, which supports customer loyalty and reduces confusion for both agents and clients. Moreover, chatbots free up human agents to handle more complex inquiries, thereby improving overall efficiency. They also facilitate data collection and analysis, allowing the company to identify common issues and improve services.

Imagine a customer who wants to know the business hours of their insurance company. He can use the company's chatbot to ask about the business hours, and the AI chatbot quickly responds with the information. Subsequently, he may ask about their policy details, and the chatbot provides the relevant information. Finally, he may inquire about the status of a recent claim, and the chatbot offers an update or escalates the inquiry to a human agent if needed. This quick and accurate response enhances the customer experience and reduces the load on customer service staff.

INSURANCE SERVICES

Figure 25: Chatbot for answering common questions

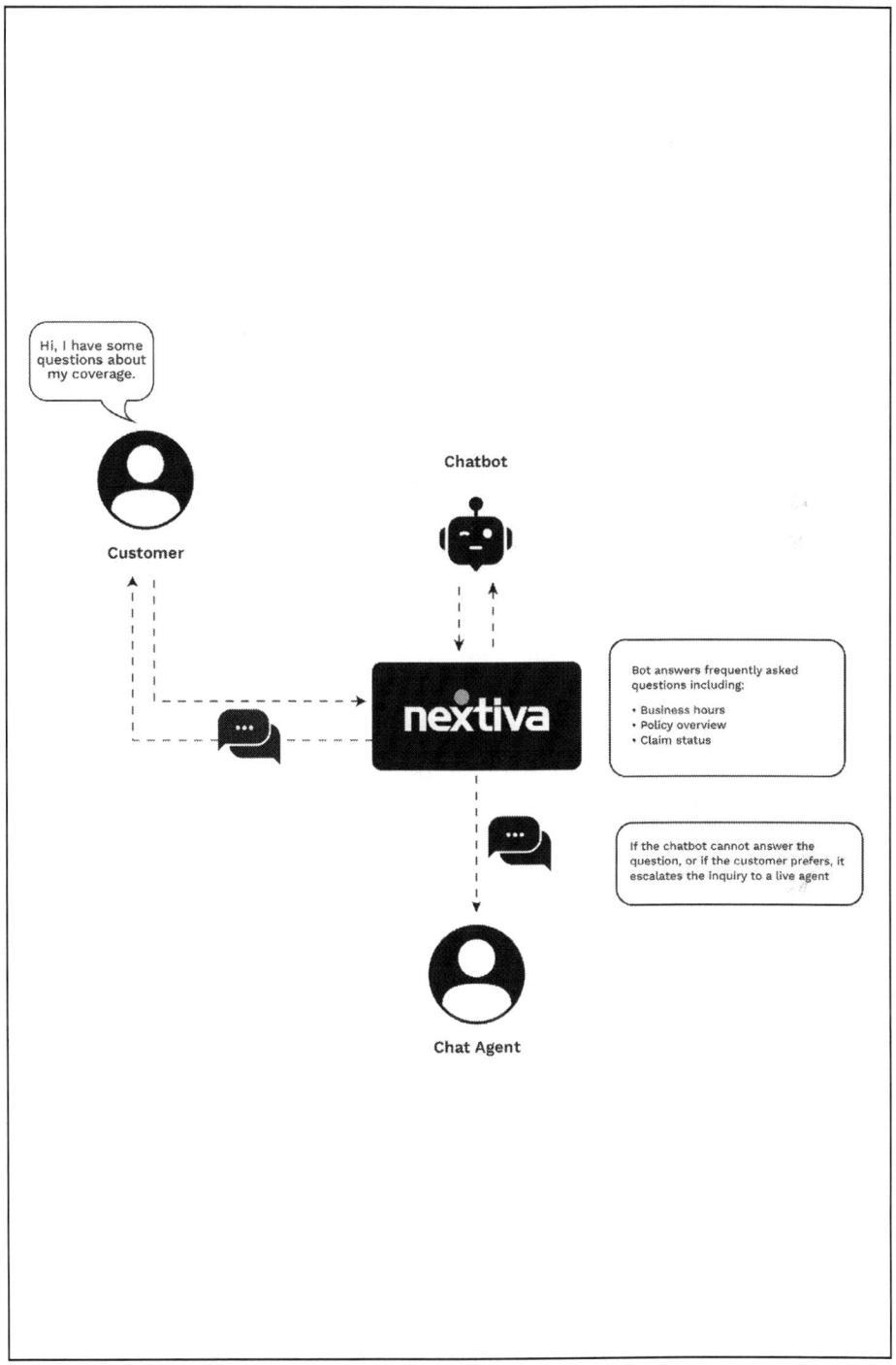

Beyond handling common inquiries, chatbots can also be programmed to guide customers through more complex processes, such as filing a claim or updating their policy details. By providing step-by-step instructions and responding to follow-up questions, chatbots ensure that customers have all the necessary information and support to complete their tasks efficiently. This not only improves customer satisfaction but also ensures that the processes are carried out correctly, reducing the likelihood of errors and subsequent complications.

Furthermore, chatbots can be integrated with other systems to provide a seamless customer service experience. For instance, they can access customer accounts to provide personalized responses based on individual policies and claim histories. This level of customization makes interactions more relevant and valuable for customers, fostering a stronger relationship between the company and its clients.

In addition to direct customer interactions, chatbots can be utilized for proactive customer service. They can be programmed to send

Table 36: Benefits of chatbots for answering common questions

Chatbot capability	Chief benefits
24/7 availability	Providing assistance outside of regular business hours is convenient for many customers
Quick response times	Reduction of average handle time for transactions removes friction for customers and produces better satisfaction scores
Consistency in answers	Ensures all customers receive the same accurate information, supporting loyalty, reducing confusion for agents and clients, and avoiding the need to restate the company's position on complex issues
Deflection from agents	Agents are freed up to handle more complex inquiries, improving overall efficiency
Data collection and analysis	Easier to collect data on and identify common issues to improve client services

reminders about policy renewals, important deadlines, or changes in policy terms. By keeping customers informed and up-to-date, chatbots help prevent lapses in coverage and ensure that customers are fully aware of their policy benefits and obligations.

Moreover, the data collected by chatbots during interactions can provide valuable insights for the insurance company. By analyzing this data, the company can identify trends and patterns in customer inquiries, enabling them to address common concerns more effectively. This information can also be used to improve chatbot performance, ensuring that responses become increasingly accurate and helpful over time.

Overall, implementing AI chatbots in the insurance industry's customer service operations is a strategic move that offers numerous benefits. It streamlines processes, enhances the customer experience, and provides valuable data for continuous improvement. As technology advances, the capabilities of chatbots will continue to grow, offering even more opportunities for efficiency and customer satisfaction in the insurance industry.

Manufacturing

IN THE MANUFACTURING sector, customer experience (CX) has become a key factor influencing business success and customer retention. As the industry shifts toward more digitized and customer-focused models, combining traditional contact center support with advanced AI and automation technologies is becoming vital. This integration allows manufacturers to deliver personalized and efficient service, improving the overall customer experience.

By utilizing AI for routine tasks, manufacturers can ensure quick responses and consistent service. Meanwhile, human agents can focus on more complex inquiries, using their problem-solving skills to address unique customer needs. This combination of automated and human support creates smoother interactions, enhancing customer trust and encouraging loyalty.

Ultimately, this approach helps manufacturers respond effectively to the evolving demands of their customers, ensuring they remain competitive and can sustain growth in a challenging market.

Top Automation Targets In Manufacturing

In the current manufacturing environment, using automation to improve customer experience is becoming essential. Order management automation can enhance transparency and efficiency by providing updates on order status and delivery times. This reduces manual tracking and eases the workload on customer service agents, allowing them to address more complex issues.

AI-powered product configuration assistance simplifies the customization process by offering real-time guidance, reducing reliance on human agents for basic queries.

Effective inventory management is critical to minimize equipment downtime and ensure operational efficiency. It provides real-time data on product availability, helping to avoid delays. Additionally, AI-driven chatbots and virtual assistants handle customer queries promptly, allowing human agents to focus on more complicated tasks. Automation in quality assurance improves the consistency and accuracy of quality data, while proactive communication through AI and IoT keeps customers informed about potential issues. Here, we will go into more detail on some of these concepts before reviewing some of the ever-present challenges in manufacturing.

Order Management Automation

Automating order management processes can improve transparency and efficiency in the manufacturing sector. By utilizing AI and advanced technologies, companies can provide timely customer updates regarding their orders, including order status, delays, and expected delivery times. This approach minimizes the need for manual tracking and reduces the number of inquiries handled by customer service, allowing agents to focus on more complex issues.

Automated order management systems also enhance coordination among departments involved in the order fulfillment process. This ensures that orders are processed efficiently, reducing the likelihood of unnecessary delays.

Additionally, automation addresses issues such as miscommunication and human error, which can lead to customer dissatisfaction and inefficiencies in operations. With real-time tracking and notifications, customers stay informed about their orders, fostering greater trust in the company.

Furthermore, the data generated by automated systems can be analyzed to identify trends and areas for improvement in the order management process. This data-driven approach facilitates continuous improvement and enhances operational efficiency over time.

Product Configuration Assistance

Product configuration can be complex, particularly in the manufacturing sector, where products are often customizable in various ways. AI-powered configuration assistants aim to streamline this process by offering real-time guidance and recommendations to customers. These tools utilize machine learning and natural language processing to better understand customer preferences and suggest relevant configuration options. By doing this, they can reduce the need for human agents to address basic configuration inquiries, allowing human resources to focus on more intricate customer needs.

Additionally, automated product configuration tools can accelerate the sales process by quickly generating quotes and validating configurations. This capability minimizes waiting times, which can lead to a more efficient sales cycle and improved customer satisfaction. The integration of AI in product configuration systems facilitates ongoing learning and adaptation, enabling them to respond to shifting customer preferences and market demands effectively. This adaptability ensures that manufacturers maintain their competitiveness in a fast-paced market environment, where customization and efficient service are increasingly important.

Inventory And Spare Parts Management

Effective management of inventory and spare parts is essential for minimizing equipment downtime and maintaining efficiency within the manufacturing sector. A systematic approach to inventory management can provide real-time data regarding product availability, which can mitigate the risks associated with delays and operational disruptions.

Incorporating automated solutions into inventory management can significantly enhance the monitoring of stock levels. These AI-driven systems can analyze historical usage data, recognize patterns, and predict future demand for various components. This predictive capability allows for timely reordering of parts, ensuring that essential items are consistently available when needed.

Automation also improves the accuracy of inventory records. Manual tracking methods are often prone to human errors, leading to discrepancies that can disrupt production schedules. By utilizing automated systems, companies can maintain more precise inventory data, which is critical for balancing supply and demand. This accuracy helps mitigate issues related to overstocking, which can tie up capital in excess inventory, as well as stockouts, which can halt production.

Moreover, automated inventory systems provide valuable insights that can enhance customer relationships. By offering transparent information regarding stock availability and order statuses, manufacturers can build trust and improve customer satisfaction. This can be particularly important in industries where timely delivery of components is crucial.

Additionally, these systems can facilitate seamless integration with other business processes, such as procurement and logistics. By aligning inventory management with these functions, companies can streamline operations, resulting in improved overall efficiency. For instance, a coordinated approach can lead to better alignment between purchasing schedules and production needs, optimizing resource utilization and reducing waste.

Overall, a well-implemented inventory and spare parts management system not only supports operational efficiency but also contributes to a more responsive and responsible manufacturing environment.

Customer Query Handling

Efficient handling of customer queries is crucial in the manufacturing sector to maintain a high level of customer service. AI-driven chatbots and virtual assistants can operate on a round-the-clock basis, addressing routine queries and providing immediate responses. This capability not only lightens the workload for human agents but also ensures that customers can receive timely and precise answers to their inquiries.

Chatbots can be configured to manage a variety of inquiries, such as requests for product specifications, shipping details, and order tracking. For more complex or sensitive issues, these systems can be programmed to escalate cases to human agents, ensuring that customers receive the appropriate level of support.

In addition to operational efficiency, incorporating AI into customer query handling promotes ongoing enhancement and personalization of service. By monitoring and analyzing customer interactions, chatbots can refine their responses and improve the relevance of the information they provide. This ongoing learning process contributes to a better customer experience, increasing the likelihood of customer retention.

Furthermore, AI-powered customer support systems can be integrated with existing business processes, including customer relationship management (CRM) systems and order management software. Such integration ensures that the customer support experience is fully streamlined, allowing agents to access relevant customer data and order history quickly. This holistic approach not only improves the effectiveness of customer interactions but also contributes to a more organized handling of customer queries.

Quality Assurance Automation

Quality assurance (QA) is an essential element of the manufacturing process. Its purpose is to ensure that products conform to specific standards and specifications required by regulatory bodies, industry standards, and customer expectations. Automation has the potential to enhance certain aspects of QA, such as inspection transcription and data summarization, which can lead to improvements in the accuracy and consistency of quality data collection.

By automating the transcription and summarization of inspection findings, the reliance on manual documentation can be reduced. This shift allows QA specialists to dedicate more time and attention to critical inspection tasks rather than spending it on administrative work. The automation of data entry and reporting means that errors associated with human intervention are minimized, thus potentially improving the reliability of the information gathered during inspections.

Additionally, automated quality assurance systems can provide insights into the production process that may not be immediately apparent through manual methods. For example, by analyzing quality data over time, manufacturers can identify patterns and trends indicating recurring issues or areas that require attention. This proactive approach enables manufacturers to make informed decisions and implement corrective actions before these issues escalate into more significant problems.

To effectively utilize automated QA systems, it is crucial for organizations to ensure that the data collected is reliable and consistently analyzed. This consistency helps maintain established quality standards while also building confidence among customers regarding the products being offered. Furthermore, automation can facilitate better integration with other business processes, such as production and inventory management. This interconnectedness creates a more comprehensive quality management system, allowing for a cohesive approach to manufacturing that encompasses all aspects of the production cycle. The careful implementation of automation in quality assurance can lead to measurable benefits in terms of efficiency, accuracy, and the ability to quickly respond to potential quality issues within the manufacturing process.

Proactive Customer Communication

Proactive communication plays an important role in building and maintaining strong customer relationships while enhancing overall customer experience. Utilizing technologies such as artificial intelligence (AI) and the Internet of Things (IoT) allows businesses to offer timely notifications and updates regarding orders, shipments, and relevant information. This approach not only helps in addressing potential issues before they occur but also keeps customers informed, thereby reducing the volume of manual inquiries and improving satisfaction levels.

Moreover, by informing customers proactively, companies can establish a sense of reliability and assurance. When clients receive timely and precise information, it fosters a trust-based relationship, making customers more likely to return for future business.

The advantages of proactive communication extend beyond customer satisfaction. It can also lead to operational efficiencies by minimizing the frequency of inbound inquiries. This reduction enables customer service agents to concentrate on more complex issues that require their expertise, which can enhance the overall quality of support provided.

Integrating AI-driven communication tools with essential business processes—like order management and inventory systems—ensures that customers receive consistent and accurate information across various channels. This integration not only streamlines communication but also enhances transparency, allowing customers to track their orders or shipments easily.

In the manufacturing sector, these advancements can significantly enhance customer service by addressing critical communication gaps. Leveraging AI and IoT technologies in proactive communication strategies can heighten transparency, boost operational efficiency, and improve customer satisfaction. These improvements ultimately contribute to long-term business success by fostering customer loyalty and repeat business.

Top Challenges In Manufacturing

In the manufacturing sector, improving customer experience presents several challenges. One major issue is the complexity of order management, where various customizable options and specifications can lead to errors and miscommunication. Real-time inventory visibility is also crucial, as outdated information can cause delays and dissatisfaction. The demand for customization puts pressure on manufacturing processes to find a balance between unique designs and operational efficiency. Effective communication is important, but customers often receive insufficient updates on order statuses, which can lead to confusion. Additionally, integrating digital tools into customer service can be difficult due to data silos and resistance to change, limiting potential improvements. Addressing these challenges is important for manufacturers who want to enhance customer experience. Here, we will go into a bit more detail on each of these before diving into some exemplary use cases that solve these issues.

Complexity In Order Management

Managing orders in the manufacturing sector often involves numerous customizable options and detailed specifications. This complexity can pose challenges for customers who may not fully understand the choices or technical requirements, leading to difficulties in accurately completing their orders. Such challenges can result in errors and miscommunication, which not only frustrate customers but also complicate the order fulfillment process for manufacturers.

A lack of a coherent and user-friendly interface can further aggravate these issues. Customers may struggle to locate necessary information or navigate complex forms, which can result in longer lead times and an increased likelihood of order errors. These complications can negatively affect the overall customer experience, making the ordering process feel inefficient. For manufacturers, this complexity can increase the workload on customer service teams, who must spend additional time clarifying orders and resolving issues.

To mitigate these problems, manufacturers should focus on simplifying the ordering process. Implementing intuitive design principles and guidance tools can assist customers in making informed decisions and streamline their workflow. Providing clear, step-by-step instructions, offering real-time feedback on order specifications, and ensuring easy navigation can all contribute to a smoother ordering experience. Simplifying the process can enhance customer satisfaction and improve operational efficiency by reducing the number of order-related issues.

Real-Time Inventory Visibility

Manufacturers face significant challenges in providing customers with accurate, updated information on inventory levels. When inventory data is not current, customers may inadvertently order items that are out of stock or on backorder, leading to delays and dissatisfaction. This lack of real-time visibility can disrupt production schedules and supply chain operations, potentially frustrating customers further.

To maintain transparency and trust, manufacturers must ensure that inventory data is consistently updated and readily accessible in a centralized format. Implementing systems that automatically refresh inventory information can help achieve this, allowing both customers and internal teams to have access to the latest data. With real-time visibility, customers can place orders confidently, knowing that the information reflects the current availability of products.

Additionally, real-time inventory visibility enhances overall supply chain efficiency. By improving coordination between production, inventory management, and customer service, manufacturers can minimize the risks of stockouts and overstock situations. This proactive approach fosters better customer relationships by aligning expectations and making order fulfillment more reliable.

Customization And Personalization

The increasing demand for customized and personalized products presents both opportunities and challenges for manufacturers. Customers expect businesses to address their individual preferences, placing pressure on manufacturing processes. To meet these expectations, manufacturers must balance unique designs with efficient production systems.

To manage personalization while ensuring operational efficiency, manufacturers can invest in advanced technologies, such as flexible manufacturing systems and scalable software. These tools can help streamline the customization process, enabling the production of tailored products without sacrificing efficiency. Implementing robust design and configuration tools also allows customers to create products that align with their specific needs.

Not meeting the demand for customization can lead to lost sales opportunities and lower customer loyalty. Customers who find their preferences unmet may choose competitors who offer more personalized options. Therefore, innovation and adaptability in production processes are essential for manufacturers aiming to remain competitive. By adopting these technologies and strategies, manufacturers can improve customer satisfaction and foster stronger relationships.

Proactive Communication

Effective communication is essential in shaping the customer experience, particularly during order fulfillment. Customers value clear information about their orders, such as status updates and anticipated delays. Unfortunately, many manufacturers face challenges establishing effective communication channels, resulting in customer confusion and frustration.

To improve the situation, manufacturers should implement proactive communication strategies. Regular updates and notifications about order statuses can significantly enhance transparency. Utilizing automated systems, such as email updates or SMS alerts, helps keep customers informed throughout the process. This approach not only builds customer confidence but also reduces inquiries and complaints related to order statuses.

Additionally, proactive communication can help prevent issues from escalating. By informing customers of any changes or delays upfront, manufacturers can manage expectations and address concerns before they become significant problems. This level of transparency is crucial for fostering trust and maintaining positive relationships with customers. Implementing these strategies can lead to a more seamless and satisfying customer experience.

Integration Of Digital Tools

Integrating digital tools and technologies into customer service operations is essential for improving the customer experience in the manufacturing sector. However, manufacturers often face challenges in adopting these solutions, including data silos, incompatible systems, and resistance to change. These issues can hinder effective integration and limit the benefits that digital tools can provide.

To address these challenges, manufacturers should focus on ensuring interoperability among systems and investing in employee training. Seamless integration of digital tools with existing systems is crucial for creating an efficient customer service operation. Additionally, comprehensive training can help employees recognize the advantages of these tools and learn how to use them effectively.

When implemented properly, digital innovations can streamline customer service operations, enhance response times, and improve transparency. They can also automate routine tasks and provide insights into customer behavior and preferences. By addressing the challenges related to integration and training, manufacturers can cultivate a more efficient and customer-focused operation, ultimately leading to higher levels of satisfaction and loyalty.

Manufacturing Use Cases

AI-driven solutions have changed several aspects of manufacturing, especially in customer support and operational efficiency. This chapter explores use cases that illustrate the impact of AI technologies. For example, chatbot support in manufacturing simplifies customer interactions and helps schedule repair personnel, check warranty statuses, and guide customers through necessary steps. These capabilities streamline the customer service process and provide timely assistance, enhancing customer satisfaction.

Other use cases include QA walkthrough transcription and summarization, IoT notifications, automated order status updates, AI-powered product configuration assistants, and platforms for checking replacement and spare parts availability. Each of these solutions addresses specific challenges in the manufacturing sector, such as reducing manual documentation, providing real-time updates, and improving product configuration accuracy.

By integrating these technologies, manufacturers can enhance operational efficiency and improve customer trust. These examples demonstrate the role of AI in promoting innovation and supporting growth in the manufacturing industry. Here, we will explore some of the most popular use cases for automation and contact centers that can be deployed for the manufacturing sector.

Chatbot Repair Scheduling

In the manufacturing sector, chatbots play a crucial role in enhancing customer support, making the experience more efficient and personalized. Customers appreciate the convenience and tailored interactions that chatbots provide, allowing them to access offers and foster relationships with vendors quickly.

Their main tasks include evaluating and securing inventory, as well as seeking assistance when needed. However, they often encounter challenges such as a lack of personalized service and a complicated ordering process.

Customer service agents aim to support sales and deliver excellent service. Their goals include providing comprehensive assistance, building strong customer relationships, ensuring a smooth order experience, and offering relevant upsells. Nonetheless, they face challenges such as balancing personalization with speed, managing complex high-value orders, and addressing gaps in technical or product knowledge.

A significant issue arises when customers expect personalized service that is not time-consuming, while agents need to balance high-touch service with efficiency. Escalations to agents can disrupt the customer experience. Chatbots can help address these challenges by handling common inquiries about products, availability, and promotions. They can also offer interactive guidance and seamlessly introduce live agents with relevant context about the customer's situation. This enables customers to receive quick answers, enhancing their experience and reducing the support burden on agents. Additionally, chatbots simplify the purchasing process, minimizing the need for live assistance while ensuring a smooth transition to live agents when required.

Furthermore, chatbots can schedule and dispatch repair personnel based on information provided by customers, such as serial numbers or other purchase details. They can check warranty status and guide

Figure 26: Chatbot repair scheduling

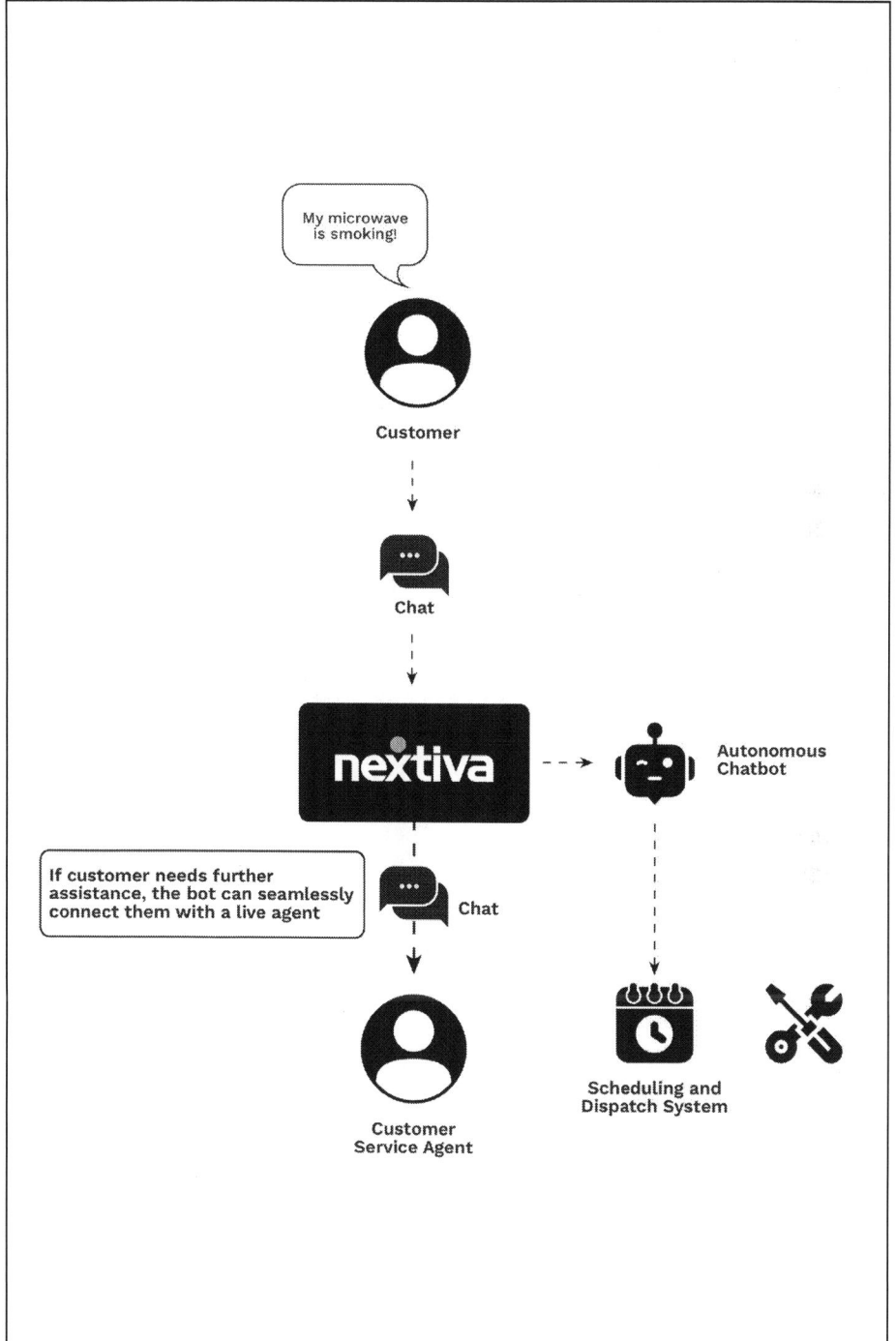

customers through the necessary steps to ensure their products are covered.

By leveraging chatbots, manufacturing companies can significantly streamline their customer support processes, enhance personalization, and ensure efficient and effective interactions. This approach leads to higher customer satisfaction and loyalty by providing quick answers, facilitating smooth transitions to live agents when needed, and ensuring comprehensive support throughout the customer journey. Additionally, chatbots can handle routine tasks such as scheduling repairs and verifying warranty information, freeing up customer service agents to focus on more complex and high-value interactions. This not only improves the overall efficiency of the support team but also contributes to a better customer experience by reducing wait times and increasing the relevance of interactions. Ultimately, integrating chatbots into customer support enables manufacturing companies to

Table 37: Benefits of chatbot repair scheduling

Chatbot repair scheduling capabilities	Chief benefits
Chatbot handling common questions about products, availability, and promotions	Allows customers to receive quick answers, enhancing their experience and reducing the support load
Chatbot providing interactive guidance	Makes it easier for customers to complete their purchases without requiring live assistance
Chatbot introducing live agents with context on the customer's situation	Creates a smooth handoff that saves time and improves the customer experience
Chatbot seamlessly connecting customers with live agents using live chat	Ensures customers do not have to repeat themselves, enhancing convenience and satisfaction
Chatbot scheduling and dispatching repair personnel based on customer-provided information	Provides efficient service and ensures quick resolution of issues

meet and exceed customer expectations, fostering stronger relationships and driving long-term success.

QA Walkthrough Transcription

In the manufacturing sector, maintaining high-quality standards and efficient reporting is essential for quality control inspectors. Their primary role is to conduct thorough inspections and accurately document their findings. Regular quality inspections, along with the analysis and reporting of quality metrics, are critical responsibilities for these inspectors. However, traditional documentation methods can be time-consuming, often diverting inspectors' attention from the inspection tasks themselves. Furthermore, different inspectors may document observations in varying ways, resulting in inconsistencies in the quality of data collected.

Quality control supervisors play a vital role in overseeing the QA process and are focused on maintaining production lines and enhancing team performance. Their primary responsibilities include reviewing and analyzing QA data to identify areas for improvement, as well as facilitating communication among different teams. These supervisors often face challenges related to ensuring uniformity across inspections and effectively interpreting the quality data they receive.

To address these challenges, the transcription and summarization of spoken quality control inspections can serve as an effective solution. By transcribing observations in real-time, the amount of time spent on manual documentation is greatly reduced. This change allows QA specialists to concentrate more on the inspection itself rather than being burdened by paperwork. Moreover, this approach ensures that all observations and findings are captured uniformly, which enhances the reliability and comparability of quality data collected by various inspectors. The transcribed documents can be shared efficiently, providing all relevant stakeholders with timely access to inspection findings and insights.

In this application of quality assurance walkthrough transcription and summarization, a QA specialist utilizes a smartphone to record spoken dialogue during a walkthrough. The data captured is transmitted to the Nextiva UCXM platform, where it undergoes processing

Figure 27: QA walkthrough transcription

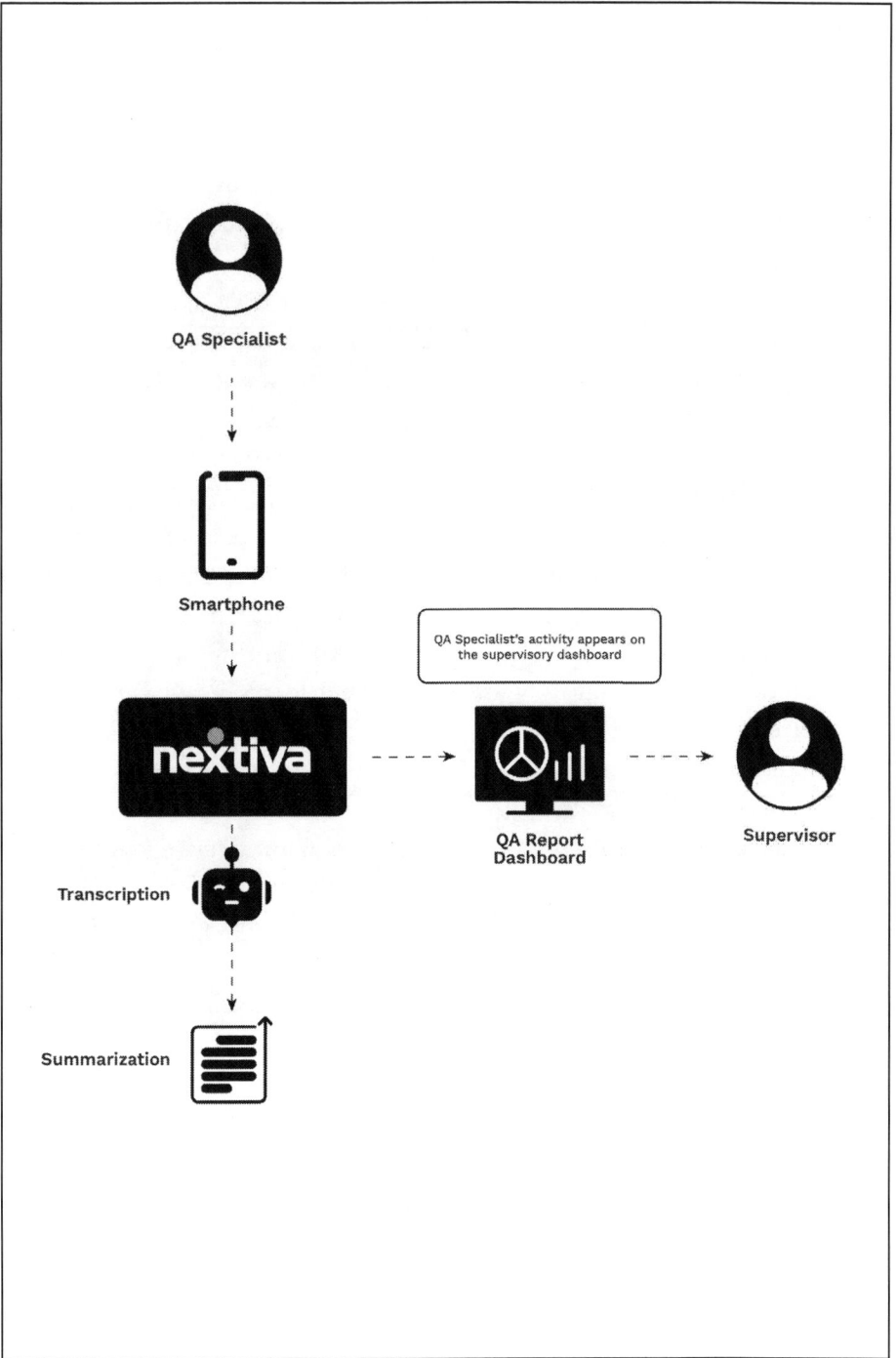

that includes transcription and summarization. The resulting data is then made available on a QA report dashboard for the supervisor. This setup allows the supervisor to monitor the QA specialist's activities, ensuring that all quality assurance processes are thoroughly documented and reviewed. Additionally, the supervisor can access the complete recording and select a quality monitoring survey to evaluate the performance of the QA specialist. This integration of technology serves to streamline QA processes, enhance the transparency of inspections, and improve oversight within manufacturing environments, which is ultimately aimed at achieving better quality control and operational efficiency.

By implementing these advanced transcription and summarization solutions, manufacturing companies can significantly enhance their quality assurance processes. This approach reduces the time QA specialists spend on manual documentation, allowing them to focus

Table 38: Benefits of QA walkthrough with transcription

QA walkthrough with transcription capabilities	Chief benefits
Transcribing observations in real-time	Reduces the time spent on manual documentation, allowing QA specialists to focus on inspections
Ensuring all observations are captured in a consistent manner	Enhances the reliability and comparability of quality data across different inspectors
Transcribed documents can be easily and efficiently shared	Provides quick access to inspection findings and insights for all stakeholders
Using a smartphone to capture spoken dialogue during a walkthrough	Streamlines the documentation process and integrates seamlessly with existing workflows
Utilizing the Nextiva UCXM platform for processing transcription and summarization	Ensures thorough documentation and review of quality assurance processes, improving oversight and efficiency

on thorough and accurate inspections. Consistent documentation ensures reliability and comparability of quality data across different inspectors, enhancing overall data integrity.

Easy sharing of transcribed documents provides quick access to critical findings and insights for all stakeholders, improving communication and collaboration. The use of smartphones to capture spoken dialogue integrates seamlessly into existing workflows, while the Nextiva UCXM platform ensures comprehensive processing and review of quality assurance activities. This integration of technology not only streamlines QA processes but also enhances transparency and oversight, leading to improved quality control and operational efficiency. Ultimately, these solutions contribute to maintaining high standards, driving continuous improvement, and fostering a culture of excellence within the manufacturing environment.

IoT-Enabled Notifications

In the manufacturing sector, IoT-driven notifications play a significant role in managing shipments efficiently. Customers require timely information to reduce disruptions in their supply chain operations. Their primary goal is to monitor inventory and shipment status accurately. Key tasks include tracking shipments and coordinating with teams and vendors. However, challenges such as revenue loss and communication issues can complicate these tasks.

Customer service agents aim to provide effective support and improve customer satisfaction. They work to communicate updates proactively and respond to customer inquiries. Their main tasks involve monitoring IoT alerts, documenting customer interactions, and resolving problems. Agents face challenges in accessing real-time data and managing difficult customer interactions.

A specific issue arises when customers need to know the arrival times of shipments for proper storage, and agents struggle to provide this information without a notification solution. Poor logistics and miscommunication can result in financial losses for customers. The solution is to integrate IoT notifications with a customer experience (CX) platform. IoT devices can monitor shipment conditions and

Figure 28: IoT-enabled notifications

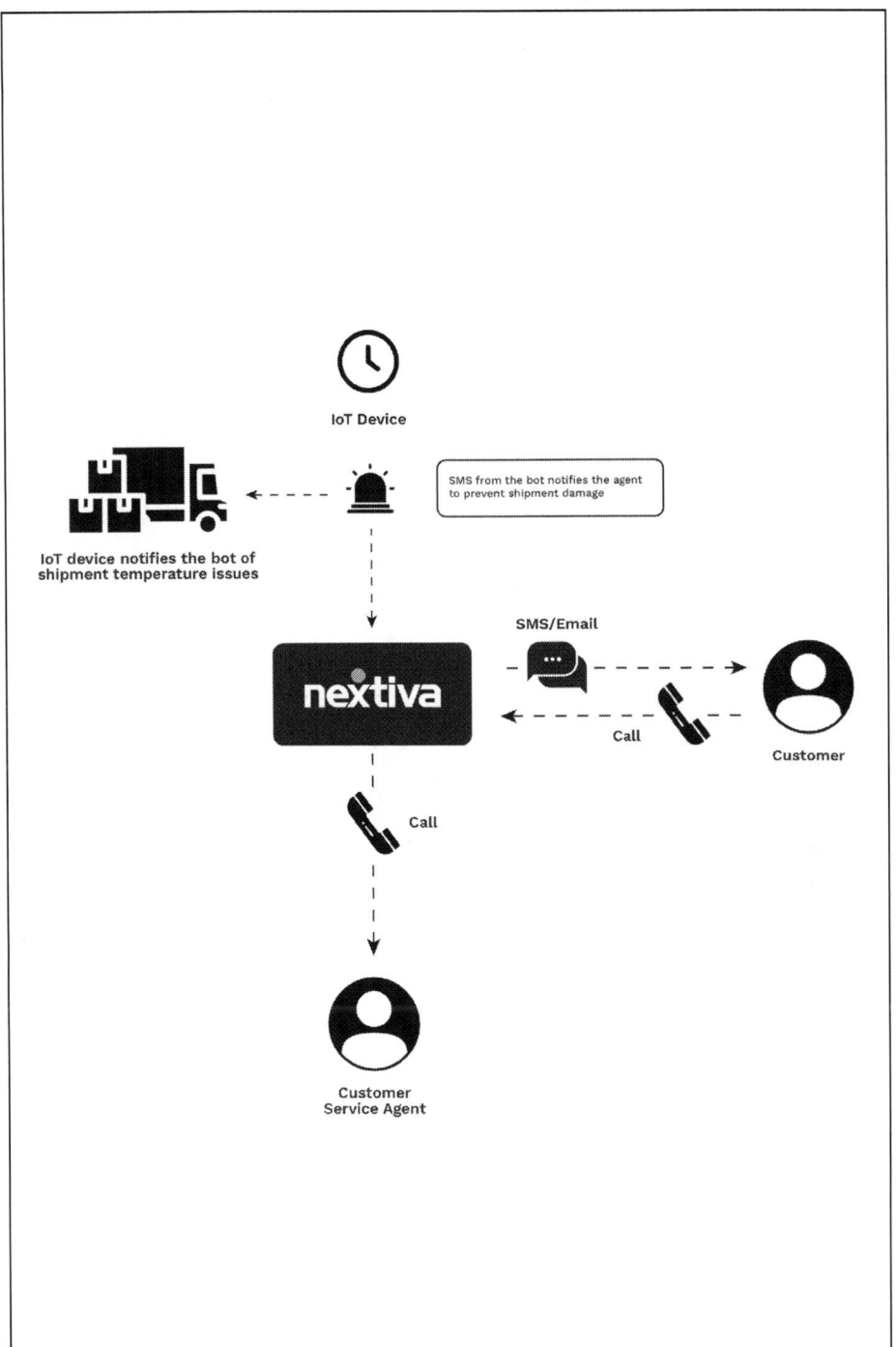

deliver real-time updates to both customers and agents, facilitating effective communication.

By utilizing IoT-driven notifications, customers and agents can receive timely updates on shipment conditions, enhancing customer engagement. This system supports proactive communication to address potential issues before they escalate, contributing to a better overall experience. Agents gain immediate access to relevant data, reducing the time spent searching for information across various systems. Integrating IoT notifications with the CX platform ensures that updates are communicated quickly, promoting reliability and efficiency.

Integrating IoT-driven solutions enables manufacturing companies to enhance supply chain management and customer satisfaction through real-time shipment updates. These notifications help prevent disruptions by ensuring products are stored properly upon arrival, which preserves quality. When coupled with customer experience (CX) platforms, this integration provides customer service agents with

Table 39: Benefits of IoT-enabled notifications

IoT-enabled notifications capabilities	Chief benefits
IoT notifications provide real-time updates on shipment conditions	Enhances customer engagement by providing timely information and minimizing disruptions
Integrating IoT notifications with the CX platform	Ensures agents have immediate access to relevant data, reducing the time spent searching for information across multiple systems
Proactively communicating with customers before issues arise	Improves customer experience by addressing potential problems early and enhancing trust
Agents and the CX system reaching out to customers with updates and solutions	Ensures customers are well-informed, improving their overall satisfaction and trust in the service

immediate access to vital information, allowing them to address inquiries efficiently and build trust with customers.

Timely updates and improved communication lead to a more positive customer experience, fostering loyalty while reducing revenue losses. Additionally, this proactive approach boosts the efficiency of support teams, creating a more responsive service. Overall, adopting IoT-driven notifications alongside CX integration empowers manufacturing companies to streamline operations, enhance data accuracy, and improve customer interactions, ultimately driving business success and growth.

Automated Order Status Updates

In the manufacturing sector, providing accurate order information is essential for ensuring smooth supply chain operations. Customers require real-time updates on shipments and delivery timelines to identify and address any delays. Their primary responsibilities include tracking shipments and inventory, coordinating with teams and vendors, and planning downstream operations. However, challenges such as limited visibility into order status, communication gaps, and production downtime risks due to delayed orders complicate these tasks.

Customer service agents strive to deliver effective support and enhance customer satisfaction. Their roles involve proactively communicating updates, responding to inquiries, and managing escalations. Key tasks include monitoring IoT alerts, documenting customer interactions, and resolving issues. However, agents often face challenges such as managing high volumes of routine queries and balancing workload between chatbot and live support, while also keeping abreast of chatbot improvements and workflow changes.

Implementing automated, AI-driven order status updates can address these challenges. Chatbots can provide customers with real-time shipment updates and potential delays, reducing the need for manual inquiries. Automated notifications can inform customers and agents about critical shipment milestones, ensuring both parties stay informed. Integrating these notifications within a unified platform facilitates communication between stakeholders, enhancing operational efficiency and customer experience.

Figure 29: Automated order status updates

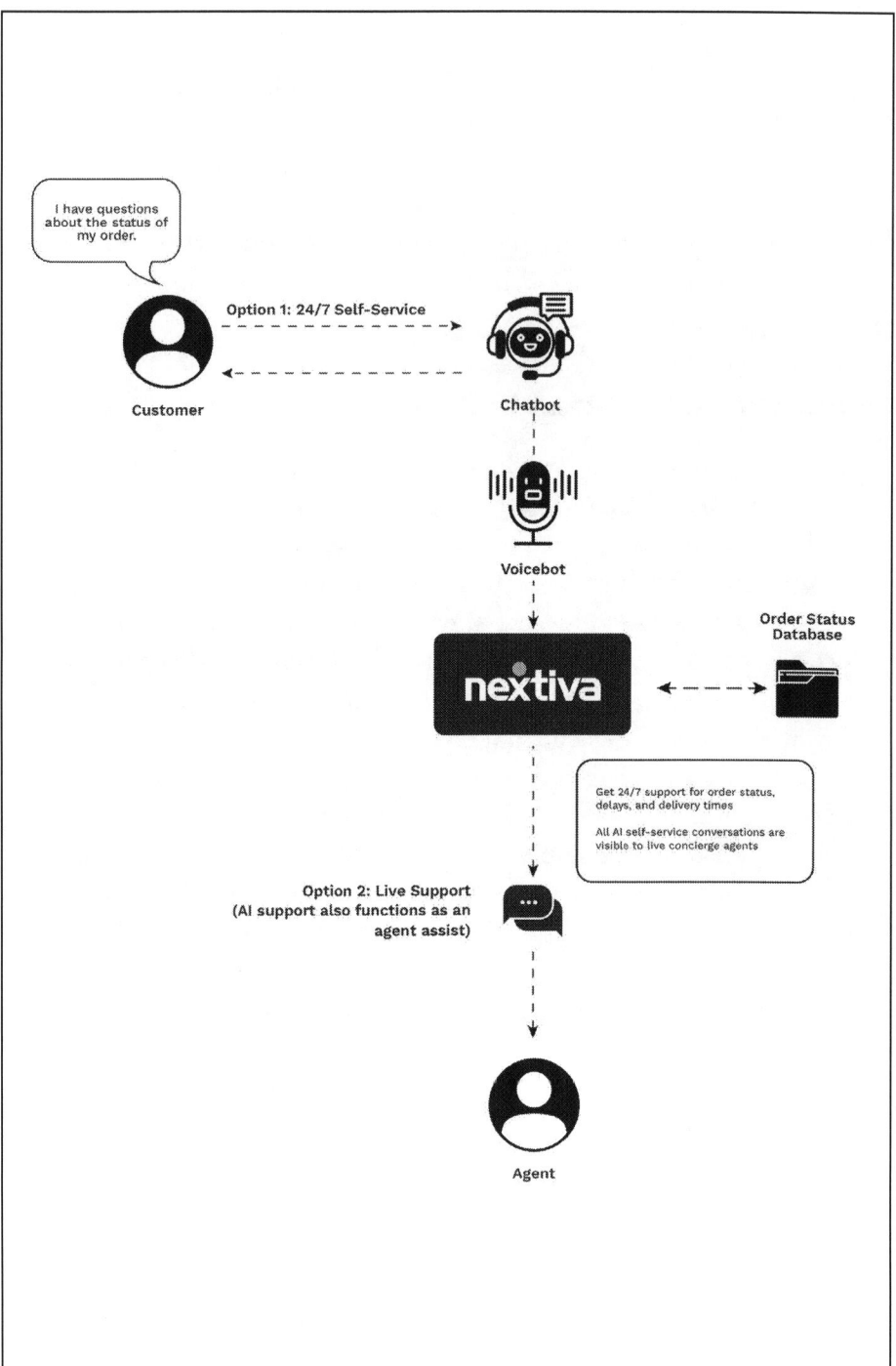

This approach offers several advantages. Proactive communication helps mitigate escalations and improves customer engagement. By automating routine tasks, chatbots free up agents to focus on more complex issues, thereby fostering customer trust and generating cost savings for the company. Furthermore, customers benefit from 24/7 self-service options and the reliability of real-time updates, which help minimize disruptions to their operations.

Leveraging automated and AI-driven updates can significantly enhance supply chain management and operational efficiency for manufacturing companies. Real-time updates from chatbots provide customers with timely order information, preventing disruptions and allowing for better planning. Automated notifications at key shipment

Table 40: Benefits of automated order status updates

Automated order status update capabilities	Chief benefits
Chatbots offering real-time updates on shipment status and potential delays	Provides timely information to customers, enhancing their experience and minimizing disruptions
Automated notifications are triggered to inform customers and agents about key shipment milestones	Ensures proactive communication, preventing issues from escalating and improving customer trust
Integration with a unified platform for seamless communication	Increases operational efficiency by ensuring all stakeholders are informed and can coordinate effectively
24/7 self-service feature via chat or voicebots	Offers customers convenient access to order information at any time, improving satisfaction
AI support system assisting live agents with relevant information	Ensures continuity in customer support and allows agents to handle more complex issues efficiently

milestones keep both customers and agents informed, promoting clear communication and reducing production downtime.

The convenience of 24/7 self-service through chat or voicebots enhances customer satisfaction by offering flexible access to order information. AI-driven support systems equip live agents with relevant data, allowing them to handle more complex issues efficiently. This combination of automated and personalized support fosters customer trust and loyalty by ensuring prompt and accurate responses. Ultimately, these technologies improve quality control, increase customer satisfaction, and strengthen the relationship between companies and their customers, driving long-term business success.

AI-Powered Product Configuration Assistant

In the manufacturing sector, an AI-powered product configuration assistant can streamline the process of configuring complex products and enhance the accuracy of chosen configurations. Customers seek to identify suitable configurations that meet their needs and budget while minimizing their dependence on support teams for basic inquiries. Their main tasks involve exploring available product options and features, confirming compatibility with existing systems, and requesting quotes based on their selections. However, customers often encounter difficulties due to limited technical knowledge, slow response times, and miscommunication, which can lead to frustration.

The virtual assistant is designed to provide immediate guidance for customers as they configure products and automate repetitive configuration inquiries. It offers round-the-clock assistance to help customers navigate product options and specifications. Utilizing natural language processing (NLP), the virtual assistant can understand customer inputs and provide relevant suggestions, collect data for escalation, and improve self-service capabilities through continuous learning. However, it may struggle with handling unusual cases or highly technical questions, ensuring smooth integration with backend systems, and fostering customer trust in automated support.

Customer service agents aim to provide expert guidance for complex configurations and effectively address escalated queries. Their goal is to ensure customer satisfaction by resolving issues promptly and

Figure 30: AI-powered product configuration assistant

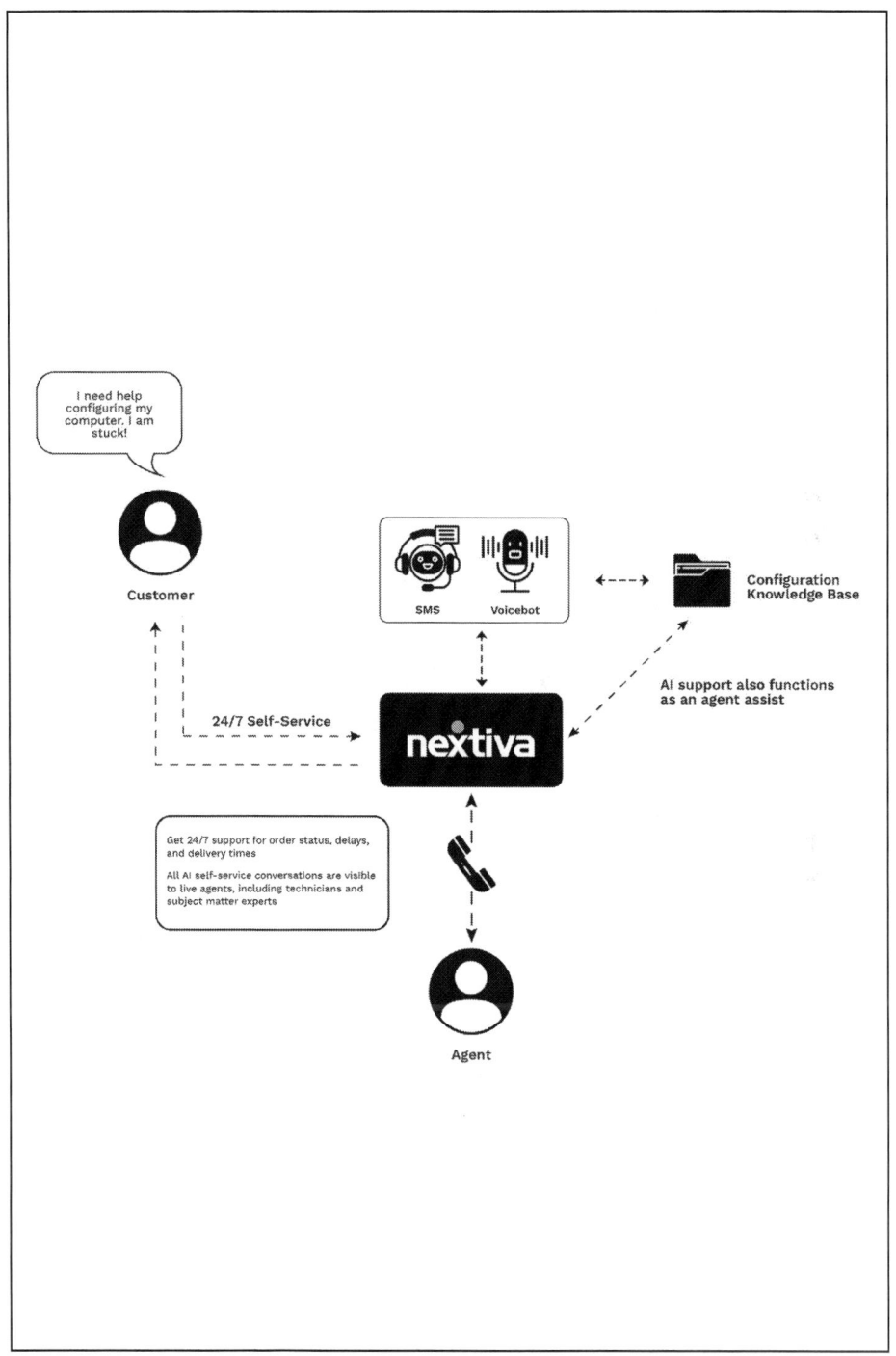

accurately, leveraging insights from the virtual assistant to enhance their support efforts. Key responsibilities for agents include managing escalations from the virtual assistant, reviewing and validating customer-selected configurations, and balancing their workload between handling escalations and completing manual tasks. Collaborating effectively with virtual assistants remains a significant challenge for customer service agents.

The primary issue is that customers often have difficulty understanding the requirements for configuring complex products, while internal support teams are overwhelmed with configuration tasks, resulting in slow response times. Errors in product selection can lead to returns, delays, and decreased satisfaction ratings. An AI-powered product configuration assistant can address these challenges by guiding customers through configurations using NLP, automating repetitive tasks, and escalating complex inquiries to human agents. Ensuring

Table 41: Benefits of AI-powered product configuration assistant

Product configuration assistant capabilities	Chief benefits
AI-powered virtual assistant guiding customers through product configurations using NLP	Provides real-time guidance, increasing customer confidence in their selections; automates repetitive configuration tasks while escalating complex queries to agents; reduces delays, accelerates sales, and improves operational efficiency
Seamlessly integrating the virtual assistant into backend systems to generate accurate quotes	Ensures accurate quote generation, saving money by reducing configuration errors
24/7 self-service support via voice and SMS bots	Offers customers convenient access to order information at any time, improving satisfaction
AI system with a configuration knowledge base assisting live agents	Ensures continuity in customer support and allows agents to handle more complex issues efficiently

this assistant integrates seamlessly with backend systems allows for accurate quote generation and enhances operational efficiency.

This solution provides several advantages. It improves customer satisfaction by offering real-time guidance, which increases customers' confidence in their selections. Automation speeds up quote generation, reducing delays and accelerating sales processes. Additionally, minimizing configuration errors builds customer trust and reduces costs.

In this use case, a customer seeking assistance with configuring a computer can access 24/7 self-service support for inquiries related to order status, delays, and expected delivery times. Support is delivered through a platform called Nextiva, which integrates with voice and SMS bots. The AI system includes a configuration knowledge base and assists live agents by making all self-service conversations visible to them, ensuring that technicians and subject matter experts can intervene when necessary. This AI support serves as both a direct resource for customers and a tool for human agents, improving the overall support experience and demonstrating how AI can enhance customer support processes.

By leveraging AI-driven solutions, manufacturing companies can boost customer satisfaction and operational efficiency. An AI-powered virtual assistant offers real-time guidance, enhancing customer confidence with 24/7 support via voice and SMS bots. This accessibility reduces reliance on human agents for basic queries, allowing them to focus on complex issues. Automating repetitive tasks streamlines processes, speeds up sales cycles, and minimizes errors in configurations with quick and accurate quotes.

The AI system also includes a knowledge base that supports live agents by providing information from self-service interactions, enabling them to resolve escalated issues more efficiently. This combination of automated assistance and human intervention enhances the customer experience, builds trust, fosters stronger relationships, and promotes long-term business success.

Replacement And Spare Parts Platform

In the manufacturing sector, the availability of replacement and spare parts is essential for minimizing equipment downtime and maintaining production schedules. Customers aim to plan replacements and repairs efficiently and require reliable updates to relay to their own clients. Their primary tasks involve searching for parts compatible with their equipment, monitoring the status of placed orders, and communicating with internal stakeholders. However, challenges such as limited visibility into inventory levels, inaccuracies in information, and delays can complicate these processes.

Virtual assistants can offer 24/7 responses to customer inquiries, thereby reducing the workload of customer service agents by providing real-time information on part availability, pricing, and delivery timelines. These assistants can handle routine questions, deliver prompt and precise information, and document customer interactions. However, they often struggle to gain customer trust in automated responses, and ensuring seamless integration with inventory systems presents an additional hurdle.

Customer service agents are vital for monitoring the accuracy of AI responses and managing escalations. Their primary objective is to enhance customer satisfaction by providing reliable information that prevents returns while addressing issues related to procurement or logistics as they arise. Balancing the handling of escalations with routine inquiries represents a significant challenge for these agents.

The core issue faced by customers is the delay in accessing necessary parts, which leads to prolonged downtime and operational interruptions. Agents frequently spend considerable time on repetitive inventory checks, causing delays in responses. Miscommunication regarding availability, pricing, or delivery times can result in frustration and erode trust. An AI-powered assistant that integrates with inventory systems can provide real-time data on parts, availability, and pricing. Chatbots or virtual assistants can effectively manage routine inquiries, allowing customers to leverage self-service options. Proactive notifications can keep customers informed about delivery times and any changes to their orders.

Figure 31: Replacement and spare parts platform

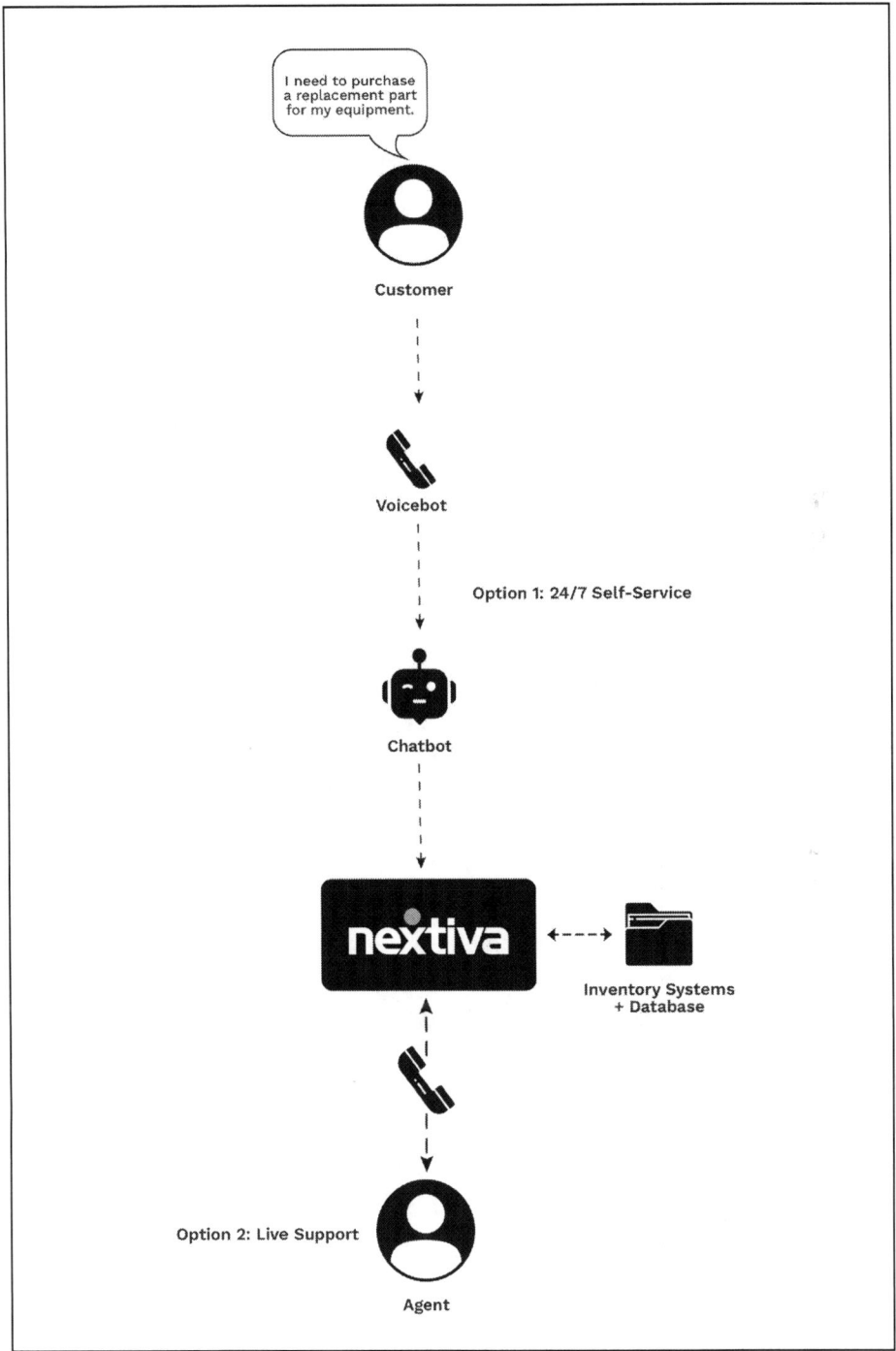

The proposed solution offers several benefits. Operational efficiency is enhanced through the automation of repetitive tasks, allowing agents to concentrate on more complex inquiries. Improved customer satisfaction is achieved via timely and accurate responses, fostering a trustworthy relationship. Access to precise information regarding availability can reduce order cancellations, ultimately enhancing the overall customer experience.

By integrating AI-driven solutions, manufacturing companies can enhance their support processes and improve customer satisfaction. The combination of AI with inventory systems provides real-time information on parts, availability, and pricing, which can reduce delays and cancellations. This is vital in manufacturing, where timely access to replacement parts minimizes equipment downtime and supports continuity in production. Additionally, chatbots and virtual assistants facilitate 24/7 self-service support for routine inquiries, easing the

Table 42: Benefits of replacement and spare parts platform

Automated replacement and spare parts system capabilities	Chief benefits
AI integration with inventory systems to provide real-time information on parts, availability, and pricing	Enhances operational efficiency and accuracy of information, reducing delays and cancellations
Chatbots or virtual assistants handle routine inquiries, enabling self-service for customers	Frees up customer service agents to focus on high-value tasks and reduces response times
Proactive notifications keep customers updated on delivery times and any changes to their orders	Improves customer satisfaction and trust by ensuring timely and accurate information
24/7 self-service option through voice and chatbots	Provides customers with convenient access to information at any time, enhancing their experience

workload on customer service agents and allowing them to focus on more complex issues.

These AI systems also track interactions and can escalate inquiries to live agents when necessary, ensuring that customer needs are addressed effectively. This collaboration between AI and human agents can enhance the quality of support while minimizing communication breakdowns. Overall, the integration of AI in support processes improves operational efficiency and enables manufacturing companies to better address their customers' evolving requirements.

Non-Profit and Education

IN BOTH THE non-profit and education sectors, enhancing the customer experience presents significant opportunities to bolster advocacy and retain clients and students. Non-profits, which often rely heavily on donor contributions and volunteer support, can benefit from improved CX by ensuring that interactions are seamless, personalized, and responsive.

By leveraging technology and automation, non-profits can streamline donor communications, manage volunteer schedules efficiently, and provide real-time updates on the impact of contributions. This creates a more engaging and satisfying experience for donors and volunteers, thereby fostering stronger relationships and encouraging continued support and advocacy.

Institutions can significantly enhance the student experience in the education sector by implementing solutions that address common pain points such as enrollment, course selection, and academic advising. Automated systems can help manage administrative tasks, provide timely information, and facilitate better communication between students and faculty. Additionally, personalized learning experiences powered by data analytics can tailor educational content to individual student needs, improving learning outcomes and satisfaction. By focusing on these areas, educational institutions can retain students by creating an environment that supports their academic journey and personal growth, ultimately leading to higher retention rates and stronger alumni networks.

Automation Targets For Non-profit And Education Sectors

Utilizing automation in non-profit organizations and educational institutions can greatly improve operational efficiency and enhance stakeholder engagement. By automating processes such as donor communications, enrollment, academic advising, and volunteer management, these sectors can offer personalized, timely, and effective interactions. This, in turn, helps strengthen relationships and boosts overall satisfaction. Moreover, adopting AI-driven analytics tools provides valuable insights into performance metrics, allowing for proactive interventions and more targeted strategies to address the needs of donors, volunteers, students, and staff.

Non-Profit Donor And Alumni Engagement

Automating donor communications in the non-profit and education sectors through AI-powered chatbots and personalized email campaigns can enhance communication efficiency. By providing timely updates about contributions and alumni or fundraising events, organizations can strengthen relationships with donors, making them feel more connected to the organization's mission. Additionally, integrating contact center engagement with live agents for complex inquiries or personalized thank-you calls can improve donor satisfaction and retention.

Education Enrollment Processes

In educational institutions, automating the enrollment and registration process can reduce the administrative burden on staff while enhancing the student experience. AI-driven systems can streamline course selection and manage prerequisites, ensuring that students are enrolled in classes that align with their academic goals and schedules. This automation minimizes errors and enhances overall efficiency, allowing staff to focus on strategic tasks and student support.

Automated Academic Advisory

Automated scheduling systems in education can facilitate timely connections between students and academic advisors, reducing wait times. AI tools can analyze student data to deliver personalized advice and identify students at risk of falling behind, enabling proactive interventions. This ensures that students receive the necessary guidance, which can improve retention rates and overall satisfaction.

Non-Profit Volunteer Management

Automating volunteer management processes can streamline the coordination of events and activities in non-profits. Automated systems can handle volunteer sign-ups, shifts, and communication, allowing staff to focus on engagement. By providing clear communication and a smoother experience for volunteers, organizations can maintain a committed volunteer base essential for their initiatives.

AI-Driven Analytics

Both non-profits and educational institutions can benefit from implementing AI-driven analytics tools to gain insights into engagement and performance metrics. For non-profits, these tools provide a better understanding of donor behavior and preferences, leading to more targeted fundraising campaigns. In education, analytics can track student progress, identify trends in academic performance, and inform decision-making to enhance educational strategies. By utilizing these insights, organizations can improve their operations and outcomes, an effective equilibrium between automation and human interaction.

Top Challenges In Non-profit And Education Sectors

Non-profits and educational institutions encounter distinct challenges that can be addressed through the strategic use of AI, automation, and contact center engagement. These sectors need to manage donor relationships, coordinate volunteers, support student engagement, and ensure effective communication while navigating complex environments to achieve their objectives. Additionally, maintaining data security and regulatory compliance is a critical concern. Advanced technological solutions can help mitigate these issues, fostering trust and enhancing efficiency across all operations.

Managing Donor Relationships In Non-Profits

In the non-profit sector, a significant challenge is managing donor relationships while maintaining personalized communication. With limited resources, providing the level of engagement and recognition that donors expect can be challenging. AI and automation can assist by personalizing outreach through automated emails, chatbots, and messages based on donor behavior and preferences. However, it is essential to ensure that these technologies integrate well with live agent support for more complex interactions, maintaining a human element in donor relations.

Coordinating Volunteers And Event Management

Another challenge for non-profits is coordinating volunteer efforts and managing events. With many volunteers and events, efficient scheduling and communication can become a burden. Automation tools can help automate volunteer sign-ups, shift reminders, and event notifications. AI-driven scheduling systems can enhance volunteer allocation based on availability and skills, while contact center engagement provides timely support and information to volunteers, improving their experience and commitment.

Supporting Student Engagement In Education

Managing student engagement and academic success poses a challenge in the education sector. Students need personalized support and timely interventions to remain on track, but providing this level of attention is resource-intensive. AI can assist by analyzing student data to identify those at risk of falling behind and suggesting personalized interventions. Automated systems can schedule advising appointments and send reminders, while live agents can provide in-depth support when necessary, ensuring that students receive timely assistance.

Enhancing Communication Among Educational Stakeholders

Another challenge in education is ensuring effective communication among students, faculty, and administration. Miscommunication can result in missed deadlines and dissatisfaction. AI-driven communication platforms can facilitate interactions by providing real-time updates, addressing frequently asked questions through chatbots, and escalating complex queries to live agents. This approach ensures that all stakeholders remain informed and engaged, reducing confusion in the educational environment.

Maintaining Data Security And Compliance

Both non-profits and educational institutions face the challenge of data security and regulatory compliance. Handling sensitive information such as donor payment details or student records necessitates robust security measures. AI and automation can improve data security by implementing encryption, monitoring for suspicious activity, and ensuring compliance with regulations such as PCI and TCPA. Balancing automation with human oversight is crucial to address security concerns and maintain trust among stakeholders.

Use Case Examples In Non-profit And Education Sectors

In both the non-profit and education sectors, automation solutions are revolutionizing how organizations tackle key challenges. For educational institutions, automated advisory appointment scheduling helps recognize when students need support from academic advisors, ensuring timely interventions and improving student well-being. Non-profits benefit from omnichannel outreach and chatbot engagement, which streamline donor interactions and simplify the donation process, ultimately strengthening relationships with donors.

Additionally, social work programs utilize advanced client care platforms for efficient onboarding and consistent communication, while AI-enabled suicide hotlines provide personalized and secure communication channels, enhancing client support and improving staff management. Automated truancy reporting systems in education track and notify student attendance, supporting collaborative efforts to maintain regular school attendance. Overall, these automation solutions improve non-profits and educational institutions' operational efficiency and effectiveness, ensuring timely and impactful support for all stakeholders. Here, we will discuss a few of these use cases as examples of how automation, AI, and contact center solutions can be useful.

Advisory Appointment Scheduling

Student affairs directors aim to provide comprehensive student services like housing, counseling, and activities. They focus on safety, academic excellence, and a positive learning environment. Key tasks include managing dorms and staff, overseeing counseling services, and organizing events. They face challenges like following regulations, ensuring security, and monitoring students.

Students are motivated to achieve their academic goals, graduate with a degree, and enjoy their university experience while forming meaningful friendships. They aim to avoid trouble, seek expert advice, and graduate on time. Their primary tasks include committing to a study plan and selecting a degree that aligns with their skills and

Figure 32: Automatic advisory appointment scheduling

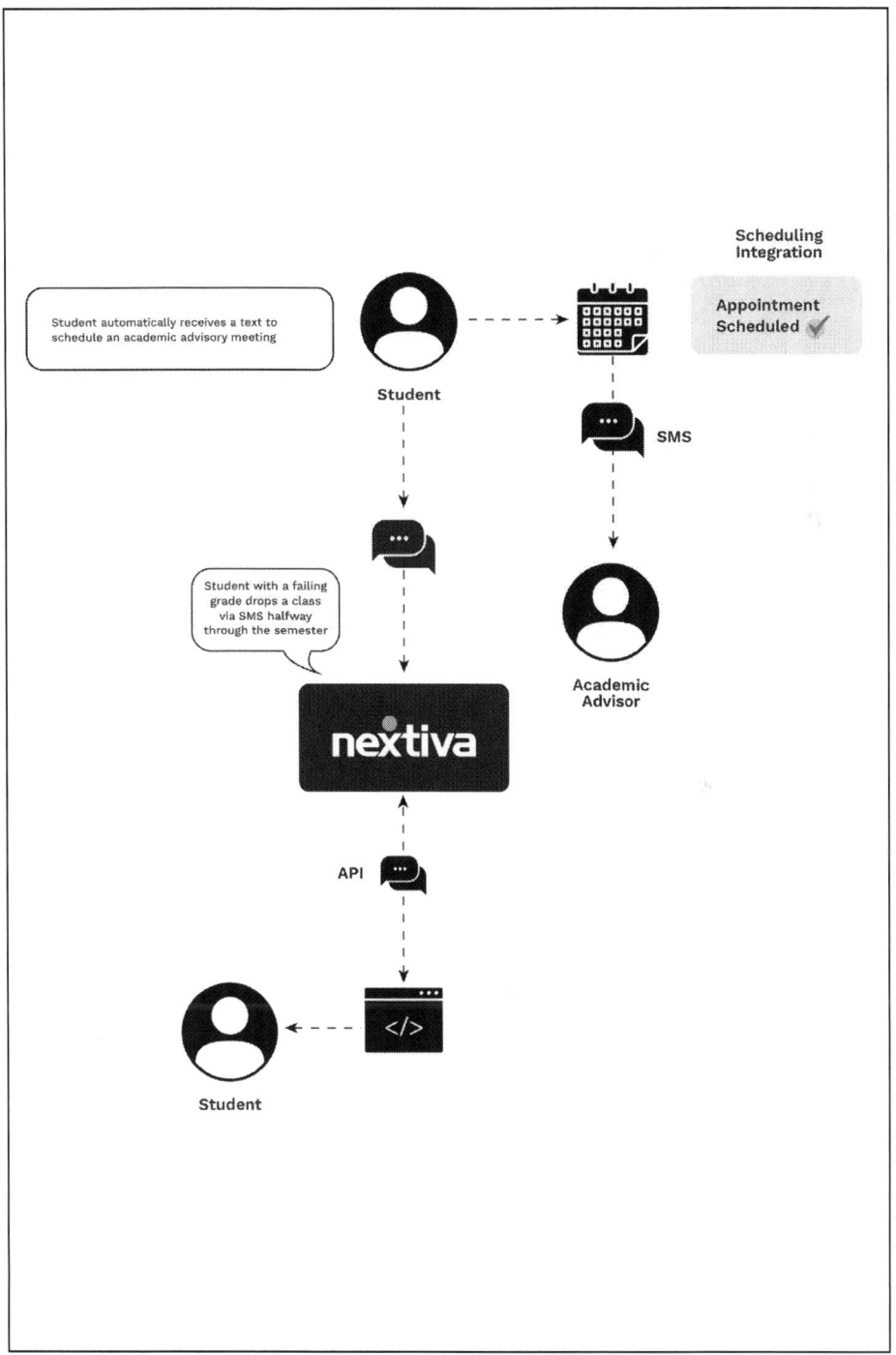

interests. However, they encounter challenges such as campus distractions, financial aid issues, and fluctuating motivation.

Academic advisors are dedicated to promoting student success, which encompasses high graduation rates and successful course completions. Their objectives are to prevent dropouts, align student plans with their goals, and enhance student satisfaction. Key responsibilities include evaluating course credits and majors and ensuring alignment with degree requirements. Advisors face challenges in managing student records and data, maintaining student motivation, and addressing inconsistencies between professors.

A notable issue is identifying when a student requires assistance from an academic advisor. Students often do not seek help proactively, and universities find it challenging to monitor all student behaviors despite their commitment to student welfare. An effective solution involves implementing automatic SMS scheduling. When a student withdraws from a class due to poor performance, it indicates a need for advisor intervention. As students are more likely to respond to SMS prompts, integrating this functionality into student information systems is essential.

The benefits of automating appointments are significant. Students receive timely and personalized support, potentially improving their satisfaction and success. Academic advisors can connect with students in need of support, and universities may reduce student dropout rates by addressing issues promptly. Moreover, automated scheduling and communication can save administrative time and help ensure that no student is overlooked, contributing to a more supportive educational environment.

Moreover, there are related capabilities and features that can further enhance this solution. For example, integrating a calendar sync feature ensures that students and advisors can easily manage and keep track of appointments. Real-time notifications can alert both parties to any changes or reminders about upcoming meetings.

Additionally, the use of a secure communication platform ensures all interactions are private and compliant with data protection regulations, further enhancing trust and confidentiality between students and advisors.

The automatic advisory appointment scheduling system for education meets the needs of students, academic advisors, and student affairs directors by providing timely support, reducing dropouts, and fostering a supportive learning environment. Key features include SMS scheduling, calendar sync, real-time notifications, and analytics tools for proactive student support. The secure communication platform ensures privacy and data protection compliance, enhancing trust and confidentiality. This approach promotes student success and well-being.

Table 43: Benefits of automatic appointment scheduling

Appointment scheduling platform capabilities	Chief benefits
Automatic SMS scheduling	Students receive timely and personalized support that increases happiness and success
Integrate SMS capabilities into student information systems	Academic advisors get connected with students who most need their support
Drop/add rapid response	Universities reduce student dropout by rapidly responding to issues
Calendar sync feature	Ensures students and advisors can easily manage and keep track of appointments
Real-time notifications	Alerts both parties to any changes or reminders about upcoming meetings
Analytics tools	Helps advisors identify patterns and trends in student behavior, enabling proactive interventions
Secure communication platform	Ensures all interactions are private and compliant with data protection regulations, enhancing trust and confidentiality

Omnichannel Outreach And Bot Engagement With Donors

Non-profit civic and social organizations face numerous challenges in their fundraising efforts. Donors are motivated to attend well-organized events and appreciate receiving recognition for their contributions. They have expectations for regular communication about upcoming events and personalized messages that make them feel valued. However, many donors struggle to stay informed about events, decide where to donate, and feel truly appreciated after making their contributions.

Volunteers play a crucial role in recruiting donors and maintaining strong relationships with them. They aim to provide excellent customer service, yet they often encounter difficulties delivering consistent communication due to limited resources. Their primary tasks involve organizing effective events and optimizing engagement with donors, which can be challenging when team coordination falters.

Membership coordinators focus on hosting fundraising events and managing volunteers to advance the organization's goals. They strive to send personalized communications and simplify follow-up processes, such as thank-you messages. However, these coordinators also face obstacles in ensuring events remain engaging for donors and in supporting the volunteer workforce while managing effective communication.

Among the primary challenges these roles face is the need to coordinate meaningful membership activities and securely maintain donor contact and payment information. Additionally, they must support the continuous growth of both the donor and volunteer base while ensuring compliance with regulations. Effective communication across multiple channels is also essential for maintaining engagement with teams and donors.

Organizations can implement several solutions to address these challenges. Automating recruitment campaigns can help raise awareness about events and opportunities to donate. Additionally, leveraging social media can enhance outreach efforts, while accessing donor contact information and sentiment history can inform better communication strategies. It is also important to securely store payment details in compliance with PCI regulations while ensuring adherence to

NON-PROFIT AND EDUCATION

Figure 33: Omnichannel outreach and bot engagement

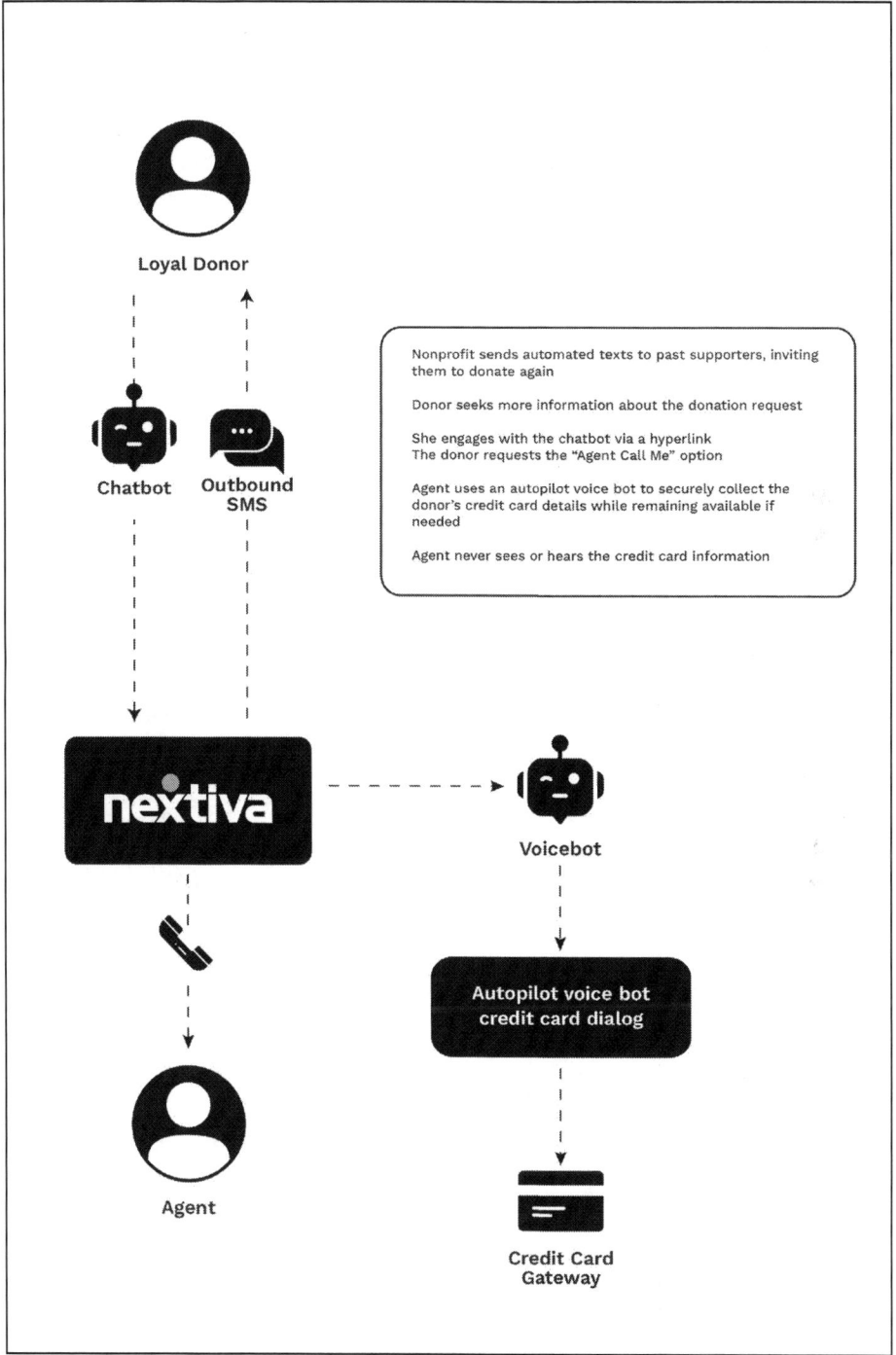

TCPA standards. By utilizing various communication methods—like inbound and outbound calling, video conferencing, web chat, and SMS—organizations can streamline interactions.

One effective approach is to use an omnichannel outreach system, which can facilitate engagement with donors through various automated channels. For instance, a non-profit could send automated SMS messages to past supporters, inviting them to donate again. If a donor wishes to learn more, they can interact with a chatbot via a hyperlink. Furthermore, if the donor requests a call from an agent, that agent can utilize a secure voicebot to collect credit card information, ensuring that the sensitive data remains confidential.

Table 44: Benefits of automated outreach

Donor outreach platform capabilities	Chief benefits
Automate recruitment campaigns to raise awareness	Maximizes social media utilization; simplifying the donation process and providing multiple ways to give makes it easier for donors to contribute more
Access donor contact info, transcriptions, and sentiment history; securely store payment details (PCI)	Full view into donor and supporter interaction history, as well as AI-powered transcription, frees up volunteers to build better relationships, fueling fundraising
Optimize outbound reach with time-saving progressive campaigns, voicemail drops, and SMS	By tailoring their outreach and engagement strategies to individual donors, non-profits can generate 40% more revenue than those that don't personalize communication
Automatic TCPA guardrails	Ensures organizational compliance with regulations and standards
Inbound/outbound calling, video conferencing, social media management, web chat, and SMS	Support multiple channels for communication with teams and donors, enhancing engagement and operational efficiency

The benefits of implementing these solutions are substantial. By simplifying the donation process and offering multiple ways to contribute, organizations can encourage donors to give more. Volunteers gain valuable insights into donor interactions, allowing them to focus on building stronger relationships. Personalized outreach strategies have the potential to generate up to 40% more revenue than non-personalized approaches. In summary, these solutions not only enhance operational efficiency and improve donor and volunteer satisfaction but also help organizations maintain compliance with necessary regulations.

Non-profit civic and social organizations face various challenges in their fundraising efforts, such as keeping donors informed and appreciated and maintaining effective communication. By implementing an omnichannel outreach system, these organizations can automate recruitment campaigns, leverage social media, and securely manage donor information, leading to increased donations and improved donor relationships. Volunteers can focus on building stronger connections, and personalized outreach can significantly boost revenue. Overall, this approach enhances operational efficiency, compliance, and satisfaction for both donors and volunteers.

Progressive Client Care Platform

In this social services scenario, three key personas emerge, each with unique responsibilities and challenges. The social services director plays a pivotal role in enhancing the training and support for caseworkers while managing client escalations and operational efficiency. Their responsibilities include budget management, community outreach, compliance adherence, and staff hiring, training, and evaluation. They face challenges such as meeting KPIs, SLAs, and compliance requirements, maintaining a strong caseworker workforce, and streamlining staff training.

Meanwhile, clients seek personalized interactions and consistent communication to feel valued and informed about their care options. Their key tasks are understanding the full scope of coaching options through regular communication and resolving issues with professional help. However, they often struggle to stay informed about changes

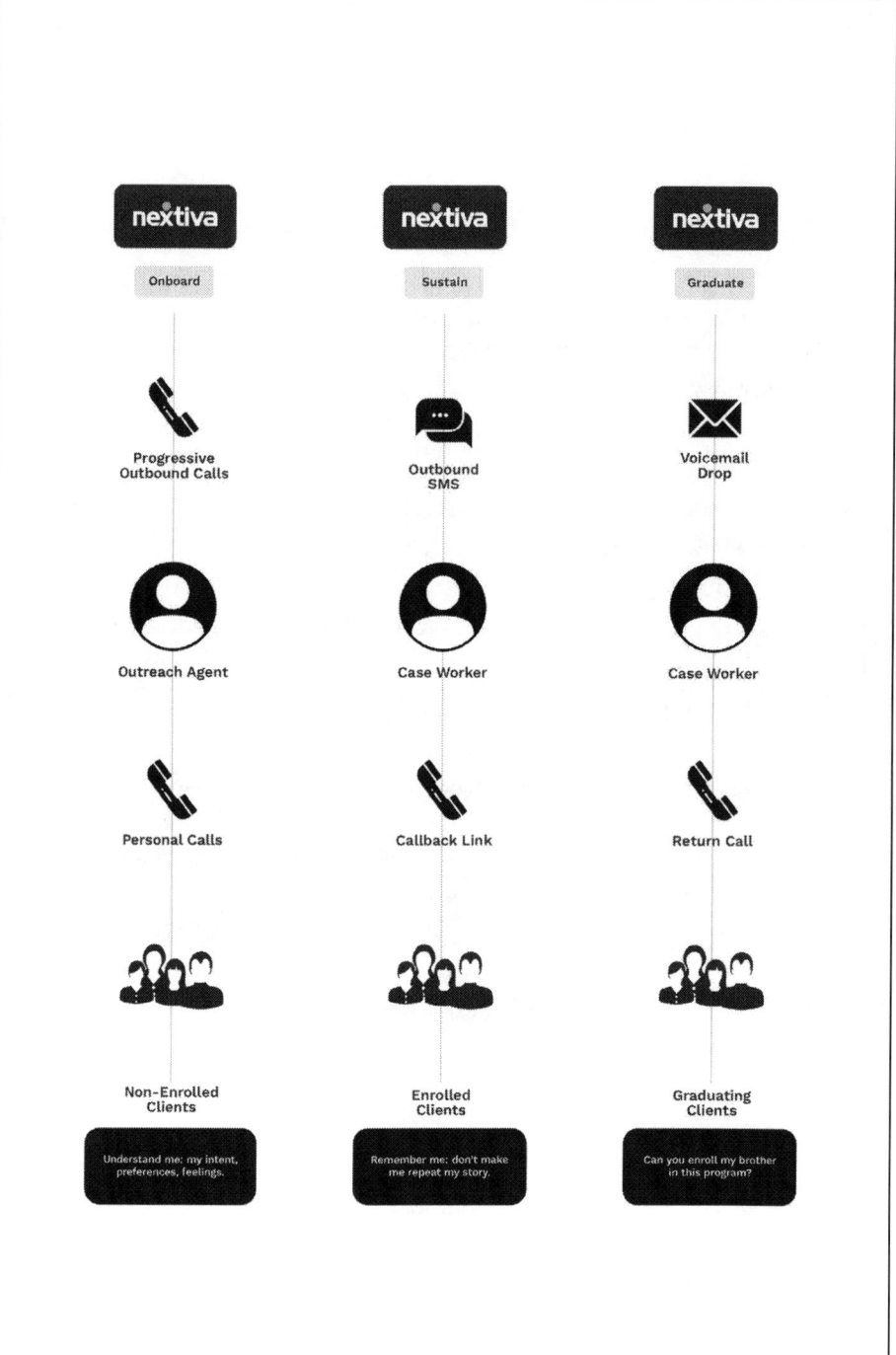

Figure 34: Progressive client care platform

to coverage, make informed decisions about their next steps, and feel well cared for.

Caseworkers serve as the crucial link between the organization and clients, striving to maintain contact and provide excellent customer service despite facing resource limitations. They aim to ensure excellent customer service using a centralized solution and deepen relationships with contact management tools. Their primary tasks involve maintaining contact with clients, alerting the client base to changes in care and coverage, and feeling supported by supervisors and leadership. Challenges include delivering consistent communication to clients and effectively communicating with teammates, often due to limited resources.

To address all of these challenges, an automated progressive client care communication system offers a comprehensive solution. It enables the semi-automation of onboarding clients who enroll in social programs. Outbound calls can be made to clients who have opted into a program and are awaiting onboarding instructions. These automated calls connect to outreach agents who guide clients through preparatory questions, capturing responses in a dynamic script for generating progress reports, augmented by AI for automatic summarization.

Once onboarded, clients are assigned a caseworker who utilizes the same system to deliver a series of automated SMS communications. Clients can respond through an SMS bot, which escalates to a live caseworker if further assistance is needed. Live SMS responses from clients are routed to caseworkers who have previously supported them. Callback links within SMS messages allow clients to request phone calls, with hyperlinks activating on the caseworker's screen to facilitate immediate communication.

Following the completion of their programs, clients participate in a voice of the customer (VOC) survey conducted by a voicebot, which guides them through a series of questions using interactive voice responses. Additionally, a voicemail can be sent automatically, directing clients to call a voicebot number to complete the survey or use a chatbot to answer the same questions. This system ensures that clients receive timely and personalized support, improving their overall experience and satisfaction. It also helps caseworkers manage their workload more efficiently and maintain better relationships with clients.

By streamlining communication and automating routine tasks, this approach can significantly enhance the effectiveness and responsiveness of social services.

Implementing a progressive client care platform can significantly enhance the efficiency and responsiveness of social services in managing client interactions. This system ensures that clients receive timely and personalized support through automated onboarding, dynamic AI-driven progress tracking, and real-time communication via SMS and voicebots. As a result, clients feel more valued and informed, leading to improved satisfaction and better outcomes.

Caseworkers benefit from a streamlined workflow, enabling them to manage their caseloads more effectively while maintaining

Table 45: Benefits of a progressive client care platform

Progressive client care platform capabilities	Chief benefits
Semi-automate the onboarding of clients with progressive outbound calls	Efficient onboarding process that ensures clients receive necessary information and support
Use AI to summarize responses in dynamic scripts	Generates detailed progress reports and improves accuracy in client tracking
Pair clients with caseworkers for automated SMS communications	Clients receive timely and personalized support, enhancing their experience and satisfaction
Integrate SMS bots that escalate to live caseworkers when needed	Ensures clients' issues are promptly addressed by familiar caseworkers, improving continuity of care
Embed callback links in SMS messages	Facilitates direct communication between clients and caseworkers, providing immediate assistance when required
Collect VOC surveys via voicebots or chatbots after program completion	Gathers valuable feedback to improve services and ensures clients feel their voices are heard

high-quality service. Additionally, directors and supervisors can monitor compliance, support their teams, and maintain operational efficiency.

Overall, this integrated approach addresses critical challenges faced by social services, creating a more supportive and effective environment for both clients and staff.

AI-Enabled Suicide Hotline

In the context of a suicide prevention hotline, both clients and hotline staff have distinct motivations, intents, tasks, and challenges that can be addressed through the effective use of AI and automation. Clients are primarily motivated by the need for immediate help and support, seeking a safe space to share their feelings, and looking for resources and guidance to cope with their distress. Their main intents include accessing resources and referrals to professional mental health services and learning about ongoing support and treatment options. Clients' top tasks involve expressing immediate concerns, sharing relevant background information, discussing coping strategies, and agreeing on follow-up actions. However, they face significant challenges, such as overcoming fear and stigma, articulating their distress, trusting the confidentiality of their communication, and maintaining consistency in seeking help.

Caseworkers, on the other hand, are driven by the desire to provide immediate support and crisis intervention, build trust and rapport with clients, and connect clients to ongoing resources and support. Their primary intents are to understand the urgency of the situation, de-escalate feelings of distress or danger, and create a safe space through active listening and empathy. Caseworkers' top tasks include assessing the immediate risk and safety of clients and providing emotional support and connection. They also face challenges, including managing the emotional intensity of their work, avoiding burnout, and ensuring effective communication under pressure.

The director of the hotline is motivated to ensure high-quality and consistent service delivery while supporting and retaining caseworkers. Their intents are to provide staff support, address challenges, and continuously review and improve service delivery. Key tasks for the

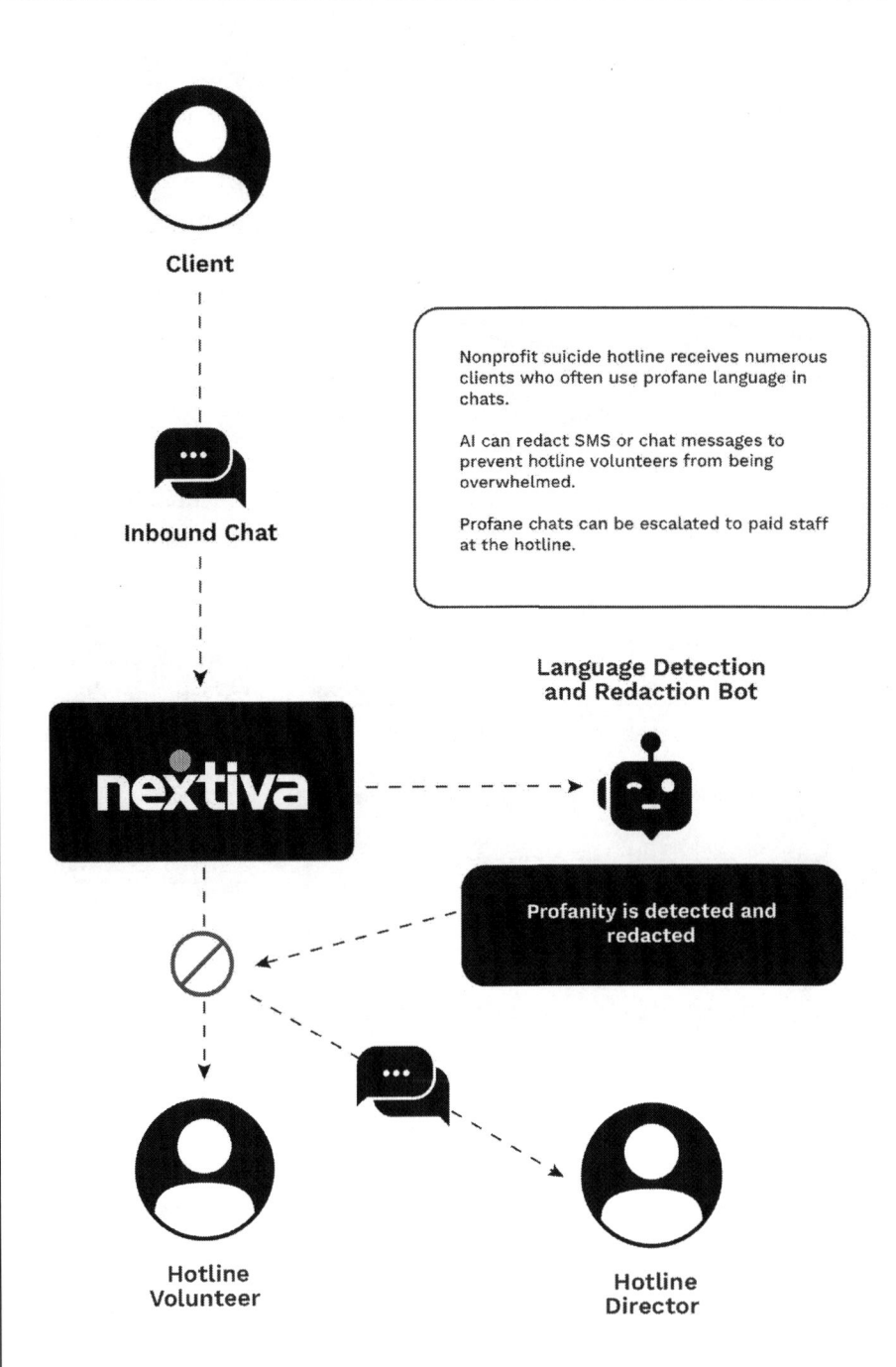

Figure 35: AI-enabled suicide hotline

director include ensuring operational efficiency and compliance, as well as providing necessary support and resources to caseworkers. The director faces challenges related to managing the emotional well-being and burnout of caseworkers and ensuring consistent quality and compliance in service delivery.

Several AI and automation solutions can be implemented to address these challenges. Maintaining the confidentiality of client communication is crucial, and this can be achieved by using AI to redact personally identifiable information (PII) automatically. AI can also

Table 46: Benefits of an AI-enabled suicide hotline

AI-enabled suicide hotline capabilities	Chief benefits
Using AI, PII can be automatically redacted	The knowledge that personal information is redacted facilitates a feeling of trust with the client, fostering deeper and more meaningful dialog
Using AI, foul language can be detected and redacted	Redacted communications allow volunteers to work longer hours without burnout or feeling of danger; supervisors can offer a second level of support and point of escalation, ensuring a safer environment for volunteers
With an omnichannel approach, all channels of communication can be used to ensure the client is communicating over the medium of their choice	Enhances accessibility and comfort for clients, fostering a supportive environment
Ability for supervisors to monitor live chat screens, take hand raises, or react to redacted material	Ensures compliance and allows real-time intervention, improving service quality and safety
Ability for directors or supervisors to barge in and take over	Directors can ensure compliance by leveraging AI and platform escalation capability

detect foul language and threats, enhancing clients' and staff's safety and well-being.

An omnichannel approach ensures that clients can communicate through their preferred medium, improving accessibility and comfort. Supervisors can monitor live chat screens, respond to hand raises, and react to redacted material in real-time. Additionally, directors or supervisors have the capability to intervene and take over communications if necessary.

These solutions provide numerous benefits. For clients, personalized communication facilitated by AI fosters a feeling of trust and safety. For hotline volunteers, the ability to redact communications using AI allows them to work longer hours without experiencing burnout or feeling endangered. Directors benefit from leveraging AI and platform escalation capabilities to ensure compliance and maintain high service quality.

Integrating AI and automation into suicide prevention hotlines enhances client support and staff efficiency. By addressing challenges like confidentiality, harmful language detection, and accessibility, these technologies create a safer environment. Clients feel more secure, volunteers can work without burnout, and directors can uphold service quality. Overall, this integration fosters trust and improves the hotline's effectiveness.

Truancy Reporting

An automated truancy reporting system is designed to efficiently track, notify, and confirm student attendance or truancy, addressing key concerns for parents, teachers, and administrators. Parents are motivated by the need to ensure their child's academic success and well-being, the safety and security of their children, and active participation in their child's education. They aim to monitor and address truancy issues promptly and collaborate with school authorities to support their child. Their top tasks include monitoring attendance reports and alerts, though they often face challenges in interpreting this data.

Teachers are motivated by the desire to promote student engagement and academic success, identify and support at-risk students,

Figure 36: Truancy reporting system

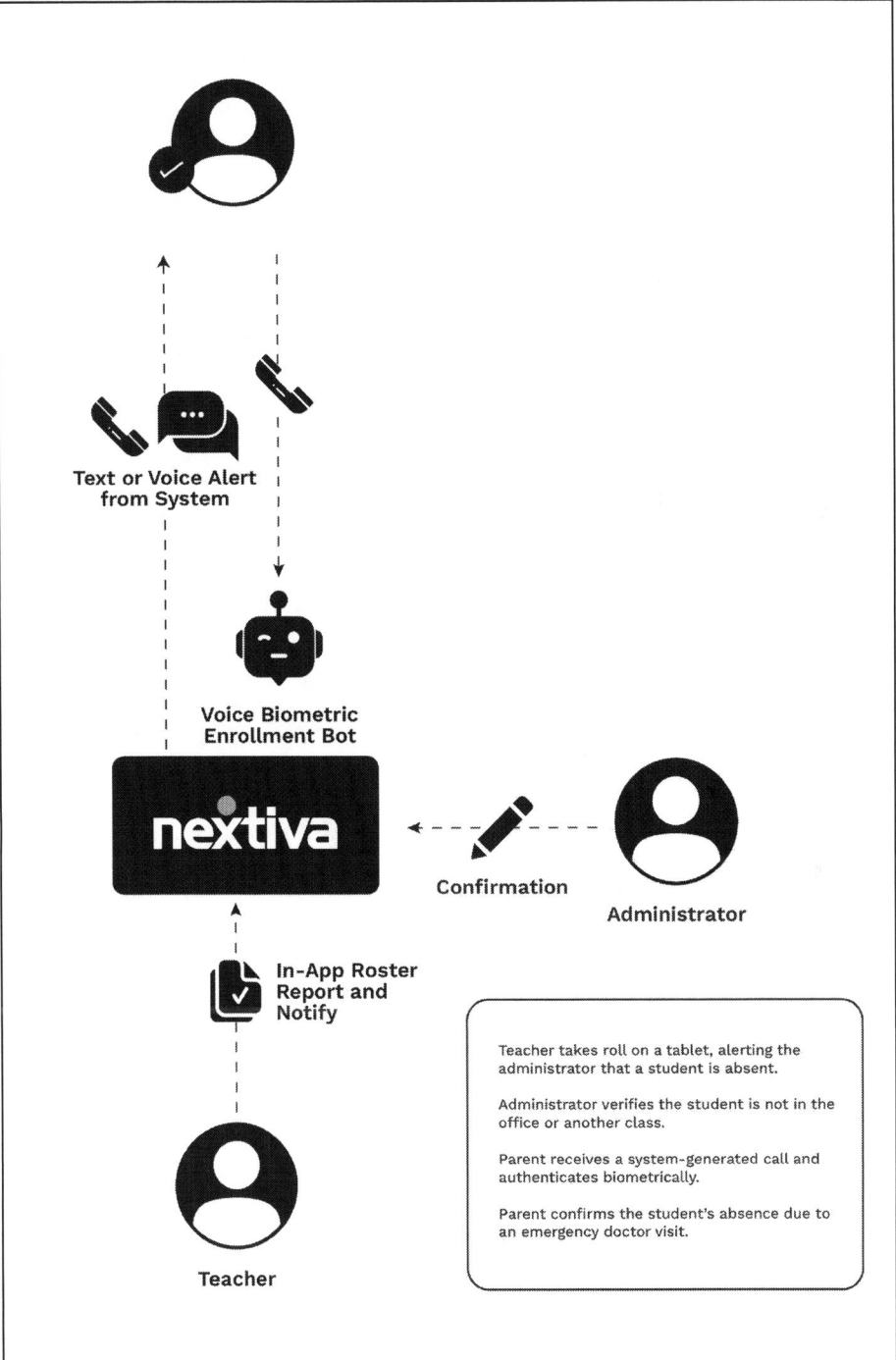

and maintain classroom management and continuity. They intend to identify and address truancy patterns and enhance communication with parents and administrators. Their top tasks involve monitoring and analyzing attendance data and communicating with parents and administrators, but they face challenges in interpreting data and implementing interventions, as well as integrating the system's use into their daily workflows.

School administrators are driven by motivation to improve student attendance rates, ensure compliance with educational regulations, and enhance school safety and student well-being. They aim to monitor and reduce truancy rates and coordinate interventions and support services. Their tasks include analyzing and interpreting attendance data and coordinating and implementing interventions, while they face challenges ensuring data accuracy and integrity and coordinating multi-departmental efforts.

Table 47: Benefits of truancy reporting system

Truancy reporting system capabilities	Chief benefits
Use of over-the-phone voice biometrics or fingerprint or face scans for smartphones	Biometric authentication ensures the fidelity of the reporting and confirmation of truancy, so reporting is fair and accurate
Omnichannel outreach to parents to alert them of student absence and ascertain authorized absence or truancy	Omnichannel approach provides convenient access to the truancy system for parents who may need to interact with the system while at work or driving
Use of an easily accessible roster checklist for teachers using smartphones or tablets	Simplifies the attendance marking process for teachers and improves efficiency
Use of transcription to capture notification dialog to ensure the school has done its part in truancy alerts	Use of AI for transcription and summarization provides an accurate audit trail and proof for administrators that they follow truancy reporting best practices

This system utilizes biometric security measures, such as over-the-phone voice biometric enrollment and smartphone or tablet fingerprint or facial recognition, to prevent students from pretending to be their parents. Teachers can easily mark attendance using a simple roster on a smartphone or tablet.

If a child is marked absent, initial notifications are sent within the app to other teachers or administrators. If no one confirms the child's presence, the system notifies the parent or guardian through various methods, including in-app notification badges, SMS alerts, or automated phone calls using a voicebot. Parents log in to the truancy application and authenticate their identity biometrically to confirm the absence or indicate truancy. Further enhancements to the system may include options for chat or voice escalation to an administrator for additional support.

An automated truancy reporting system efficiently tracks and manages student attendance by utilizing biometric security measures and omnichannel notifications. Parents, teachers, and administrators are motivated by different aspects, such as academic success, student engagement, and regulatory compliance. They each have specific intents and tasks aimed at reducing truancy and improving student well-being.

The system's solutions, including biometric authentication and AI-driven transcription, offer significant benefits, ensuring accurate reporting, ease of use, and robust communication among all stakeholders. This comprehensive approach fosters a supportive and effective environment for addressing and managing student truancy.

Retail Goods And Services

IN TODAY'S RETAIL landscape, automation, AI, and live customer support enhance customer experience. The retail sector offers a vast array of products, transforming corner stores into expansive supermarkets with banks, eyewear services, bulk purchasing options, curbside pickup, and home delivery. The rise of boutique clothing stores online and in malls highlights the diversity of retail options available.

With the widespread use of smartphones, improving customer service presents both opportunities and challenges. Retailers must navigate multiple communication channels and cater to a savvier consumer base demanding personalized service. This chapter will delve into the primary targets for automation, the challenges enterprises face in implementing advanced customer experience (CX) solutions, and popular use cases in retail today.

Top Automation Targets In Retail

Retail executives are increasingly integrating automation and contact center technologies to refine customer experiences and enhance operational efficiencies. Journey orchestration and breadcrumbing help guide customers through personalized shopping experiences, while mobile technologies and geo-fencing offer targeted promotions based on location. Advancements such as visual interactive voice response (IVR) systems and abandoned shopping cart recovery tools significantly reduce customer wait times and increase conversion rates, highlighting major focus areas for automation. Customer engagement and assistance are enhanced through sophisticated tools like size calculators and timely reminders about sales and reservations, deepening customer connections and transforming how retailers interact with their customers.

Furthermore, automation in delivery and fulfillment improves coordination and timeliness through dispatch and field service automation, flexible delivery options, and efficient rain check management. Operational efficiencies are also optimized with voice of the customer (VOC) technologies, process automation, multi-site intelligent routing, and special event management automation.

AI-powered chatbots provide real-time assistance and personalized recommendations, bridging the gap between online efficiency and in-store personalization. Live customer support remains crucial for addressing complex issues, ensuring every customer query is addressed with care, thus fostering loyalty and enhancing customer satisfaction.

Journey Orchestration And Breadcrumbing

Executives are focusing on integrating automation and contact center technologies to refine customer experiences and enhance operational efficiencies. Journey orchestration and breadcrumbing navigate customers through personalized shopping experiences effectively. Mobile technologies and geo-fencing capabilities offer targeted promotions based on customer location, further personalizing the shopping experience.

Advancements such as visual interactive voice response (IVR) systems and solutions to eliminate waiting queues are reducing customer wait times. Abandoned shopping cart recovery tools re-engage customers, increasing conversion rates. These developments collectively signify a major focus area for automation within the retail sector.

Customer Engagement And Assistance

Customer experience practitioners are integrating advanced automation and contact center technologies to enhance customer engagement and support. Shopping assistance tools like size calculators help customers find what they need efficiently. Sophisticated communication strategies, such as timely reminders about sales and reservations, keep customers informed and connected.

Personalized marketing promotions and dynamic pricing strategies enhance campaign effectiveness and deepen customer connections. This approach marks a significant direction in retail automation, transforming how retailers interact with customers.

Delivery And Fulfillment

Retail executives are implementing dispatch and field service automation for better coordination and timeliness. Delivery notifications keep customers informed about order status, fostering trust and satisfaction. Flexible delivery options, such as home or curbside services, cater to diverse customer needs.

Layaway plans and efficient rain check management provide additional purchasing avenues, demonstrating responsiveness to customer financial planning. This comprehensive approach to automation refines customer service and operational efficiency, reinforcing the retailer's market position.

Operational Efficiency And Automation

The implementation of voice of the customer (VOC) and process automation technologies streamlines feedback collection and workflow improvement. Multi-site intelligent routing and virtualization improve service delivery, while real-time mobile and web lead curation enhances customer engagement. Special event management automation simplifies planning and execution, creating engaging customer experiences.

These technologies represent a pivotal area of investment, delivering substantial improvements in customer satisfaction and operational efficiency. Automation within the retail sector optimizes resource allocation and enhances customer interactions.

Process Automation

Automated inventory management systems monitor stock levels in real-time, automate reordering, and forecast future needs based on sales data. This approach ensures high-demand products are available while reducing overstock situations. Automation also enhances customer service by managing routine inquiries and processes such as returns.

By automating repetitive tasks, businesses can allocate human resources more effectively, focusing on complex and unique customer concerns. Integration of automation within the retail sector optimizes operational efficiency and contributes to a more dynamic and responsive retail environment.

Security And Compliance

The retail industry is adopting advanced authentication systems and biometric security protocols to safeguard customer data. These initiatives strengthen protection against unauthorized access and ensure compliance with data protection regulations like GDPR and CCPA. Integration of fraud detection systems proactively identifies and mitigates fraudulent activities.

Recall notification and management tools enable prompt and efficient handling of product recalls, ensuring adherence to safety regulations. These advancements enhance security, ensure compliance, and foster customer trust within the retail sector.

Artificial Intelligence (AI)

AI-powered chatbots serve as the first point of contact for shoppers, offering real-time assistance and personalized recommendations based on browsing history. Machine learning algorithms analyze extensive datasets to predict consumer behavior, optimize pricing strategies, and customize marketing campaigns.

AI also enhances the shopping experience by identifying complementary products and encouraging additional purchases. This integration of AI redefines retail dynamics, bridging the gap between online efficiency and in-store personalization, ultimately setting a new standard for customer satisfaction and business performance.

Challenges With Automation In Retail

The retail sector has experienced significant transformations, with large supermarkets and online shops increasingly supplanting small local stores. This shift has introduced convenient services like curbside pickup and home delivery, catering to the evolving needs of modern consumers. The rise of digital-native brands and direct-to-consumer models has intensified competition, compelling traditional retailers to continuously innovate to stay relevant. The growing integration of AI and automation technologies offers opportunities for enhancing operational efficiencies and customer experiences, but it also brings challenges, particularly in terms of privacy and security. Ensuring strict adherence to data protection laws while effectively balancing data-driven insights while safeguarding customer privacy remains a complex task for retail executives.

As the retail landscape becomes more complex, mobile and multichannel challenges have come to the forefront. Retailers must optimize their services for mobile devices, necessitating responsive websites and user-friendly mobile apps. Social commerce requires seamless integration between social media platforms and e-commerce sites for effective marketing, direct sales, and customer service. Real-time customer support across various channels demands advanced contact center technologies and the efficient deployment of AI-powered chatbots and virtual assistants. However, maintaining the accuracy and personalization of automated systems requires ongoing updates and a careful balance with human touchpoints to ensure high customer satisfaction. The evolution of retail is also characterized by ethical consumerism, where transparency in sourcing and sustainability practices is critical for building trust and loyalty among increasingly savvy consumers.

Multichannel Challenges

Optimizing services across multiple channels is challenging. Integrating social media with e-commerce is complex and constantly evolving, affecting marketing, sales, and customer service. Keeping up with these changes is difficult for practitioners. Additionally, offering real-time support requires advanced contact center technology.

Implementing AI-powered chatbots and virtual assistants efficiently manages inquiries, but maintaining accuracy and personalization requires ongoing updates. Balancing automation with human touchpoints is key to high customer satisfaction.

Savvy Consumers

Informed and demanding consumers expect personalized service and seamless interactions across all touchpoints. Retailers must leverage data analytics to tailor offerings and stay ahead of trends. Ethical consumerism requires transparency in sourcing and sustainability practices to build trust and loyalty.

Managing online reviews and ratings is essential for maintaining a positive reputation. Implementing robust CRM systems helps track interactions and ensure timely follow-ups, building a community of loyal customers who advocate for the brand.

Implementation Challenges

Implementing advanced CX, automation, and AI solutions requires significant investment in technology and training. Integration with existing infrastructure can be complex, but the benefits of improved efficiency, enhanced customer satisfaction, and increased sales are worthwhile. Upgrading legacy POS systems to be compatible with AI and automation tools requires careful planning.

Retailers must continuously update systems and processes, fostering a culture of innovation. Collaboration with technology partners and startups drives innovation and helps retailers stay ahead of the curve.

Data Privacy And Security Concerns

Retailers gathering large amounts of customer data for personalization must ensure compliance with data protection regulations. Strong cybersecurity measures are essential to protect customer information and maintain trust. Balancing data-driven insights with privacy protection is an ongoing challenge.

Retailers must educate customers about data usage and protection, fostering trust and transparency. Ethical data practices and clear communication are key to maintaining customer loyalty.

Inventory Management And Supply Chain Integration

Automation and AI revolutionize inventory management by predicting demand and optimizing stock levels. Integrating these technologies into supply chain systems can be challenging due to multiple suppliers and systems. Real-time inventory tracking requires investment in IoT devices and advanced analytics, ensuring accurate data flow between stores, warehouses, and online platforms.

Employee Training And Adaptation

Introducing advanced technologies requires comprehensive training programs for staff. Addressing concerns about job displacement and emphasizing the enhancement of roles through technology is crucial. Creating a culture of continuous learning and innovation helps employees adapt to changes.

Employee feedback and involvement in the implementation process foster acceptance and ensure successful technology adoption. Investing in training and development is essential for long-term success.

In summary, the retail sector has seen significant transformation, with large supermarkets and online shops replacing small local stores. This evolution introduces conveniences like curbside pickup and home delivery. The rise of omnichannel retailing integrates online and offline operations, providing a seamless customer experience.

The competitive landscape has intensified with digital-native brands and direct-to-consumer models, pushing traditional retailers towards constant innovation. While AI and automation present privacy and security challenges, balancing data-driven insights with protecting customer privacy remains crucial. The retail sector's transformation exemplifies its commitment to enhancing customer service and operational efficiency.

Top Automation Targets In Retail

Abandoned Shopping Cart Recovery

Online shopping cart abandonment is a significant issue, with 70% of carts abandoned globally without the customer completing a purchase, leading to lost sales revenue. Customers frequently abandon carts due to various challenges, including complex checkout processes, high shipping costs, concerns about delivery speed, lack of preferred payment options, website errors, mistrust of the website, window shopping, lack of urgency, and comparison with competitors.

To address these challenges, the solution involves the use of breadcrumbs and automation. Tracking customer preferences, history, and shopping cart contents with breadcrumbing enables the system to send automated offers when a shopping cart is abandoned. These offers can be sent via SMS, email, proactive chat, or outbound call, providing an option to connect with an agent for questions or purchase assistance.

The motivation, intent, tasks, and challenges differ for customers, agents, and bots in this scenario. Customers are motivated by their need to find suitable deals and make purchases that make sense, but they face challenges such as indecision and needing a reason to buy now. Agents are motivated to understand customer needs and provide personalized assistance to help them complete purchases, but they

Figure 37: Abandoned shopping cart recovery

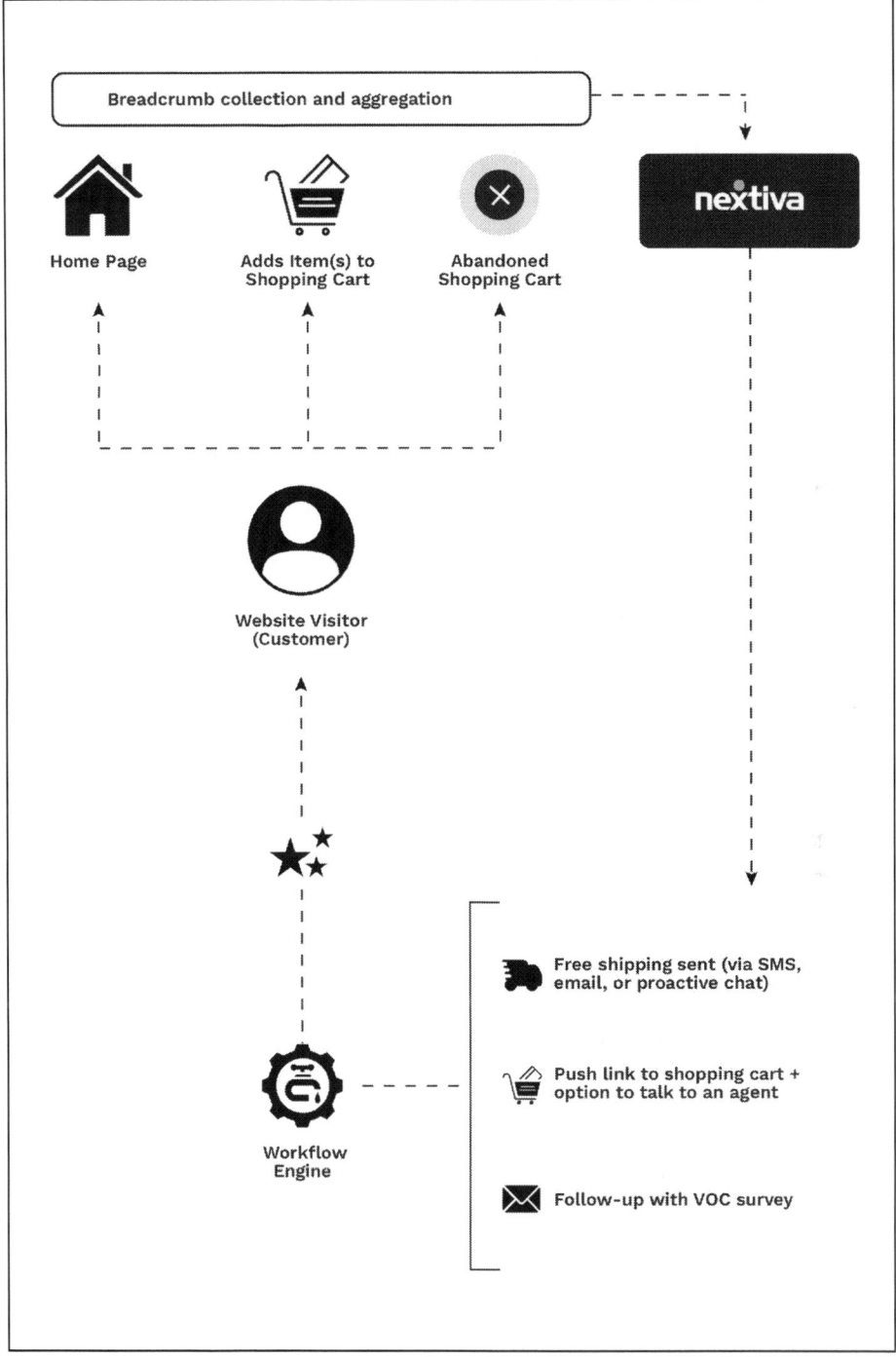

require visibility into customer preferences, search history, and shopping cart contents to be effective. Bots are programmed to prevent cart abandonment and provide a frictionless shopping experience that increases conversion rates. They track customer preferences, history, and activity and send automated offers when a cart is abandoned.

There are several benefits to this approach. For customers, simple cart recovery through clicking a link and frictionless buying with offers that incentivize purchase, such as discounts or free or expedited shipping, make the process smoother and more appealing. For businesses, this approach leads to a 10% to 20% increase in sales from recovered abandoned shopping carts. Agents benefit from having a full view of customer interactions, which helps them provide better assistance when they intervene.

The illustration demonstrates a common shopping cart abandonment solution. When a customer abandons their shopping cart, the UCXM platform starts a recovery process. The platform collects and aggregates breadcrumb data to monitor the visitor's behavior. It manages a recovery journey using a workflow engine, providing multiple communication modes based on the customer's preference.

The system can send a free shipping offer via SMS, email, or chat. The bot provides a link to the customer's abandoned cart and an option to talk with an agent. The UCXM system can also follow up with a voice of customer (VOC) survey. This strategy re-engages customers, recovers lost sales, and improves satisfaction through personalized, timely interactions.

In summary, journey orchestration and breadcrumbing can be effectively used to re-engage customers who abandon their shopping carts. This strategy involves automated messaging, feedback surveys, and live agent interactions, which prompt customers to reconsider their transactions.

For customers, this solution simplifies cart recovery by providing easy re-engagement through clickable links and offers that incentivize purchases, such as discounts or free shipping. Businesses benefit from a 10% to 20% increase in sales from recovered abandoned carts. Additionally, agents gain a comprehensive view of customer interactions, enabling them to assist more effectively.

Table 48: Benefits of abandoned shopping cart recovery

Cart recovery benefits	Chief benefits
Track customer preferences, history, and shopping cart contents with breadcrumbing	Provides a comprehensive understanding of customer behavior, enabling personalized and effective recovery strategies
Send automated offers when shopping carts are abandoned (via SMS, email, proactive chat, or outbound call)	Increases the likelihood of purchase completion by providing timely and relevant incentives to customers
Provide an option to connect with an agent for questions or purchase assistance	Ensures that customers receive personalized support when needed, improving their shopping experience and satisfaction
Journey manipulation for conversion	By re-engaging customers with automated messages and incentives, the system helps convert abandoned carts into completed purchases
Customer engagement aspect	Personalized interactions through live chat and tailored incentives create a more satisfying customer journey
Customer journey insights	Feedback from surveys provides critical data to understand customer behavior and improve future interactions

Mobile And Geo-Fencing Solutions

In the retail sector, the incorporation of geo-fencing technology can be a great aid to customer service, contact center operations, and field service management. With a combination of geo-fencing and a unified customer experience management platform, retailers can offer highly personalized experiences through mobile apps, automated systems, and in-car telemetry. Customers benefit from tailored recommendations and promotions, while retailers can send real-time notifications about sales or offers when customers enter specific areas.

This approach enhances the shopping experience and drives sales by providing customers with offers that align with their preferences and past behaviors.

These technologies also bring significant advantages to the automotive and field service sectors. For instance, integrating in-car telemetry with geo-fencing can provide drivers with real-time updates on traffic conditions and nearby services. In field service operations, geo-fencing helps manage the locations of field workers, optimizing routes and ensuring safety. Overall, combining AI and geo-fencing enhances operational efficiency and safety, benefiting customers, contact center agents, and field service personnel alike. Use cases in this area set a new standard for the intersection of automation and enhanced mobility applications.

Geo-fencing technology is revolutionizing contact centers' operations, enhancing efficiency and customer satisfaction. Contact centers can offer personalized and expedited service by integrating real-time location data into their workflows. For instance, when a customer contacts a center regarding an order pickup, agents are immediately informed of the customer's proximity to the store through geo-fencing, enabling them to respond more effectively and streamline the customer's experience. Implementing automation via geo-fencing optimizes operational procedures.

These automated systems can notify staff when a customer enters a predefined geographic boundary, such as a store parking lot, allowing the staff to prepare for the customer's arrival by having their online order ready for curbside pickup.

Integrating in-car telemetry and geo-fencing technologies marks a significant advancement in delivering auto services to drivers on the move. Combining these tools creates a solution that detects issues with a vehicle's engine in real-time. The system can pinpoint the nearest service stations equipped to handle the specific problem and guide the driver to the chosen location. This interaction between a car's telemetry and geo-fencing technology enhances the driving experience by minimizing the time and stress involved in dealing with unexpected vehicle issues.

In summary, combining AI and geo-fencing technologies in various sectors improves customer service, safety, efficiency, and

Table 49: Benefits of mobile and geo-fencing automation

Mobile and geo-fencing automation capabilities	Chief benefits
Geo-fencing enabled personalization	Tailors offers and notifications based on customer location and preferences
Live agent tie-ins mean contextual efficiency	Reduces wait times and streamlines operations through real-time data and automation
Enhanced behavioral insights	Geofencing solutions are useful in combining valuable data on customer behavior and preferences, aiding in better decision-making and strategy formulation
Enhanced mobile engagement	Improves customer satisfaction through timely and relevant interactions tied to their specific location, helping the consumer to save time, gas, and effort
Personalized restaurant recommendations	Tailored restaurant recommendations based on user preferences saves time and frustration for travelers
Mobile on-the-go convenience	Easy navigation and reduced effort in finding suitable dining options can be useful in establishing affinity for a favored brand
Time-of-day scheduling; improved travel experience with personalized and timely suggestions	Time-of-day scheduling can be fine-tuned for the habits and preferences of the consumer, increasing customer satisfaction
In-car telemetry and geo-fencing for auto service	Quick identification and navigation to the nearest suitable service station; timely resolution of vehicle issues, reducing the risk of breakdowns; automated notifications and real-time guidance for a hassle-free experience
AI-assisted field service	Optimized routes and automated data capture reduce time spent on manual tasks; AI verification of deliveries ensures accurate inventory updates; streamlined processes allow technicians to focus on core tasks, improving overall productivity

convenience. Retailers can offer personalized experiences through mobile apps and send immediate notifications about sales or offers when customers enter a specific area. Integrating in-car telemetry with geo-fencing provides drivers with real-time updates on traffic and nearby services, while geo-fencing helps manage the locations of field workers to optimize routes and ensure safety. Overall, these technologies enhance operational efficiency and safety for customers and field service personnel.

Customer Service Queue Management

Automation processes, AI, and seamless integration with contact center infrastructure can improve queueing applications. Improved queueing includes allowing customers to request a callback or switch to a different communication channel when wait times are long. Applying AI in this context can also help reduce customer frustration and wait times, ultimately leading to higher satisfaction and loyalty. In this section, we will explore how visual IVR and hold-free queueing can be creatively used to enhance various aspects of the retail customer service experience. This will benefit both customers and retailers by increasing efficiency, personalization, and convenience.

These queue management technologies aim to improve the often-frustrating experience of waiting for customer service by making it more user-friendly and efficient. Visual IVR solutions offer customers an intuitive menu of service options accessible via websites or mobile apps. These systems analyze previous interactions and preferences to dynamically adjust the menu and provide a personalized and context-rich experience for individual customers. This simplifies the process for customers and equips live agents with relevant information, reducing the need for customers to repeat themselves.

Improving customer experience is crucial, and one way to do this is through hold-free queueing. This approach provides alternatives to waiting on hold, such as allowing customers to request a call-back during long wait times or using visual IVR prompts on mobile apps to choose other communication methods, like self-service options or chatting with an agent. This flexibility is particularly helpful for customers who cannot wait on hold, such as those who are driving. By

Figure 38: DialMyApp example of visual IVR

capturing caller ID and preferences, the system can smoothly transition the customer to a more convenient communication channel, enhancing both safety and satisfaction. Moreover, this approach is cost-effective for businesses since outbound calls are generally cheaper than inbound toll-free calls.

For instance, visual IVR solutions offer a user-friendly menu of customer service options for customers to access on a website or mobile app. These applications can customize the service options based on the customer's past preferences and behavior. This ensures that the customer's journey begins with a focus on their needs. The menu options can be adjusted in real-time, creating a dynamic experience. This not only enhances the customer experience with relevant information but also provides customer preferences and completes tasks for live customer service agents if needed, reducing the need for customers to repeat themselves.

These applications are very helpful in the retail sector, especially when a customer is unable to complete a task without live assistance, despite no fault of their own. It's common for consumers to have preferred communication channels. This information can be stored in the contact center so that when a person calls or requests a chat, the brand understands that the customer may be initiating communication through a non-preferred channel. This could happen when the person is frustrated with a bot and wants to switch to live assistance or if the person is driving and cannot text for safety reasons, opting for a phone call instead.

Hold-free queueing can be achieved in various ways. For instance, a customer waiting in a voice queue can be given the option to receive a callback instead. Before offering this, a notification about the long wait time and the option not to hold but have the system call back when an operator is available can be made. In this scenario, visual IVR prompts can be used in a mobile app to display the wait time and provide buttons for the customer to select alternative communication options. For instance, one button may be used to request a call back, while another may be used to attempt self-service over the phone.

An alternative approach involves "side-car communication." In this scenario, a customer who is on hold may choose to switch to a different communication channel where agents are available. This can be made possible through automation and visual IVR, allowing the customer to press a button that says, "Try chat instead." For mobile customers, they can be asked, "Would you like us to queue you up for a chat agent? You can say yes and let us know when it would be safe or convenient to start that conversation. We see you are driving, and we don't want you to have an accident." The customer could then respond with, for instance, "Yes, I'd like to switch to a chat agent, and you can connect me in two minutes so I have time to pull off the highway."

This approach benefits the customer by providing convenience and minimizing wait times. It also enhances safety. Additionally, the enterprise benefits from capturing the customer's caller ID. This allows the system to prompt the customer for preferences either over the phone or via mobile visual IVR and subsequently terminate the toll-free call. Calling the customer back is also more cost-effective for the enterprise, as outbound calls are cheaper than inbound, toll-free ones.

In summary, there are significant benefits of leveraging process automation, AI, and integration with existing contact center infrastructures for retail sector customer service. You can use automation to significantly streamline queue management. Central to this enhancement are visual IVR and hold-free queueing technologies, which aim to revolutionize the customer experience by minimizing wait times, reducing customer frustration, and obviating the need for callers to repeat information. These technological advancements offer personalized, context-enriched interactions and provide customers with alternatives to waiting on hold, such as call-back options and additional channels of communication. The integration of these technologies not

Table 50: Benefits of customer service queue management

Customer service queue management capability	Chief benefits
Visual IVR and personalization	Personalized shopping recommendations can be based on a customer's past purchases and browsing history. This enhances the shopping experience by offering tailored suggestions, increasing customer satisfaction and sales.
Hold-free queueing enhanced issue resolution	Hold-free queueing allows customers to request a call-back or switch to a chat agent when wait times are long. This approach reduces customer frustration and wait times, leading to higher satisfaction and loyalty.
Call-back safety and convenience	Integration of mobile apps with geo-fencing with visual IVR can provide real-time updates and alternative communication options. This ensures drivers receive timely assistance without compromising safety, enhancing the overall customer experience.
Dynamic service menus	Visual IVR systems can dynamically adjust service menus based on customer preferences and historical behavior. This provides a more intuitive and efficient service experience, reducing the time and effort required to find the right assistance.
Cost-effective customer support	By capturing caller ID and preferences, automation-powered retail apps can terminate toll-free queued calls and initiate cheaper outbound calls. This reduces operational costs for the enterprise while maintaining high levels of customer service.

only elevates the customer experience through increased efficiency, personalization, and convenience but also presents tangible advantages for retailers by optimizing operational efficiencies.

These innovations serve to enhance customer convenience and safety while simultaneously presenting cost-saving opportunities for businesses by reducing inbound, toll-free call expenses. Through these technologies, a more user-friendly and efficient future in retail customer service is in reach.

Loyalty Program Automation

Loyalty program automation is essential in retail for addressing customer, agent, and program manager motivations and challenges. Customers seek personalized rewards and a seamless experience to feel valued and recognized for their loyalty. They aim to track and redeem rewards efficiently, providing feedback to enhance the overall experience. However, they often struggle with managing, understanding, and using benefits before they expire and ensuring their loyalty is accurately rewarded. Agents are motivated to provide excellent customer service by assisting customers with their points and ensuring a positive experience. They help customers understand the loyalty program benefits and resolve any issues promptly and accurately. Agents face challenges managing high volumes of inquiries and ensuring accurate and timely resolution of customer issues.

Loyalty program managers aim to streamline the management of loyalty programs to reduce workload and enhance program effectiveness through automation. They leverage AI to provide personalized rewards and ensure programs run smoothly with accurate tier adjustments and reward distribution. The key tasks for managers include overseeing the program's operation and performance, analyzing customer data to refine offerings and strategies, and managing routine tasks to keep the program engaging and relevant to evolving customer preferences.

The problem with managing loyalty programs manually is that it can be time-consuming and prone to errors. Traditional programs often lack personalization, leading to lower engagement and satisfaction among customers. Additionally, manual processes can delay reward tier adjustments and distributions, negatively impacting the overall customer experience. The solution lies in loyalty program automation, which leverages AI to customize rewards, automate tier adjustments, enhance guest engagement, and send notifications via SMS, in-app messages, or email. Using AI, businesses can analyze customer data to offer personalized rewards and experiences, making loyalty programs more engaging and effective.

Automation also streamlines program management, reducing employee workload and improving operational efficiency. Customer benefits include personalized rewards, timely tier adjustments, a seamless experience, and more frequent use of rewards. Business benefits encompass increased customer satisfaction, operational efficiency, more frequent visits, higher retention and loyalty, and data-driven insights. Employees and supervisors benefit from visibility into customer loyalty points and offers.

Including QR codes on physical receipts or product packaging enables customers to easily scan the code and provide feedback through a mobile-friendly survey. This approach seamlessly connects physical and digital realms, allowing customers to effortlessly share their thoughts on a product or service by using their mobile devices. The primary advantage of this method is that it offers a convenient way for customers to share feedback through their mobile devices, thereby closing the gap between physical and digital interactions.

Augmenting automated routines with live operator intervention adds a vital human element to the feedback collection and analysis process. Automated systems are adept at handling routine feedback efficiently, but live operators are essential for dealing with complex feedback and offering personalized assistance. For instance, when a customer provides negative feedback or raises specific concerns, a live operator can engage with them to understand the issues more deeply and propose customized solutions. This human interaction ensures customers feel appreciated and that their concerns are swiftly addressed.

Live operators also have a role in proactively contacting customers who have left feedback, particularly when the feedback suggests major issues or dissatisfaction. This engagement allows operators to discuss

Figure 39: Loyalty program automation

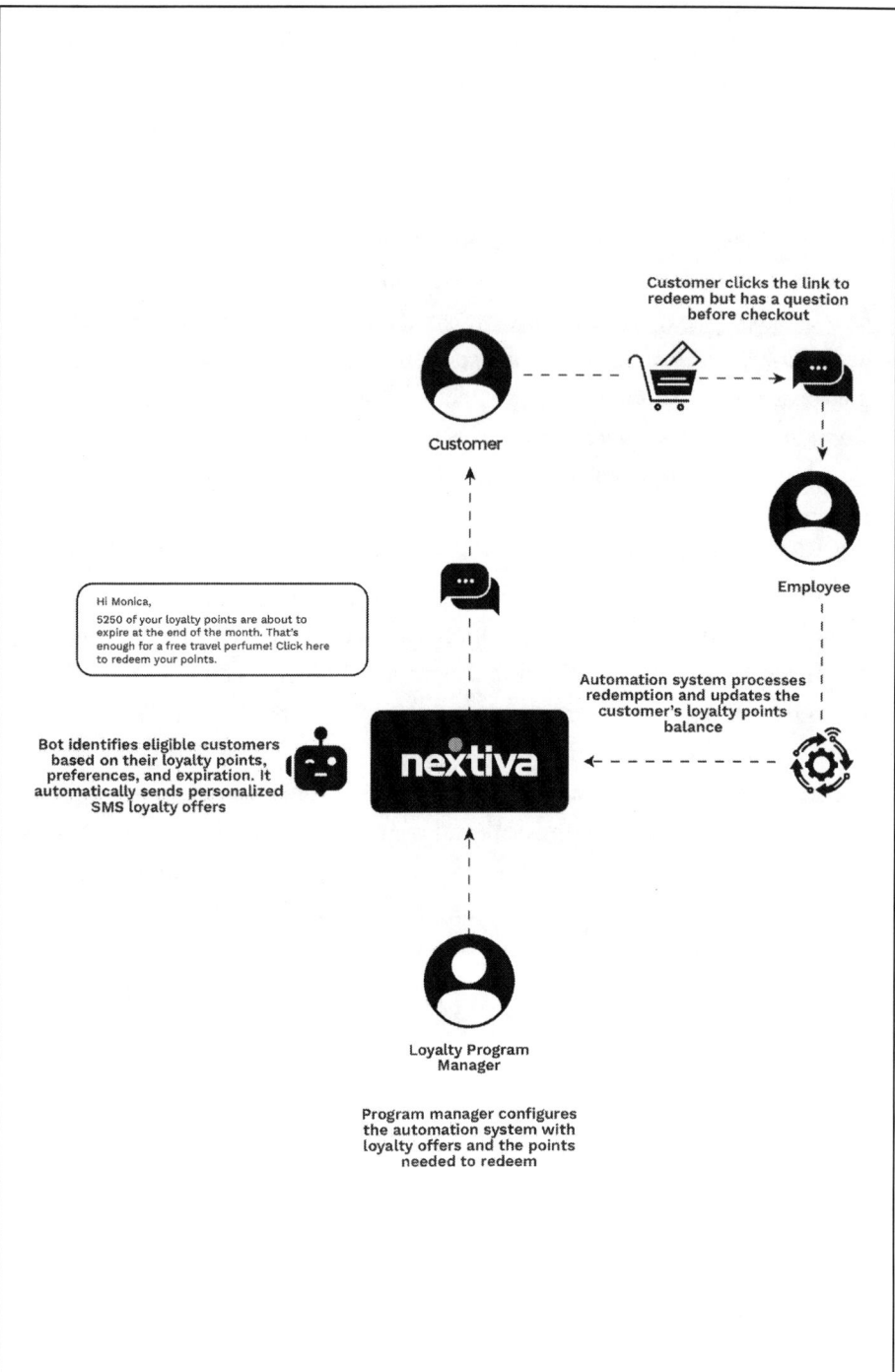

the customer's concerns, offer reassurances, and present solutions, thus managing expectations and minimizing frustration.

Additionally, live operators are invaluable when feedback requires a nuanced understanding or immediate action. If feedback reveals a recurring problem with a product or service, operators can quickly escalate the issue to the appropriate departments for resolution. This prompt action guarantees that customer feedback leads to concrete improvements in products and services.

Combining automated feedback collection with live operator intervention strikes an optimal balance in customer service. While automated systems efficiently compile and analyze feedback, live operators address complex issues with a personal touch, ensuring customer satisfaction. This combined approach significantly enhances the customer experience, ensuring that feedback is not only gathered but also effectively acted upon.

The diagram on the left illustrates a retail use case for loyalty program automation using a UCXM platform. The bot identifies eligible customers based on their loyalty points, preferences, and expiration dates. It then sends personalized SMS loyalty offers to these customers.

The customer receives an SMS that reads:

"Hi Monica, 5,230 of your loyalty points are about to expire at the end of the month. That's enough for a free travel perfume! Click here to redeem your points."

The customer clicks the link to redeem the points but has a question before checkout. The customer reaches out with a question, and an employee assists the customer. The automation system processes the redemption and updates the customer's loyalty points balance.

Meanwhile, the loyalty program manager configures the automation system with loyalty offers and the points needed to redeem them. This use case demonstrates how the UCXM platform can automate the management of loyalty programs, enhancing customer experience by ensuring timely redemption of loyalty points and personalized offers while also efficiently streamlining the workflow for employees and program managers.

In summary, automated loyalty programs and feedback collection systems are vital tools in capturing customer insights across various touchpoints, including post-purchase and during interactions. These

Table 51: Benefits of loyalty program automation

Loyalty program automation capabilities	Chief benefits
Track and redeem loyalty rewards efficiently	Enables customers to take full advantage of their benefits and feel valued and recognized through timely offers
Provide personalized recommendations and support	Ensures customers understand the benefits and use the loyalty program effectively, enhancing their overall experience
Leverage AI to provide personalized rewards and experiences	Keeps the loyalty program engaging and relevant to customers, improving satisfaction and retention
Automate tier adjustments and reward distribution	Reduces the workload on employees and improves operational efficiency, ensuring accurate and timely updates
Streamline management of loyalty programs	Enhances the effectiveness of the program, making it easier to oversee and refine offerings and strategies
Send notifications (SMS, in-app, email) for rewards and tier adjustments	Keeps customers informed and engaged, increasing the likelihood of reward usage and program satisfaction
End-of-call IVR surveys	Immediate and relevant feedback, ensuring timely insights into customer satisfaction
In-call agent-guided surveys	Real-time feedback collection and immediate issue resolution, improving customer satisfaction
In-app feedback prompts	Captures feedback in real-time within the app, providing immediate insights into user experience
Social media monitoring	Provides insights from organic customer interactions on social media, capturing unfiltered opinions

systems utilize methods such as visual IVR for surveys post-call, AI-summarized contact center conversations, and more direct approaches like IVR surveys, SMS, email hyperlinks, and in-call surveys to collect valuable data. This data informs on customer satisfaction, leading to continuous service improvement. The deployment of these tools, by providing timely and convenient feedback mechanisms, not only helps in gathering critical insights but also in conveying a sense of value to the customers.

Additionally, the technology extends to capturing detailed feedback through emails, real-time calls or chats via dynamic scripts, in-app after certain actions, and through monitoring social media for brand mentions. Pop-up surveys on websites, feedback through digital and physical receipts, and QR codes are other innovative ways of bridging the gap between physical and digital feedback collection.

To complement the automated systems, live operators are deployed for handling complex feedback and offering personalized customer service. This blend of automation and human interaction significantly enhances customer satisfaction levels, ensuring that the feedback collected is effectively utilized for improving services and resolving issues promptly.

Journey Orchestration And Use Of Breadcrumbs

Journey orchestration involves combining human expertise with technology to enhance customer interactions. The key components for successful journey orchestration include breadcrumb aggregation, which involves collecting and analyzing data from various customer interactions to create a complete view of the customer journey.

Additionally, a workflow engine incorporates this breadcrumb data into its execution of tasks and processes, enhancing operational efficiency and ensuring smooth customer interactions. The workflow engine may rely on its hosting unified customer experience platform to use intelligent routing so that customer inquiries are directed to the most suitable resources or agents based on specific parameters, ensuring efficient interactions.

When live assistance is required, the UCXM system may use agent tooling to provide customer service professionals with access to resources for managing customer interactions effectively. Such resources may include AI-assisted knowledge base access and summarization of notes, for example.

The UCXM platform serves as the system of record for all customer interactions. It collects, stores, and manages customer data from various sources, enabling personalized customer experiences. A well-curated knowledge base offers quick access to solutions for common queries, enhancing self-service and support efficiency.

A fair amount of process automation is used in journey orchestration, which is useful for automating repetitive tasks, boosting operational efficiency, and allowing human resources to focus on more complex activities.

Surveys and voice of the customer tools capture direct feedback from customers, providing insights for improvement. Insights and reporting analyze data from customer interactions to guide strategic decisions and enhance customer engagement. Artificial intelligence improves customer interactions with technologies like chatbots, predictive analytics, and personalized recommendations.

Maintaining a persistent or semi-persistent session with the customer ensures continuous monitoring of web or mobile sessions, facilitating a seamless return if there is a disruption.

The "multi-segmented journey" diagram illustrates how journey orchestration collaborates with third-party systems to collect "breadcrumbs" and ensure a cohesive customer journey. This is especially relevant in retail transactions, where customer authentication is crucial.

It all starts with a customer navigating a specific webpage. If further assistance is needed, the customer can initiate a voice call, connecting them with an agent. The voice call is guided by an interactive voice response (IVR) system, which directs customers through options. If the IVR cannot resolve the issue, it can escalate to an agent for personalized assistance.

Customer authentication with a third-party IVR system may involve credit card payments or biometric verifications, ensuring transaction security. Breadcrumbs collected during the journey provide insights into customer interactions. After the transaction, customers are encouraged to provide feedback through a survey. The collected feedback, along with breadcrumb data, is sent via an API to update

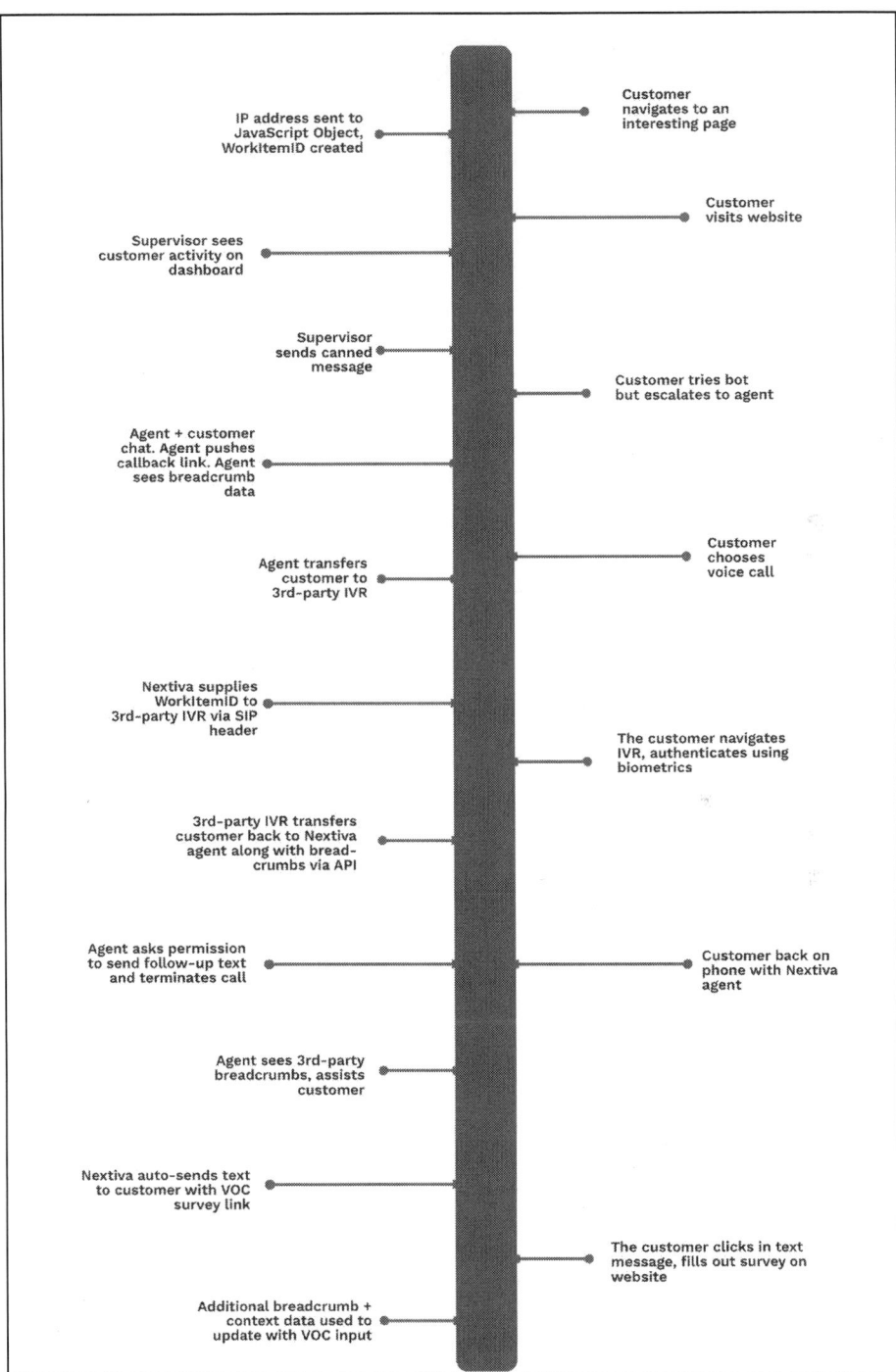

Figure 40: Multi-segmented journey example

Table 52: Benefits of journey orchestration

Journey orchestration and breadcrumb capability	Chief benefits
Automated navigation and interaction	Efficient and seamless initiation of the customer journey is ensured through smooth navigation and the availability of voice call functionality
Interactive voice response	The IVR system is adept at navigating customers through a spectrum of choices, diminishing the necessity for direct engagement with agents, and thereby accelerating the resolution of issues
Escalation to live agent	Offering the capability to transfer interactions to a live representative guarantees that clients obtain tailored support as necessary, thereby enhancing total satisfaction levels
Third-party authentication	Secure authentication through credit card payments or biometric verifications ensures that transactions adhere to industry standards and regulations
Breadcrumb collection	Collecting data points throughout the journey provides insights into customer interactions, preferences, and behaviors, enabling continuous improvement and personalization of services
Feedback collection	Gathering feedback through surveys is essential for understanding customer satisfaction levels and identifying areas where improvements can be made
Data integration and analysis	Integrating breadcrumbs and feedback into the customer data platform ensures a comprehensive record of the journey, facilitating ongoing analysis and optimization
Real-time monitoring	Supervisors have the capability to observe the progression of operations in real-time, enabling immediate oversight and intervention when necessary. This ensures a continuous enhancement of the customer experience.

the customer data platform, maintaining a comprehensive record of the journey. Supervisors use dashboards to monitor real-time customer journeys, ensuring consistent oversight and improvement of the customer experience.

Overall, the orchestration of this multi-segmented journey ensures that customers enjoy a seamless experience while the company captures valuable data at each step of the process. This methodical approach to journey orchestration emphasizes the importance of customer engagement, data integration, and continuous improvement in delivering exceptional customer service.

Order Tracking And Updates

The automation of order tracking and updates offers significant capabilities to improve the customer experience. Automated order tracking allows customers to use systems such as visual IVR for real-time tracking of their orders, including updates on status from processing to delivery. This transparency builds trust and reduces customer anxiety, leading to a positive shopping experience and improved satisfaction, which encourages repeat business.

In addition to automated systems, live operator intervention plays a crucial role. Personalized assistance by live operators is essential when customers have specific questions or issues that the automated system cannot address. They help explain delays or offer solutions, ensuring customers feel valued. Live operators handle complex inquiries, such as changes in delivery address, promptly and accurately, preventing issues from escalating.

Proactive communication by live operators demonstrates high customer care, helps manage expectations, reduces frustration, and enhances loyalty. Automated systems also enhance communication through outbound SMS notifications and push notifications, keeping customers informed about their order status, such as when an order is shipped or delayed. This convenience enhances the overall customer experience.

Automated delivery notifications via emails, SMS, or app-based push notifications inform customers when their order is out for delivery and once it has been delivered. This ensures customers are prepared to receive their orders, reducing missed delivery attempts. Live operator intervention, such as confirmation calls for high-value items, ensures customers are available to receive their orders, decreasing missed deliveries and enhancing satisfaction.

When issues arise, live operators promptly resolve them, scheduling redeliveries or processing returns as needed. This maintains customer trust and satisfaction. Following delivery, reaching out to verify customer satisfaction with a brief survey or thank-you call fosters a stronger relationship, encouraging feedback for service improvement and promoting loyalty and repeat business.

Sending SMS notifications and push notifications provides real-time updates directly to customers' cell phones or through mobile apps, including delivery windows and special instructions. These notifications keep customers engaged and informed throughout the delivery process, enhancing their overall experience.

Table 53: Benefits of automated oder tracking and updates

Order tracking and updates	Chief benefits
Automated order tracking	Transparency builds trust and confidence in the retailer; helps reduce customer anxiety and uncertainty, leading to a more positive shopping experience; enhances their overall satisfaction and encourages repeat business
Live operator intervention	A human touch can turn a potentially negative experience into a positive one
Proactive communication	Proactive communication demonstrates a high level of customer care and helps manage customer expectations, reducing frustration and enhancing loyalty
Notification of delivery	Notifications can be sent via email, SMS, or push notifications, ensuring that customers receive timely updates
Follow-up communication	Helps build a stronger relationship with the customer, fostering loyalty and repeat business

In summary, real-time order tracking through websites, mobile apps, and automated phone systems enhances the customer experience by fostering trust and reducing anxiety. Live operators handle specific queries and complex issues, ensuring proactive communication and customer value. Automated systems send SMS and push notifications for timely updates on order status and delivery. This balance of technology and human interaction optimizes customer engagement.

Dispatch, Field Service, And Field Sales Automation

Dispatch applications for tablets and handheld devices enable field service technicians to access real-time job details, customer information, and special instructions directly. These tools feature interactive maps that guide technicians efficiently to destinations, reducing travel time and enhancing service delivery. Access to detailed job information and customer history allows technicians to prepare thoroughly and deliver high-quality service.

Field service staff can utilize technologies like QR codes and geo-fencing for automated information capture on-site. This includes scanning QR codes for product information and using geo-fencing to track job locations. Automated data capture reduces errors, ensuring accurate information collection.

Support for complex tasks is provided through centralized help desk experts who offer step-by-step guidance. This support enhances technicians' ability to perform their job accurately, improving customer satisfaction.

Field sales personnel can improve their efficiency through mobile applications with agent-facing shopping carts. These applications assist in onboarding customers by providing visual IVR-type assistance, capturing necessary information quickly and easily, and improving the customer experience.

Mobile applications are useful for field service personnel in various fields, such as landscaping, home repairs, or pest mitigation. They enable effective interaction with customers, accurate estimates, and efficient scheduling of follow-up visits, improving communication and service delivery.

A system may be configured to connect to a live help desk for expert intervention. Dynamic scripting allows live help desk agents to offer real-time support, guiding technicians through troubleshooting steps and providing additional information from an extensive knowledge base. Proactive support includes monitoring field technicians' status, offering alternative routes or extra resources to ensure timely job completion.

Technology enhances collaboration between field service and centralized contact center staff by allowing seamless data sharing and real-time support. Field staff collect data onsite using mobile devices, making it instantly available to centralized agents for analysis. This empowers agents to provide informed support, facilitating better decision-making. AI-powered knowledge bases offer detailed troubleshooting steps and the ability to elevate issues, ensuring technicians receive support tailored to their immediate needs.

Live help desk agents support field sales personnel during customer onboarding by addressing inquiries and technical challenges in real-time. This ensures a smooth process and improves customer satisfaction. Centralized agents facilitate customer interactions for field service personnel, verifying requirements and coordinating follow-up visits to ensure successful service delivery.

In summary, dispatch applications for tablets and handheld devices are enhancing field service and sales operations with real-time access to job details, customer information, and maps. This technology improves efficiency by optimizing travel times and enhancing customer service quality. Features like QR codes and geo-fencing support precise on-site data capture, including measurements and photos, thus improving accuracy and reducing errors. Centralized help desk expertise further supports field personnel, contributing to accuracy and customer satisfaction.

For field sales professionals, these applications streamline the customer onboarding process with tools like agent-facing shopping carts and visual IVR assistance, making the capture of customer details and navigation through onboarding steps more efficient. This enhances both customer experience and operational efficiency. Additionally, the integration of live help desk support with dispatch and sales automation elevates operational capabilities. Real-time troubleshooting,

Table 54: Benefits of automated dispatch and field service

Dispatch and field service automation capabilities	Chief benefits
Dispatch apps for tablets and other handhelds	Access to detailed job information and customer history allows technicians to prepare adequately and deliver high-quality service
Live help desk intervention	Dynamic scripting ensures that technicians receive consistent and accurate support, enhancing their ability to help remotely resolve issues on-site
Help desk contextual assistance	Ensures that technicians receive relevant support tailored to the specific situation, improving problem resolution
Automated information capture in the field	Streamlined data collection makes it easy for technicians to capture and record information accurately and efficiently
Agent-facing shopping carts	Mobile applications with agent-facing shopping carts simplify the onboarding process, making it quick and easy for sales agents to capture necessary information and complete the process

proactive monitoring, and seamless data integration between field staff and contact centers improve decision-making and support provision, ensuring high service quality and customer satisfaction.

Home And Curbside Delivery

Automated routines for home and curbside delivery have significantly transformed customer interactions with businesses by offering enhanced convenience and efficiency. These systems allow customers to place and schedule orders online or through mobile applications, selecting either home or curbside delivery options at times that best fit their schedules.

Customers benefit from real-time order tracking through automated tracking systems, receiving updates on the delivery status from preparation to dispatch and arrival. Automated notifications keep customers informed throughout the delivery process, thus enhancing transparency and minimizing anxiety.

For curbside pickups, automated systems direct customers to designated parking spaces for order collection. Detailed instructions provided by these notifications improve the curbside pickup experience by reducing wait times and ensuring a seamless process.

Live operators offer personalized assistance with specific delivery-related inquiries or concerns, such as changes in delivery schedules or special instructions. This personalized service effectively addresses customer needs and enhances satisfaction.

The integration of mobile technologies boosts the capabilities of delivery personnel. Mobile apps provide real-time updates on delivery routes, customer instructions, and scheduling changes, ensuring efficient order deliveries. QR codes and geo-fencing technologies confirm deliveries and capture proof of delivery, thereby minimizing errors.

Customer interaction with delivery personnel via mobile apps facilitates real-time feedback and additional instructions, improving communication and the overall delivery experience. Centralized data sharing between contact centers and delivery personnel ensures effective coordination. Contact center agents can access real-time data to assist delivery personnel and enhance decision-making.

Knowledge base applications enable contact center agents to quickly locate pertinent information and support delivery personnel. Dynamic scripting allows agents to provide real-time support, guiding delivery personnel through troubleshooting processes.

Proactive monitoring by contact center agents involves tracking delivery statuses and contacting delivery personnel if delays or issues are identified. By offering alternative routes or resources, timely delivery completion is ensured, further increasing customer satisfaction.

In summary, the use of automated routines for delivery services has improved interactions between businesses and customers. Incorporating flexible scheduling, real-time tracking, and automated notifications enhances convenience and transparency. This integration optimizes the delivery process and minimizes wait times.

Table 55: Benefits of automated home and curbside delivery

Home and curbside delivery	Chief benefits
Order placement and scheduling	Enables customers to schedule delivery times that are convenient for them, providing flexibility and convenience
Real-time tracking and notifications	Reduces anxiety for customers and improves the overall experience
Mobile apps for delivery personnel	Ensures that orders are delivered promptly and correctly
Centralized data sharing and knowledge base access	Assists delivery personnel effectively, improving decision-making and problem-resolution
Dynamic scripting	Ensures that delivery personnel receive consistent and precise support, enhancing their ability to resolve issues on-site

Live operators provide a personalized touch, addressing complex queries and special requests. This human element, along with mobile technology for delivery personnel, ensures better communication and efficient navigation. Centralized data sharing and proactive monitoring guarantee timely and accurate support, enhancing customer satisfaction and streamlining the delivery process.

Automated Personalized Offers

Automated personalized offers can leverage AI to analyze customer data and preferences, enabling businesses to create and send tailored offers that resonate with individual customers. By automating this process, businesses ensure that customers receive relevant and timely offers via SMS, email, or in-app notifications, enhancing their overall experience and engagement. This method boosts conversion rates, leading to increased sales and fostering customer loyalty. Behavioral segmentation in email marketing allows marketers to segment customers based on unique behaviors like purchase history and browsing patterns, making communication more relevant and engaging.

Personalized offers provide key benefits to both customers and businesses. Customers receive offers tailored to their preferences and behaviors, enhancing their shopping experience and making them feel valued. For businesses, this results in increased engagement, operational efficiency, and valuable data-driven insights into customer preferences. Agents and supervisors benefit from visibility into campaign offers sent to customers and reduced human error through the automation of manual offer delivery.

In retail, personalized marketing and shopping assistance significantly enhance customer engagement and drive sales. AI-powered chatbots analyze a customer's past purchases and browsing history to suggest products that align with individual preferences, creating a personalized shopping experience. These assistants provide real-time interaction with instant responses and tailored recommendations, making the shopping process more efficient and enjoyable. Unlike human counterparts, these virtual assistants are available 24/7, offering consistent customer support regardless of time zones. Chatbots can support multiple languages, breaking down language barriers and allowing businesses to reach a wider audience, enhancing accessibility and enabling businesses to cater to a global customer base effectively.

Additionally, email marketing campaigns leverage insights on shopping behavior to send personalized product recommendations directly to customers' inboxes. This approach boosts conversion rates, leading to increased sales and fostering customer loyalty. Behavioral segmentation in email marketing allows marketers to segment customers based on unique behaviors, enhancing the relevance of communication and increasing customer engagement.

Product availability alerts keep customers informed and engaged through SMS and push notifications, increasing the likelihood of purchases and improving customer satisfaction. Personalized alerts ensure customers receive relevant updates without being overwhelmed. Cross-channel integration of alerts ensures messages reach customers wherever they are, maintaining consistent communication and reinforcing the brand's presence. Customer feedback through these alerts

Figure 41: Automated personalized offers

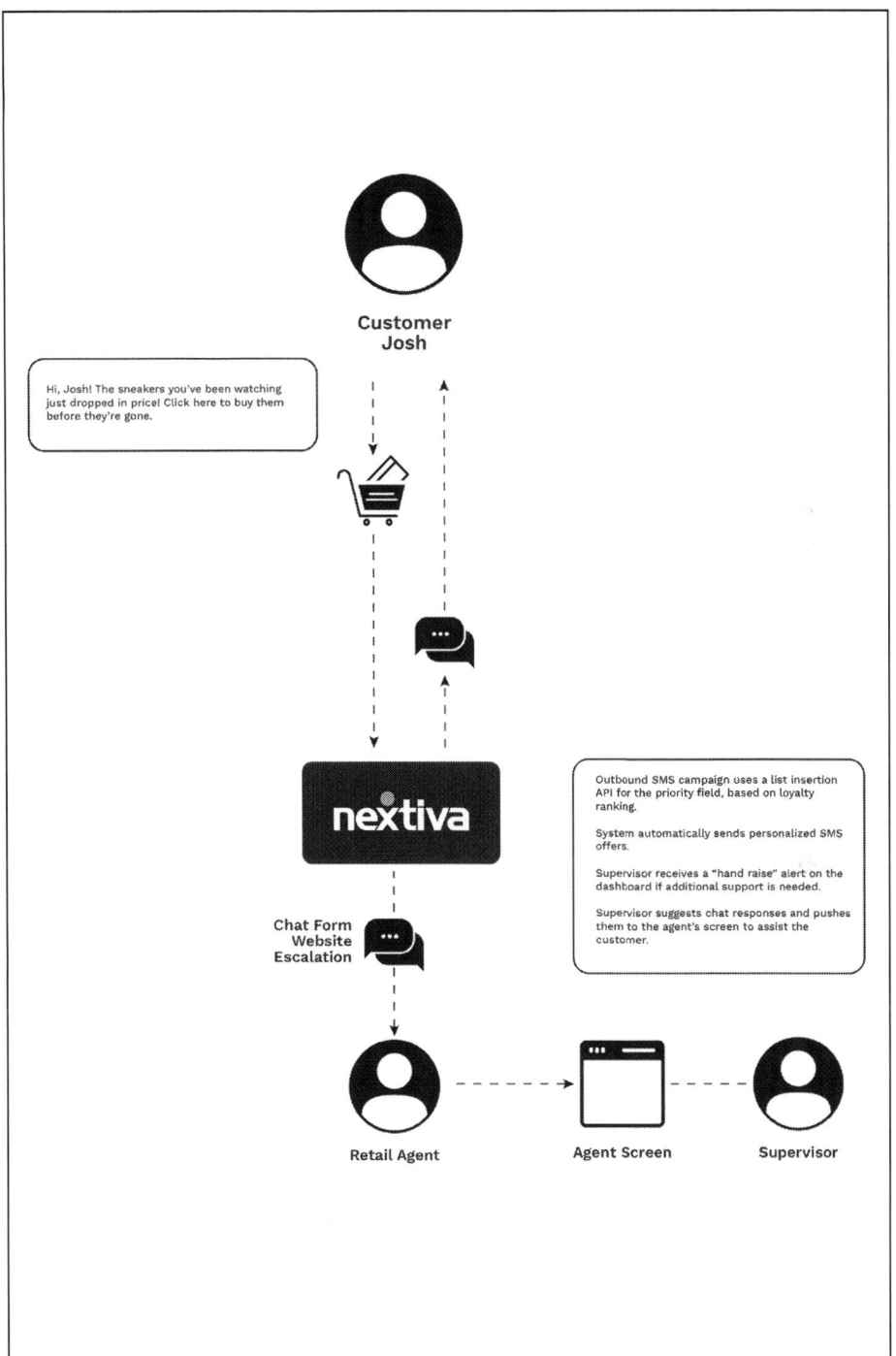

helps retailers understand preferences and guide inventory and product decisions.

In this illustration of a personalized offer scenario, a customer named Josh receives a personalized SMS message:

"Hi Josh, the sneakers you've been watching just dropped in price! Click here to buy them before they're gone."

This message is sent through the UCXM platform. The UCXM platform uses a list insertion API for the priority field based on loyalty ranking, automatically sending personalized SMS offers. If Josh escalates the chat from the website, it is routed to a retail agent via the UCXM platform.

The retail agent receives the escalated chat and handles Josh's inquiries. Meanwhile, the supervisor monitors the situation through the dashboard, where they can see the agent's screen. The supervisor can push suggested chat answers to the agent, ensuring that the customer receives accurate and timely responses. This process highlights how the UCXM platform can enhance customer engagement by providing personalized offers and efficient customer service escalation.

In summary, the use of automated personalized offers is a powerful way to create tailored offers for individual customers. This process ensures relevant and timely offers via SMS, email, or in-app notifications, enhancing customer experience and engagement. It boosts conversion rates, increasing sales and fostering loyalty. Behavioral segmentation in email marketing helps marketers segment customers based on behaviors like purchase history and browsing patterns, making communication more engaging.

AI-powered chatbots and personalized campaigns enhance customer engagement and drive retail sales. Chatbots analyze past purchases and browsing history to suggest products that align with preferences, offering real-time interaction and recommendations. Available 24/7, they provide consistent support and break language barriers, reaching a global audience. Email campaigns that use shopping behavior insights to send personalized recommendations and product alerts further boost conversion rates and loyalty. These technologies ensure consistent communication, improve satisfaction and guide inventory decisions through valuable feedback.

Table 56: Benefits of automated personalized offers

Automation of personalized offers capabilities	Chief benefits
Automated personalized offers leveraging AI	Tailored recommendations make the shopping experience more enjoyable and relevant for customers; personalized suggestions can lead to higher conversion rates and increased sales and can foster customer loyalty and repeat business
Automated delivery of offers via SMS, email, or in-app notification	Enhanced customer engagement and experience
Behavioral segmentation in email marketing	Increased relevance and effectiveness of communication
UCXM platform for priority-based offer delivery and customer service escalation	Efficient customer service and accurate, timely responses
Monitoring and support through the UCXM platform's dashboard	Improved visibility and support for agents and supervisors
Product availability alerts	Keeping customers informed about product availability increases the chances of a purchase; timely alerts ensure that customers do not miss out on products they want to buy

Store And Dealer Locators

Both chatbots and interactive voice response (IVR) systems can assist customers in finding dealers or stores. These automated solutions provide quick and accurate information based on the customer's location and buying intent. While these systems ensure process efficiency, live operators are available for personalized assistance as needed.

Mobile applications that use GPS data can automatically locate nearby stores or dealers, displaying a list of the closest locations with directions and contact details. This integration offers instant and relevant information, and live operators are available to provide real-time assistance through the app.

The incorporation of QR codes on marketing materials is a straightforward and inexpensive addition to a dealer locator scenario. These enable customers to receive store or dealer information by scanning, which then directs them via navigation apps to the nearest location for a streamlined experience. Live operators can handle follow-up questions or additional assistance.

SMS-based services allow customers to request store or dealer locations, triggering an automated response with the relevant details. This method accommodates users who prefer text communication, offering quick access to location information. Live operators enhance this service with personalized support.

Geo-fencing applications help customers find products in stock at nearby stores when their preferred location is out of inventory. The application detects the customer's location and suggests alternative stores where the product is available. Live operators offer additional support for inventory-related inquiries, ensuring accurate and up-to-date information.

Centralized oversight of store matches enhances customer service by directing calls back to the corporate contact center if the store does not respond, ensuring that customers receive assistance. Live operators manage rerouted calls, providing necessary information and connecting with another store. This system aims to improve customer satisfaction with reliable support.

The addition of intelligent routing and skill-based agent assignment ensures effective engagement by matching customers with suitable agents. Combined, these strategies ensure a seamless customer journey and maximize conversion potential.

In summary, various digital tools such as interactive voice response (IVR) systems, mobile apps, QR codes, and SMS outreach significantly enhance customer service by enabling efficient location of dealers or stores. IVR systems offer automated guidance based on zip code input, while mobile apps leverage GPS for nearby store detection.

Table 57: Benefits of store and dealer locator systems

Store and dealer locator capabilities	Chief benefits
IVR-based dealer or store locators	Provides quick and accurate store or dealer information while allowing for personalized assistance when needed
In-app solutions using GPS data	Reduces the time it takes for an answer and reducing friction for the customer
QR code scans with automation routines	Avoids typing errors and provides a smooth experience for the customer
SMS-based outreach	Quick and convenient information via SMS means users on the go can get what they need quickly without having to log in to an application or website, making it better for consumers who do not have smartphones
Geo-fencing applications for inventory management	Ensures a more seamless shopping experience when inventory is limited
Centralized oversight of store matches	Ensures customers receive assistance even if their initial contact attempt fails, providing reliable and consistent support
Intelligent routing and agent skill assignment	Live agent support acts as a safety net to capture customers who otherwise may have gone to a competitor out of frustration

QR codes provide instant access to store information, and SMS outreach allows for direct requests. Additional support via live operators ensures a personalized service. Contact centers further optimize customer engagement through intelligent routing and tailored outreach strategies, fostering improved experiences and higher conversion rates.

Product Returns And Recalls

In the retail sector, efficiently managing product returns and recalls is essential for maintaining customer satisfaction and trust. By incorporating automation and contact center technologies, retailers can streamline these processes, thus enhancing convenience for customers.

Tools such as visual IVR, mobile applications, AI-driven notifications, and dynamic agent scripting ensure a seamless and responsive experience. These technologies simplify the steps involved in returns and recalls, provide timely updates, and offer personalized assistance, thereby improving the overall shopping experience.

Visual IVR applications facilitate the return and exchange process through step-by-step instructions, engaging users in dialogues to identify reasons for returns, such as size, color, or damage issues. The application gathers necessary product information and offers solutions like account credits, RMA numbers, shipping labels, or item pickups. This technology not only makes the return process more convenient for customers but also reduces the workload on customer service agents. Retailers like Amazon and Zappos have successfully implemented these systems to enhance customer satisfaction.

Real-time return status notifications keep customers informed about their return progress. Delivered through outbound IVR messages, SMS, or in-app alerts, these notifications update customers on return approvals, replacement dispatches, and delivery timelines and even suggest complementary products. This proactive communication significantly improves the customer experience.

When automated processes are insufficient or more personalized assistance is necessary, the system can escalate the issue to live operators. This feature allows a smooth transition from automated interaction to live agent support without interruption. Equipped with comprehensive data from previous interactions, live agents can provide informed suggestions and efficiently navigate the return process, ensuring complex issues are resolved smoothly and maintaining customer satisfaction.

Efficient recall management is critical for customer safety and brand trust. Using mail distribution with QR codes, customers can access detailed recall information via a designated landing page. IVR systems with natural language processing enable customers to verbally provide product codes and receive safety information. Mobile applications further simplify this process by allowing customers to scan recalled items for instant information. This ensures customers receive accurate and timely recall notifications, thereby enhancing their overall experience.

In summary, streamlining product returns and recalls in the retail sector is essential for enhancing customer satisfaction and trust. By integrating automation with contact center technologies, such as visual IVR, mobile apps, and AI-driven notifications, the return and recall processes become more efficient and user-friendly. This approach ensures timely and personalized customer support and simplifies the escalation to live agents when necessary, avoiding redundancy and improving issue resolution.

Table 58: Benefits of automated product returns and recall

Automated product returns and recall capabilities	Chief benefits
Visual IVR apps	Simplifies the return process, making it highly convenient for customers and significantly reducing the workload on customer service agents
Real-time return status notifications	Ensures customers remain engaged and well-informed throughout the return journey, significantly enhancing the overall customer experience
Escalation to live assistance	Ensures complex return issues are resolved smoothly and efficiently, safeguarding the customer's experience and satisfaction
Recall management	Ensures customers receive accurate and timely information, enhancing their overall experience and safety
Automated return authorization	Expedites the return authorization process and reduces the workload on customer service agents
Proactive recall alerts	Ensures customers are informed promptly, enhancing their safety and trust in the brand

Additionally, employing innovative recall management strategies, like snail mail with QR codes, natural language processing, and mobile apps, facilitates quick access to recall information and smooth return authorization, thereby improving customer safety and the overall shopping experience.

Language Translation And Intelligent Routing

In the retail environment, different personas, such as customers, agents, and supervisors, have unique motivations, intents, tasks, and challenges. Customers are motivated to make purchases to fulfill needs or wants and are curious to discover options and pricing. Their intent is to find suitable deals within their criteria and decide on a purchase when it makes sense. They primarily shop around in search of the right deal and compare options in the marketplace. However, language barriers make it difficult for customers to research and purchase products and get help in their native language.

Agents are motivated by understanding customer needs and providing personalized assistance. They aim to help customers make purchases and understand their needs and wants. Their main tasks include educating customers on options, resolving customer concerns, and helping complete purchases. However, agents face challenges such as not being skilled in speaking the customer's language, slow online translation tools, and a lack of resources to transfer customers to someone else.

Supervisors are motivated to support both agent and customer experiences to ensure smooth operations and maintain service levels. Their intent is to help agents assist their customers and promote a positive experience for both agents and customers. Supervisors' top tasks include providing over-the-shoulder support to agents as needed and monitoring queues and agent interactions. They face challenges such as lacking visibility into customer interactions because of language barriers and needing agents to assist customers more quickly.

The problem arises when shoppers who speak different languages need help, but it's too difficult to research and get help in their native language. Businesses often need to help customers in multiple languages but may not have enough skilled agents to assist, especially

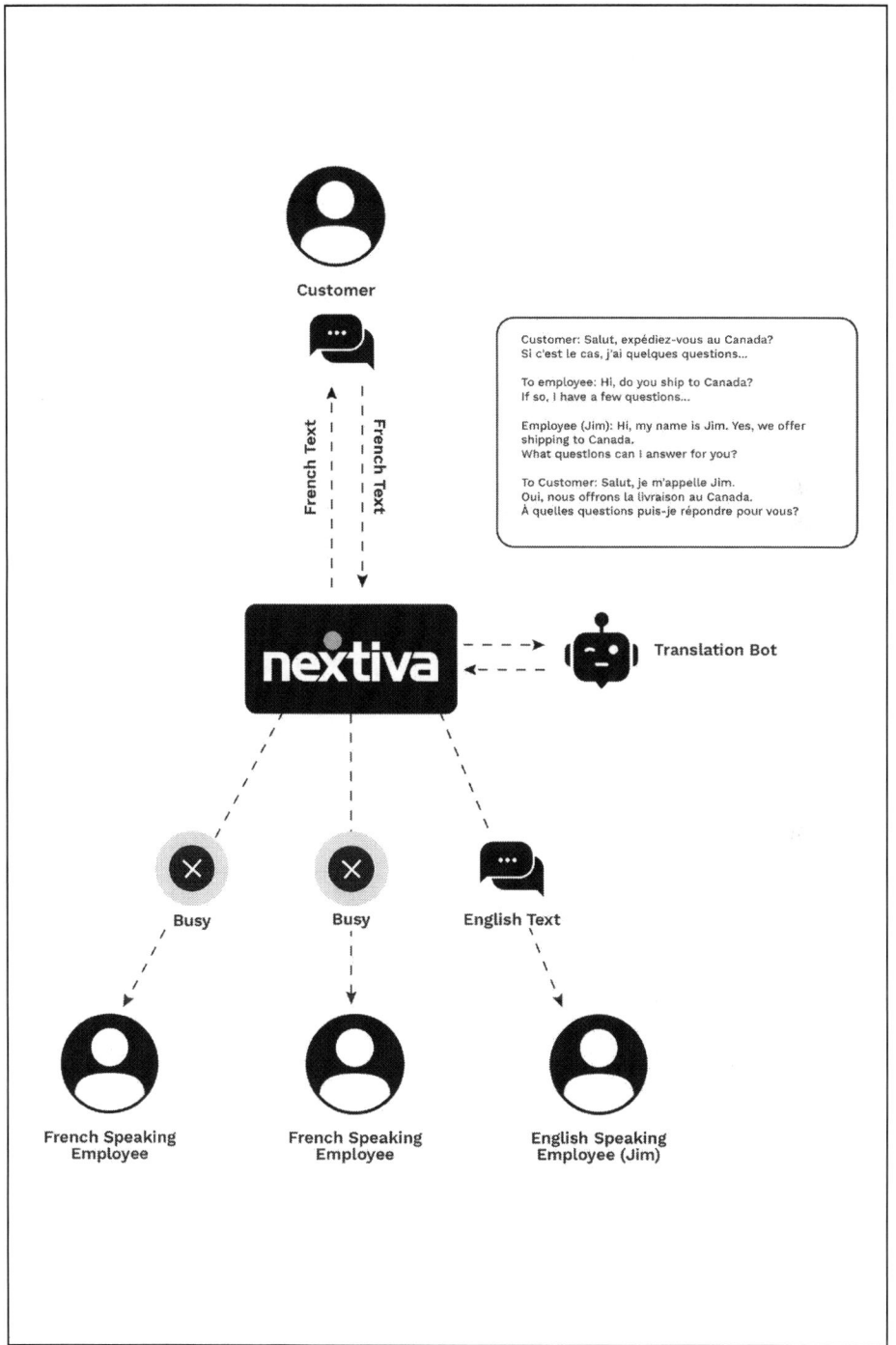

Figure 42: Language translation and intelligent routing

during seasonal demand peaks and valleys. Online translation services are too slow and require manual copy-and-paste operations, which adds to the delay.

The solution uses a language detection and translation bot for live chats. The UCXM platform checks agents' language skills using a workflow engine. If no agents are skilled in the identified language, the bot translates the text for both the agent and the customer. This ensures customers get help in their native language and agents can assist effectively.

The illustration depicts a retail scenario in which a customer who speaks French sends a message that reads:

"Salut, expédiez-vous au Canada?..." This translates to, "Hi, do you ship to Canada?..."

Since there are no French-speaking employees available, the UCXM platform uses a translation bot to facilitate communication.

Table 59: Benefits of language translation and intelligent routing

Language translation and intelligent routing capabilities	Chief benefits
Detection of language used for initial dialog turn	Ensures the customer receives assistance in their native language, reducing friction and making it easier to get help
UCXM workflow checks "skills" of agents available for identified language	Efficiently matches customers with agents who can assist in their language, improving connection times and customer satisfaction
A language translation bot is utilized when there are no available customer service representatives with the necessary language skills to assist the customer	Allows businesses to serve more customers regardless of language spoken, making economical use of available agent resources
Language conversion used bi-directionally for the remainder of the dialog turns	Maintains consistent communication in the customer's native language, enhancing the overall experience and ensuring accurate assistance

The customer's message is translated into English and sent to an English-speaking employee.

The employee responds in English:

"Hi, my name is Jim. Yes, we offer shipping to Canada. What questions can I answer for you?"

This response is then translated back into French for the customer:

"Salut, je m'appelle Jim. Oui, nous offrons la livraison au Canada. À quelles questions puis-je répondre pour vous?"

This setup demonstrates how a UCXM platform equipped with AI-based language detection and translation can enhance customer engagement. The support real-time language translation allows customers and agents to communicate effectively despite language barriers.

In short, language translation and intelligent routing benefit everyone. Customers face less friction and get help faster in their native language. Businesses use agent resources efficiently and serve more customers. Agents provide better service in the customer's language, while supervisors can better monitor interactions.

Language detection ensures customers are directed to the right resources initially, setting a positive tone. The UCXM workflow matches agents with the right language skills to customers, improving satisfaction.

When agents with the necessary language skills are unavailable, a translation bot helps, allowing businesses to serve all customers efficiently. Bi-directional language conversion during the dialog maintains consistent communication, enhancing the experience and ensuring accuracy.

Overall, these capabilities streamline customer service, foster stronger relationships, and lead to better outcomes by reducing language barriers.

Service Providers

WITHIN THE COMMUNICATIONS and service provider industry, there's a growing trend toward automation to boost efficiency and improve customer experience. Service providers aim to enhance network capacity and service quality while cutting costs.

Traditionally, phone companies, cable providers, and other communications firms have led in adopting automation. Recently, artificial intelligence is becoming more common. This section will explore key automation targets for these providers.

Top Automation Targets For Service Providers

Many organizations now use a hybrid work model, combining in-person and remote work. Digital transformation supports this, allowing a dispersed workforce to manage communications without disrupting voice services. Cloud-based customer experience (CX) solutions blend voice and digital tasks.

Traditional centralized contact centers are becoming less relevant. Remote agents using cloud-based tools provide greater flexibility and improve workforce management. A distributed workforce offers benefits like better access to talent and easier crisis management.

Claims that human agents will soon be replaced by automated bots are exaggerated. Current AI technology is not yet advanced enough. However, there is a shift toward digital channels, especially among younger generations. Despite this, phone interactions remain important, as shown in the accompanying diagram.

Omnichannel Customer Experience Strategies

In today's consumer landscape, customer experience strategies are focusing more on digital channels like SMS, chat, email, and automated bots instead of traditional voice calls. This shift is not just to reduce call traffic but to match consumer preferences. AI chatbots and self-service options for simple queries are gaining popularity. However, it's important to deploy these tools effectively to avoid customer dissatisfaction. Bots should not try to mimic human interaction poorly, as it can lead to a negative experience.

Digital-First Approach

A digital-first approach offers many benefits. Service agents can manage multiple digital interactions at once, reducing labor costs. Digital channels also help avoid the frustration of waiting in call queues, improving customer satisfaction. These platforms can also resolve issues faster on the first contact due to predictive capabilities. This means agents have better resources, such as knowledge bases and historical data, to help customers.

Adopting a digital-first strategy can improve customer satisfaction. However, it's crucial to offer choices to customers. Forcing digital channels on customers who prefer human interaction can lead to dissatisfaction. A balanced approach is essential, prioritizing digital channels while respecting customer preferences.

SERVICE PROVIDERS

Figure 43: Generational cohorts and digital channels

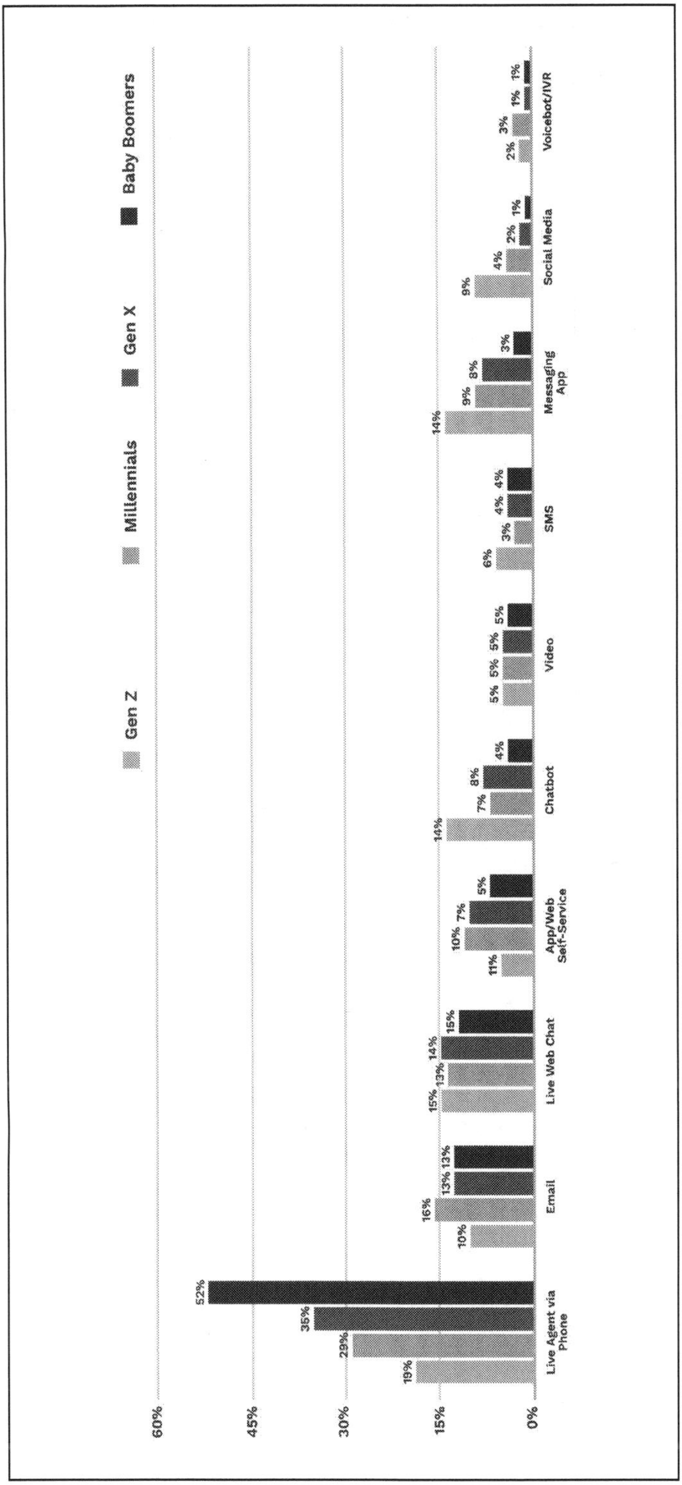

Channel	Gen Z	Millennials	Gen X	Baby Boomers
Live Agent via Phone	19%	29%	35%	52%
Email	10%	16%	13%	13%
Live Web Chat	15%	13%	14%	15%
App/Web Self-Service	11%	10%	7%	5%
Chatbot	14%	7%	8%	4%
Video	5%	5%	5%	5%
SMS	6%	3%	4%	4%
Messaging App	9%	9%	8%	3%
Social Media	9%	4%	2%	1%
Voicebot/IVR	3%	2%	1%	1%

261

Virtual Contact Centers And Data Security

Service providers that are adopting virtual contact centers face challenges with data privacy, authentication, and secure communication. Security officers ensure interactions across all digital platforms are protected.

Despite these issues, providers are committed to improving customer security and privacy while enhancing the user experience. They are adopting technologies that ensure secure customer interactions without compromising convenience. An example is "Secure Payment Agent Assist" technology, which securely handles credit card data.

Sales Strategies And Agent Training

Service providers are refining their sales strategies and agent training programs to align with customer expectations and technological advances. Automation, empathy, and precise training help CSPs stay competitive and deliver superior customer experiences.

Providers are increasingly integrating more automation into contact center operations to streamline sales processes. Automated lead scoring helps identify and prioritize prospects, and AI-powered recommendations guide agents to relevant products or services.

There is also a focus on training programs for agents, covering digital skills, empathy, and automation technologies. Training in CRM systems, chatbots, and virtual collaboration tools ensures agents handle digital interactions effectively. Emotional intelligence training helps agents understand and respond to customer needs, building trust and rapport.

Effective use of automation tools is key in modern customer service workflows. Training programs empower agents with the skills needed to excel in a digital environment, delivering exceptional customer experiences. Factors like customer demographics, service offerings, and market dynamics influence these training decisions. For example, reducing legacy applications and simplifying workflows can enhance revenue growth and improve the overall customer experience.

Challenges With Automation For Service Providers

In today's rapidly evolving telecommunications landscape, the integration of automation into the operations of communications service providers (CSPs) presents a multifaceted set of challenges, particularly in the realms of security and regulatory compliance. As CSPs increasingly lean toward automation to enhance efficiency and service delivery, the deployment of artificial intelligence and automated processes introduces a new spectrum of risks and vulnerabilities. These complexities not only threaten the integrity of sensitive customer information but also expose network infrastructures to potential breaches, underlining the imperative for rigorous security measures and compliance with prevailing regulations.

Security Measures And Regulatory Compliance

CSPs face many challenges with automation, especially in security and regulatory compliance. As they adopt automation, the risks to customer data and network security increase. It is crucial to use strict security measures and adhere to regulations like GDPR, HIPAA, and PCI DSS. Implementing strong access controls and advanced encryption is essential. Regular compliance checks help identify and fix potential issues.

Technical Intricacies And Organizational Readiness

CSPs must handle various technical issues like integrating old systems with new ones. Managing these different systems requires careful planning. Organizations need to address skill gaps and cultural resistance to automation. Training IT teams and having strong leadership at the executive level are vital for successful automation.

Initial Investment And ROI Challenges

Automation projects require a significant initial investment, including costs for systems, training, and maintenance. Calculating the return on investment (ROI) is complex due to indirect benefits like increased efficiency and reduced errors. To improve ROI, CSPs should focus on projects that align with their strategic goals.

Scalability And Flexibility Challenges

Scalability is a major challenge. As CSPs grow, their automation systems must handle tasks more efficiently. Effective resource allocation and dynamic adjustment to workload changes are crucial. CSPs should avoid vendor lock-in by choosing flexible solutions that integrate with existing systems.

Managing Change In Automation And AI

Adapting to automation and AI can cause employee resistance. CSPs need comprehensive training programs and clear communication about the benefits of automation. Leadership support and cross-functional collaboration are essential. Addressing change management involves engaging staff, explaining automation benefits, and fostering a supportive culture.

Despite these challenges, careful planning, targeted approaches, and regular evaluation can help CSPs succeed in automation. The goal is to improve operations while ensuring customer satisfaction.

Top Automation Use Cases For Service Providers

Service providers are increasingly using AI and automation to improve efficiency and the customer experience. They are leveraging various automation use cases to streamline operations and provide personalized support. Key areas include automating customer inquiries and agent-assist solutions, which enable faster and more accurate responses to customer queries. Additionally, automating notetaking and summarization reduces the administrative burden on agents, allowing them to focus on complex interactions. Personalized offers and recommendations powered by AI ensure that customers receive relevant promotions and suggestions.

Automation also extends to retention desk functions and self-service options, enabling customers to resolve issues independently. Handset, gateway, and device upgrades, along with upsell opportunities, are optimized through automation, leading to increased sales and customer loyalty. Billing and payment assistance, as well as the automation of billing queries and disputes, simplifies financial interactions for customers. Customer sentiment analysis provides insights into customer experiences.

Effective complaint resolution and timely customer reminders and notifications are part of the range of AI and automation use cases, helping service providers maintain high service levels and foster positive customer relationships. In this section, we will explore some of these use cases in further detail.

Automating Customer Inquiries

Customer inquiries encompass a range of questions or requests for information from customers, including billing discrepancies, service interruptions, and plan details. These inquiries can be submitted through various channels, such as customer service hotlines, emails, live chats, social media, or in-person interactions. Prompt and efficient resolution is crucial to maintaining customer satisfaction and trust.

The application of AI in interpreting customer inquiries represents a significant advancement. For instance, when a customer inquires about network issues or billing, an AI system analyzes the input using NLP models to understand the intent and context, facilitating a tailored response.

AI can quickly navigate extensive knowledge bases, extracting relevant information efficiently. This capability enhances workflow by optimizing knowledge retrieval from recent publications, FAQs, and internal guides, significantly improving information management.

Professionals are increasingly leveraging data from customer profiles and CRM systems. AI technologies extract insights from databases, ensuring responses are precise and contextually relevant. For example, AI-driven systems can pull details from technical specifications and service offerings within vast archives.

In automating customer inquiries, AI's ability to recognize intent and integrate knowledge is vital. This involves analyzing the inquiry to provide a tailored response based on individual account details and recent industry developments.

Enhancing issue resolution speed is another benefit of automation. Customers can engage with chat or voicebots instead of waiting in queues, efficiently managing routine inquiries and freeing human agents for more complex issues.

AI systems improve over time by learning from each interaction, adjusting algorithms to enhance accuracy and operational efficiency. For instance, when addressing a network coverage complaint, the AI system analyzes data from cell tower locations and coverage maps to provide a well-informed response:

"We apologize for the network challenges in your area. Our team is working on a resolution. Meanwhile, here are steps you can take to improve your experience."

This approach ensures a consistent and efficient resolution process, maintaining high service levels and fostering positive customer relationships.

In summary, CSPs can use automation and AI to improve customer service. They can better interpret queries related to network, billing, or troubleshooting, providing swift, tailored responses. AI excels by efficiently accessing and analyzing vast knowledge bases, surpassing human speed and accuracy capabilities. This includes using data from customer profiles and historical interactions stored in CRM systems and employing large language models for insights.

Automating customer inquiries with AI's intent recognition and comprehensive knowledge results in personalized service experiences. AI's iterative learning from each interaction enhances its accuracy, empathy, and efficiency. For example, it strategically handles network coverage complaints using extensive information for informed responses. By automating responses and accessing knowledge sources, service providers can improve customer satisfaction and revolutionize customer experiences.

Table 60: Benefits of automated customer inquiry use cases

Automated customer inquiry capability	Chief benefits
Customer intent detection	Enhances customer satisfaction by ensuring responses are specifically aligned to individual needs
Knowledge base access	Streamlines workflow and improves knowledge discovery
Leveraging data insights	Enables precision in responses and strategic decision-making based on comprehensive data analysis
Automating inquiry responses	Boosts efficiency by providing accurate solutions tailored to specific customer concerns
Speed to resolution	Reduces wait times and improves customer experience by efficiently managing routine inquiries
Adaptive learning	Continuously improves in precision, empathy, and operational efficiency, ensuring better outcomes in future interactions

Agent Assist Using Knowledge Bases And Summarization

Communications companies and their global customer service centers are now employing advanced technology to automatically document and summarize conversations. This technology, driven by AI, simplifies post-call tasks for customer service representatives. Traditionally, agents would devote considerable time to transcribing call details and updating customer records.

With the advent of automated call summarization AI tools, this process has become significantly more efficient, generating concise summaries through conversation analysis. This innovation not only reduces the time required for documentation but also enhances the accuracy of these summaries.

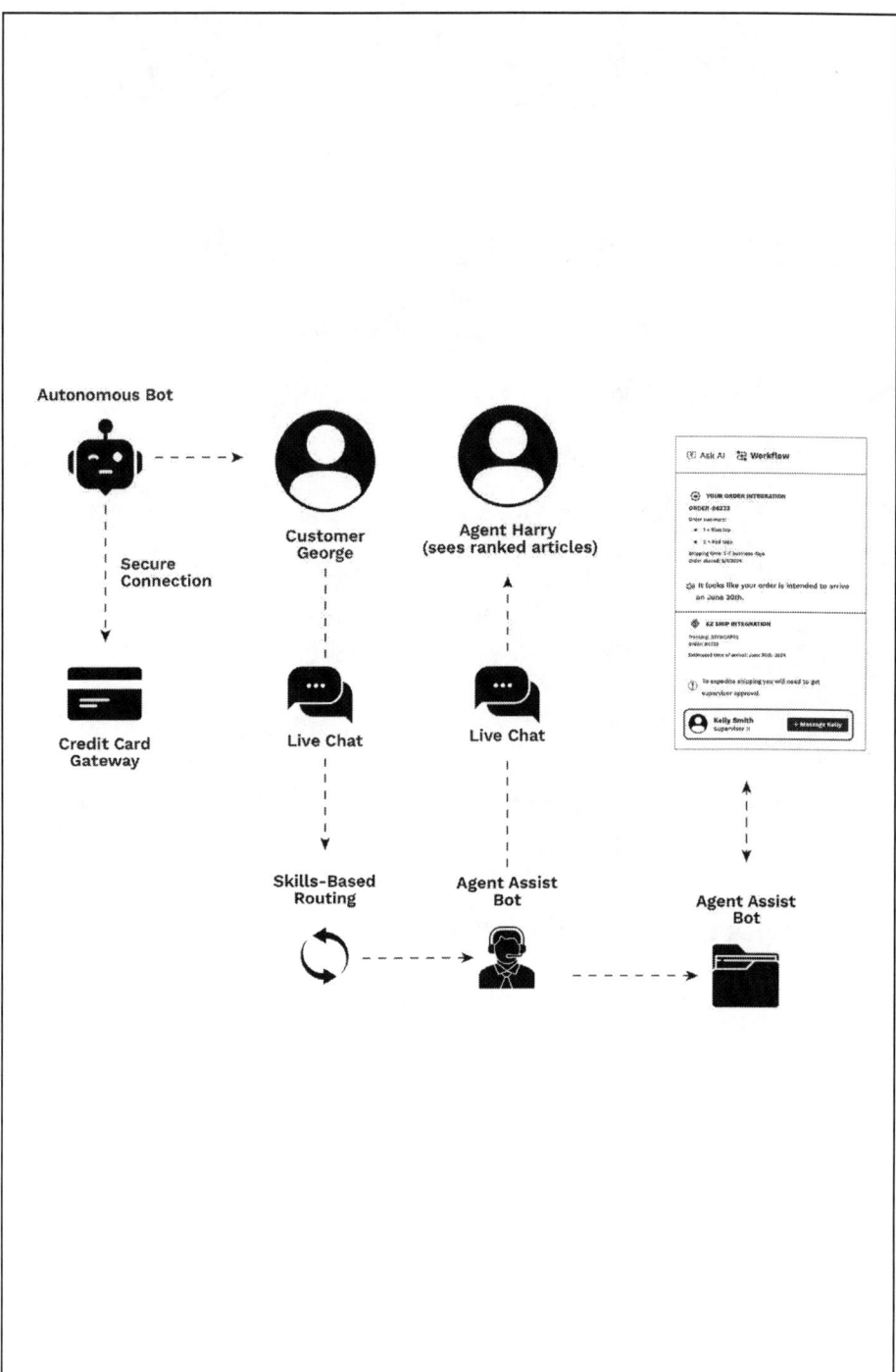

Figure 44: Use of knowledge base with live assistance

Providing agents with immediate access to relevant information empowers them to respond effectively to customer inquiries, particularly those of a technical or complex nature. Agent assist bots can seamlessly retrieve and prioritize pertinent knowledge base articles for the agent. An advanced unified customer experience management (UCXM) system can utilize ongoing dialogues to fetch appropriate articles.

This automation also facilitates the transfer of customer information between agents and ensures compliance with regulatory requirements. By automating these processes, customer service centers operate more efficiently, promoting customer satisfaction.

The implementation of automated notetaking, summarization, and knowledge base article retrieval can substantially enhance the efficiency of contact centers managed by communication service providers (CSPs). Through the integration of AI and automation, CSPs can streamline workflows, maintain accurate documentation, and improve customer interactions, ultimately enhancing overall service delivery.

In the domain of customer service, agents engage in dynamic interactions with customers daily. These engagements necessitate active listening, quick decision-making, and the ability to capture crucial information. However, traditional notetaking practices during these conversations can be time-consuming and impede the agent's ability to fully understand and address customer needs.

Balancing active listening and accurate documentation is challenging for customer service representatives. They need to empathize with customers and provide assistance while ensuring essential details are recorded accurately. Automating note-taking and summarization offers significant benefits.

Firstly, it improves documentation accuracy. AI-generated notes capture critical information, summarizing previous interactions, customer preferences, and resolutions. Secondly, it enhances efficiency by generating real-time summaries of key points and action items, allowing agents to focus on interactions. Thirdly, AI systems often include sentiment analysis, flagging customer emotions like frustration or satisfaction, and identifying keywords for prioritization.

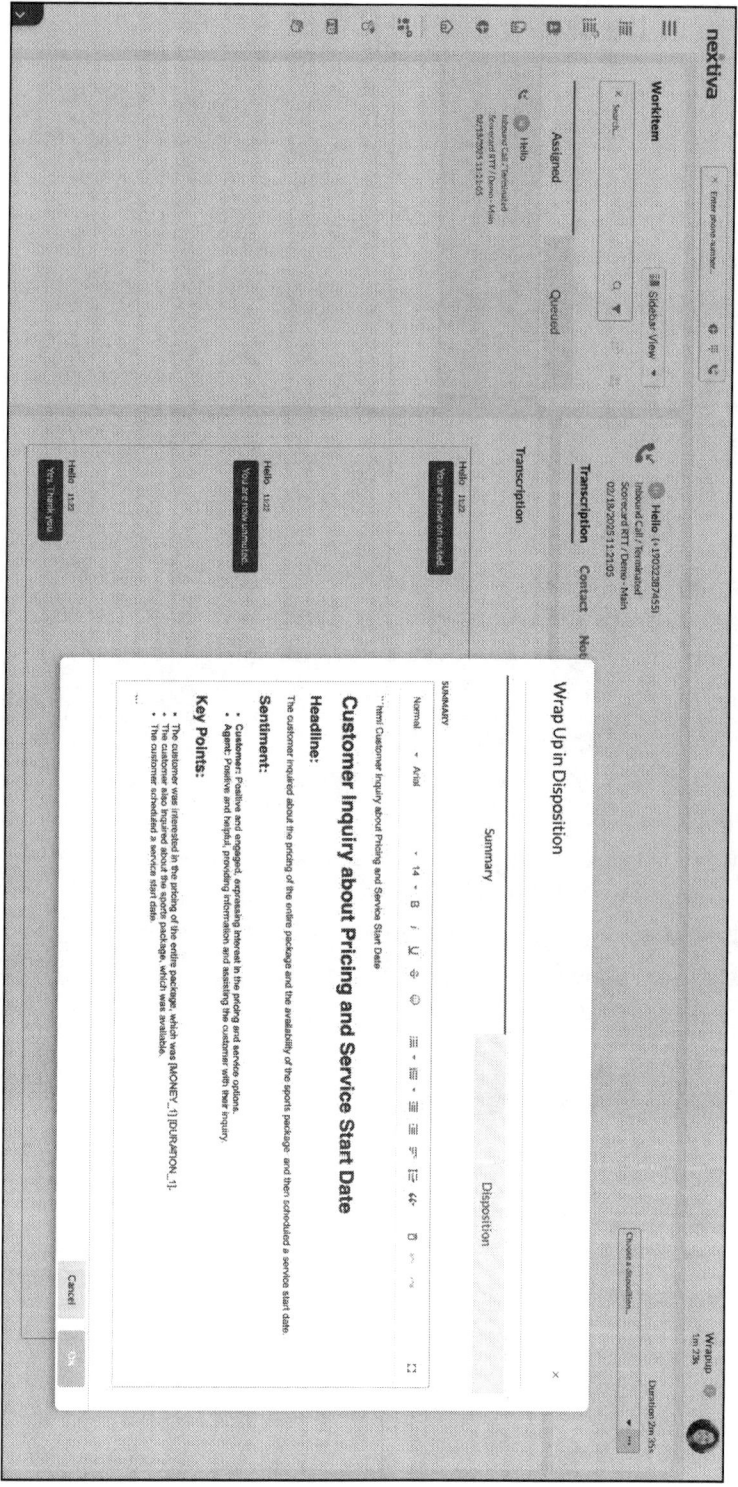

Figure 45: Transcription and summarization

Storing summaries in a CRM system ensures consistency and accessibility for future reference, benefiting not only agents but also supervisors conducting history searches. By utilizing AI, CSPs streamline workflows, reduce manual effort, and maintain accurate records. The future of customer service lies in integrating human expertise with AI to enhance efficiency and customer satisfaction.

Table 61: Benefits of automated notetaking and summarization

Automated notetaking and summarization capability	Chief benefits
Automated notetaking	Increases documentation accuracy; saves time for agents, enhancing efficiency
Summaries and contextual notes	Provides relevant context (e.g., account history, customer preferences); summarizes essential details and action items from conversations
Real-time assistance	Keeps agents focused on interactions while capturing key information
Sentiment analysis flags customer emotions (frustration, satisfaction)	Identifies urgent matters for prioritized response
CRM system integration	Facilitates consistent follow-up and service; enhances the accessibility of customer interaction histories for all agents
Workflow automation	Streamlines processes; improves efficiency and customer interaction quality
Balancing active listening and personalized assistance	Helps agents capture vital information without detracting from customer engagement

Personalized Offers And Recommendations

Without a doubt, personalized offers and recommendations yield a multitude of impactful use cases. These encompass tailoring customer interactions and support to perfectly match individual needs and preferences. By harnessing customer data, service providers can truly grasp each customer's unique requirements and anticipate their needs. The beauty of personalization is its diverse manifestations, from engaging through preferred channels to providing spot-on product recommendations derived from purchase and search history. It's all about creating meaningful connections and enhancing the overall customer experience.

Major telecommunications providers such as Comcast, Verizon, and Telefonica understand the importance of tailoring offers to align seamlessly with their customer-centric approaches. These personalized offers demonstrate a deep understanding of individual needs, going beyond simple transactions. Imagine a scenario where a customer uses a mobile application and is presented with a customized service plan recommendation meticulously suited to their unique usage patterns, preferences, and historical interactions. It's like having a knowledgeable personal assistant who can anticipate and cater to your requirements effectively.

The growing expansion of customer bases presents a significant challenge in the manual creation and management of personalized offers, leading to increased complexity and a higher risk of errors. The substantial volume of personalized recommendations requires a more efficient approach to handling this process. The use of decision engines is crucial in automating key aspects of this process, ensuring the timely delivery of relevant offers during customer engagements, including website visits, phone calls, and chat sessions that require swift decision-making.

The real-time assessment of customer data and preferences is of utmost significance. Through the use of AI and automation, telecommunications service providers (CSPs) can adeptly handle the intricacies and sheer volume of data they encounter on a daily basis. AI has the capacity to untangle this complexity, revealing patterns that inform personalized recommendations.

These tailored offers underscore the company's recognition of each customer's unique needs. Customers who receive personalized recommendations feel genuinely appreciated and acknowledged, leading to heightened overall satisfaction levels. Relevant offers also serve as strong catalysts for upselling, cross-selling, and customer retention, ultimately resulting in increased revenue.

The incorporation of automation reduces manual workload, allowing staff members to focus on more intricate and strategic aspects

Table 62: Benefits of AI-powered personalization

AI-powered personalization capability	Chief benefits
Customized interactions	Enhances the customer experience by matching interactions with individual preferences and needs
Diverse personalization	Leads to meaningful connections with customers
Automated offers	Reduces complexity and error risk in personalizing offers, ensuring efficiency in customer engagement
Real-time data assessment	Ensures the relevance of offers through a timely understanding of customer preferences
Voice of the customer	Personalized recommendations make customers feel appreciated, boosting their overall satisfaction levels
Upsell, cross-sell suggestions	Enhances customer retention and increases revenue
Workload distribution	Automation allows staff to focus on strategic tasks instead of mundane ones, decreasing agent burn-out
Sales and support automation	Faster service issue resolutions

of their roles. Additionally, automation can intricately craft tailored messaging and conduct lead scoring, freeing up salespeople to concentrate on high-value customers.

Personalized offers are extended through virtual assistants and bots, adeptly managing routine inquiries, providing appropriate plans, and processing transactions through automation sequences. Personalization goes beyond sales and encompasses addressing complaints and troubleshooting, resulting in expedited resolution times for service-related issues.

In essence, AI-driven personalized recommendations and support play a decisive role in propelling CSPs to deliver exceptional service.

Retention Desk Functions

In the world of companies that provide communication services, a "Retention Desk" is a special team in the call center dedicated to keeping customers from leaving. They identify customers who might be thinking about canceling their service or switching to a competitor and reach out with offers, discounts, or different plans to retain them. The goal is to address any issues and offer better solutions, reducing customer loss.

AI and decisioning engines enhance responses to customers wanting to discontinue service by considering customer history, previous complaints, and special packages that may appeal to them. AI also helps escalate transactions to supervisors and retention specialists based on customer intent.

Effective retention strategies lower customer churn and safeguard revenue. Personalized responses demonstrate empathy and understanding, enhancing satisfaction. Predictive analytics identifies potential churners by analyzing customer history, usage patterns, and complaints. Timely intervention is achieved through alerts sent to retention specialists, which is crucial in retaining valuable customers.

Tailoring responses to individual needs is important. When customers express a desire to leave, AI can recommend special packages, discounts, or incentives based on their preferences and behavior. Escalation decisioning helps handle critical cases efficiently. AI

SERVICE PROVIDERS

Figure 46: Use of automation in retention desk scenario

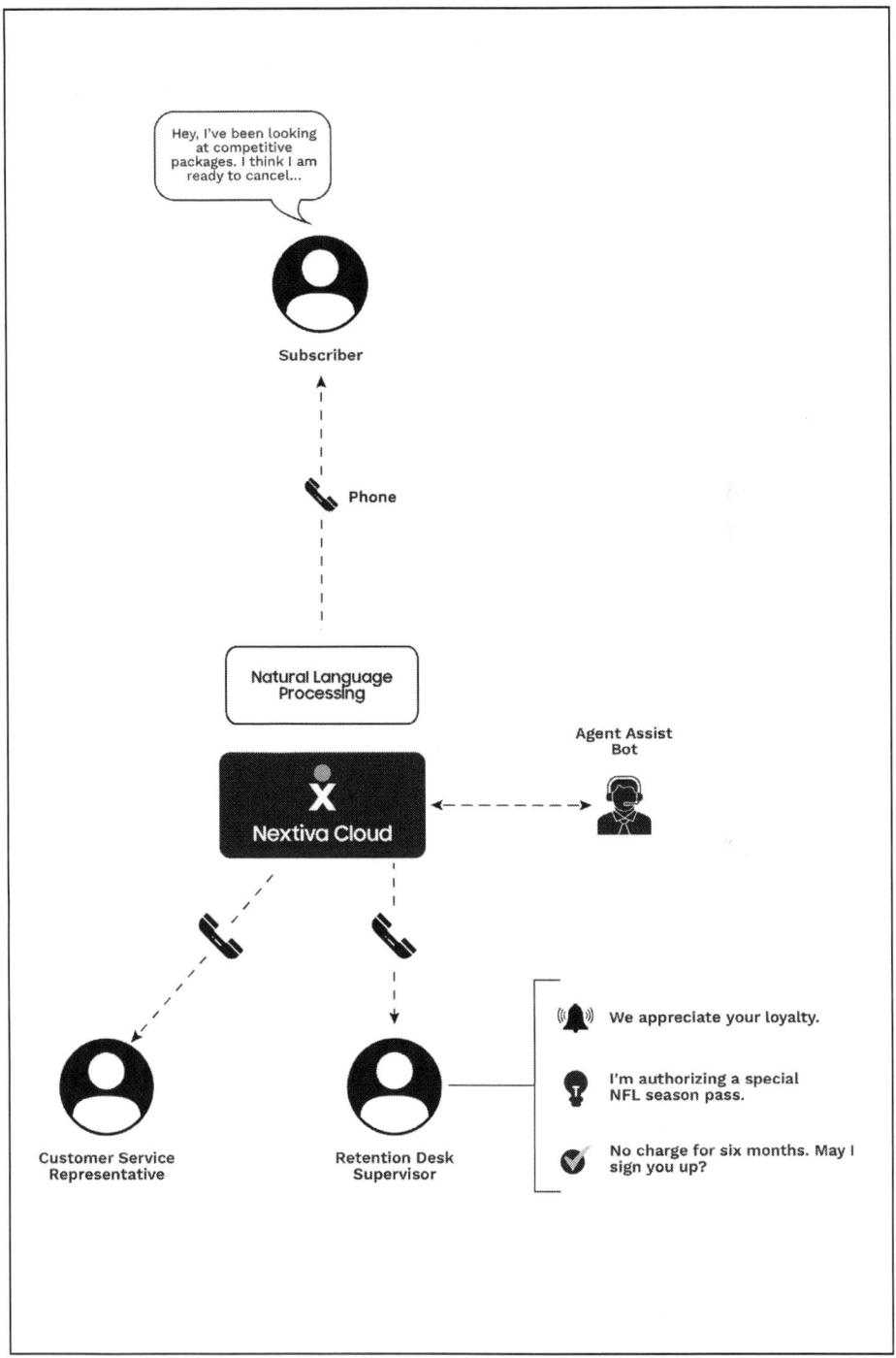

Table 63: Benefits of retention desk use cases

Retention desk capability	Chief benefits
Predictive analytics	Timely and proactive retention efforts, leading to a reduction in customer churn
Customized responses through AI	Enhances customer satisfaction by demonstrating empathy and understanding
Escalation decisioning	Optimizes retention desk operations and improves efficiency and response times
Deployment of AI and decisioning engines	Safeguards company revenue through reduced customer churn

evaluates urgency based on issue severity, customer history, and potential impact, ensuring prompt attention to high-priority matters.

In summary, AI and process automation can elevate retention desk functions in the communications and service provider industry. They provide an overview, address challenges, outline benefits, and propose resolutions for retention desk use cases, enhancing customer satisfaction and reducing churn.

Self-Service Options

Self-service options provided by communications companies allow customers to find information, complete tasks, and solve problems on their own, without needing to talk to a customer service representative.

These options cover a wide range of tools such as FAQ pages, detailed help centers, community forums where users can discuss, mobile applications, chat services powered by artificial intelligence, and automated phone systems.

The main aim of these tools is to make it easier and more convenient for customers to get the help they need whenever they need it, without waiting. This not only makes things faster and more efficient for customers but also helps companies save money by reducing the number of staff needed to handle customer queries directly, all while keeping customers happy and engaged with the service.

Let's explore how AI and process automation enhance self-service options in the communications and service provider industry.

Figure 47: Business agent bot at TATA PLAY

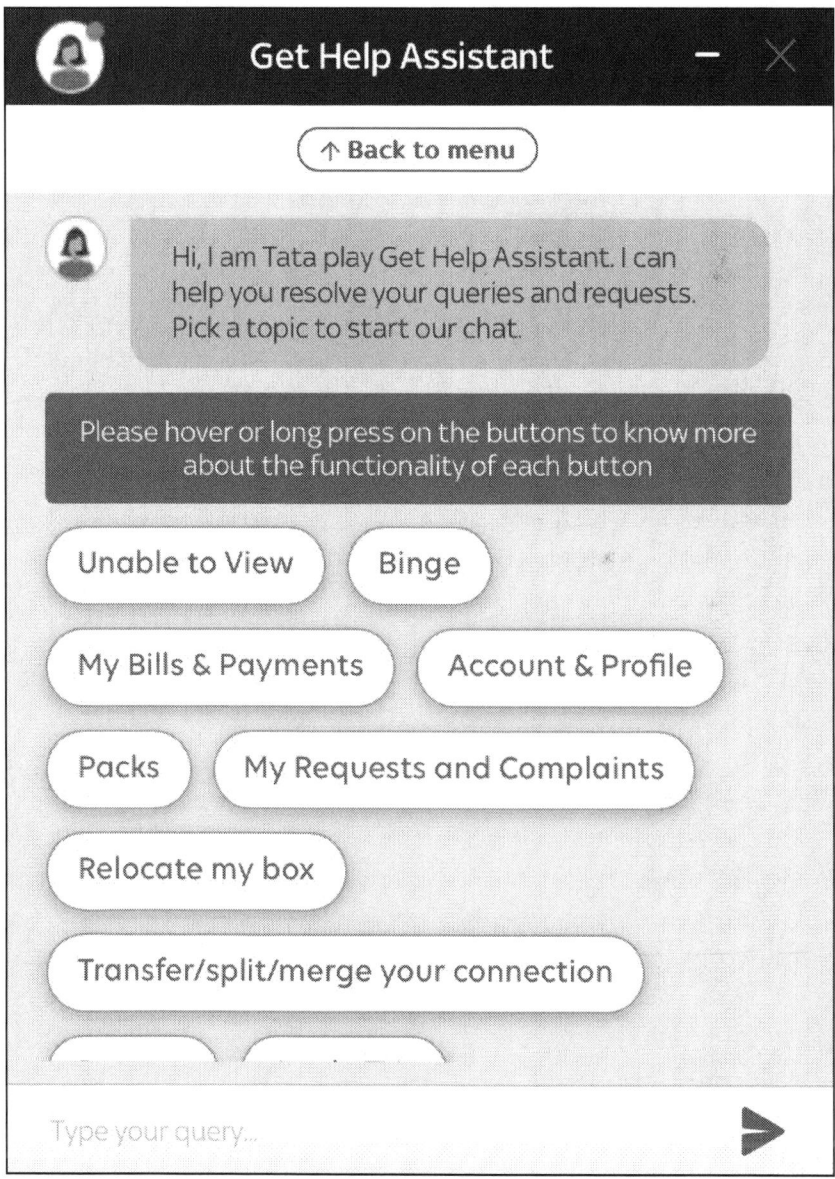

AI-powered self-help portals and chatbots allow customers to find answers independently, reducing the need for agent intervention.

Traditional customer support relies heavily on human agents, leading to high operational costs, longer response times, and potential errors. Customers increasingly expect quick, convenient, and 24/7 self-service options.

By implementing AI-powered self-help portals and chatbots, companies can improve customer satisfaction, reduce agent workload, and enhance overall service quality.

Chatbots do a pretty good job of handling routine queries and providing instant responses that would be resource-intensive for human agents. This may include guiding users through troubleshooting steps and providing accurate information. For instance, when a customer asks about data usage or billing details, an AI chatbot can instantly provide relevant answers.

Self-help portals and knowledge bases also provide answers to common questions independently of agents. CSPs routinely maintain comprehensive knowledge bases where users can find step-by-step instructions for setting up devices, troubleshooting network issues, or managing accounts. Customers can often find answers without contacting support, which can be satisfying for customers who do not want to talk to an agent.

The top CSPs use chatbots to assist customers with account inquiries, plan changes, and technical troubleshooting. Users can interact with the chatbot via the website or mobile app, which offers faster resolution and reduced reliance on human agents.

In summary, self-service options offered by communications companies have revolutionized the way customers find information, complete tasks, and solve problems independently. These options encompass a range of tools, including FAQ pages, detailed help centers, community forums, mobile apps, AI-powered chat services, and automated phone systems. The primary intent is to provide round-the-clock assistance, greatly enhancing efficiency and customer satisfaction by minimizing the need for direct interactions with customer service representatives. This not only accelerates issue resolution but also reduces staffing costs significantly.

Moreover, the integration of AI and process automation has further elevated the effectiveness of these self-service options. AI-driven portals and chatbots enable customers to obtain answers without involving human agents, leading to higher satisfaction rates and alleviating the workload on support staff. Traditional support systems, which heavily rely on human agents, often come with high operational costs, longer response times, and the possibility of errors. In contrast, AI-powered tools adeptly manage routine queries, deliver instantaneous responses, and guide users through troubleshooting steps.

Additionally, self-help portals and comprehensive knowledge bases provide detailed instructions for resolving common issues. By leveraging these advanced technologies, companies can ensure faster problem resolution and offer a more fulfilling customer experience. This seamless support system, governed by AI and automation, not only meets but often exceeds customer expectations, thereby fostering a more loyal and satisfied user base.

Table 64: Benefits of self-service use cases

Business agent (bot) self-service capability	Chief benefits
FAQ pages	Quick access to common questions and answers, saving time for both customers and support teams
Self-service bots	Quick access to commonly asked questions, account balance, and other data allows customers to complete tasks 24/7 at their own pace (bolstering customer choice often equals better customer satisfaction)
Detailed customer portals	Comprehensive information on services and troubleshooting, enabling customers to solve issues independently
Community forums	Peer support and shared solutions, fostering a user community and reducing reliance on direct customer service

Billing And Payment Assistance

The incorporation of artificial intelligence (AI) into chatbot systems has significantly transformed the approach of communication service providers toward handling billing inquiries, payment reminders, and payment processing. Over the last decade, these providers have consistently pushed the boundaries to enhance customer experiences through innovative solutions, marking substantial progress in this domain.

In these use case examples, we explore the potential of AI and process automation within the communications and service provider industry, with a specific emphasis on billing and payment assistance. It is intriguing to examine how industry leaders such as AT&T, T-Mobile, DISH Network, and Comcast can harness the capabilities of automation and AI to truly revolutionize their operations in this aspect.

The billing and payment procedures within the telecom sector are notably intricate, involving a multitude of complex transactions, inquiries, and reminders. Manual handling of these tasks often results in inefficiencies, errors, and delays. However, the integration of AI and automation presents an opportunity for companies to streamline these processes, ensure accuracy, and elevate overall customer satisfaction.

Customers frequently encounter queries and concerns regarding their bills, such as understanding charges, due dates, or payment methods. AI-driven chatbots provide an ideal platform for companies to offer 24/7 support for billing inquiries, delivering immediate responses and freeing up human agents to focus on more intricate tasks. For example, if a customer raises concerns about an unexpected charge, a chatbot can promptly analyze historical data, identify the issue, and explain it to the customer, thereby enhancing the overall customer experience.

Timely reminders regarding upcoming payments are crucial to ensure prompt collections. Through automation, consistent reminders can be dispatched without manual effort, thereby reducing late payments and optimizing cash flow. Personalized payment reminders via SMS or email efficiently ensure that customers are reminded of

SERVICE PROVIDERS

Figure 48: Nextiva secure payment agent assist

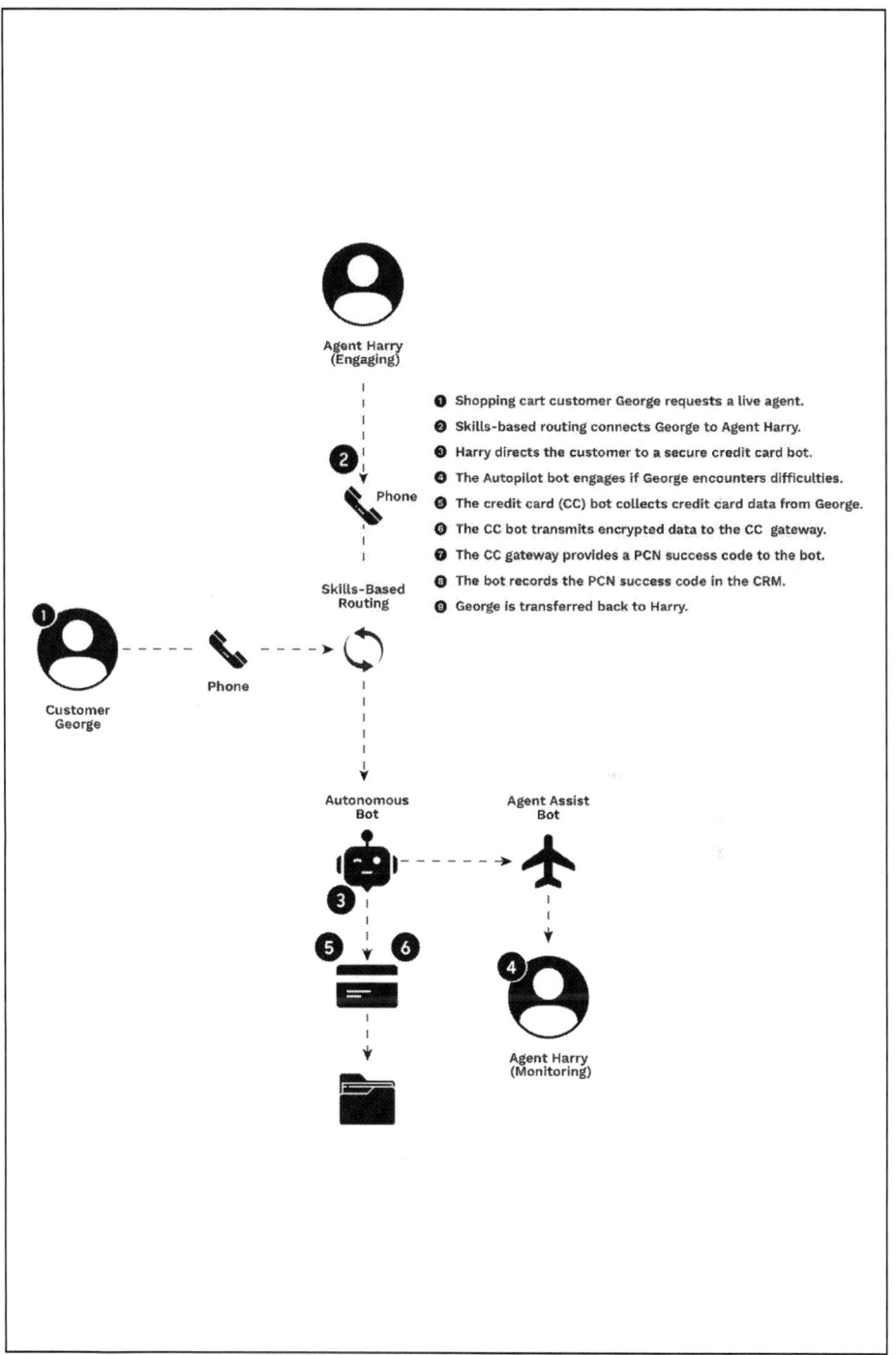

their upcoming payments, thereby providing them with a seamless and positive experience.

AI also plays a pivotal role in automating payment processing, which often involves manual data entry, verification, and reconciliation. By leveraging automation, errors are minimized, and payment processing is expedited. AI algorithms have the capability to match payments to invoices, identify any discrepancies, and update accounts in real-time, ensuring seamless processing, leading to improved efficiency and accuracy in the overall billing and payment processes.

In summary, the integration of AI and automation empowers telecom companies to efficiently manage billing and payment processes, resulting in cost savings, heightened accuracy, and elevated customer

Table 65: Benefits of secure billing and payment assistance

Billing and payment assistance capability	Chief benefits
AI and automation application to integration strategy	Streamlines processes; ensures accuracy; elevates customer satisfaction
AI-driven chatbots for billing inquiries	Provides 24/7 support; frees human agents for complex tasks; enhances customer experience
Automation of payment reminders	Reduces late payments; optimizes cash flow
Personalized payment reminders via SMS/email	Ensures timely payments; enhances customer experience
Automating payment processing with AI	Minimizes errors; expedites payment processing
AI for predictive analytics	Identifies customers at risk of non-payment; enables proactive interventions
AI-driven dispute resolution	Expedites resolution process for billing disputes; improves customer relationships; saves resources

experiences. By embracing these technological advancements, CSPs can position themselves competitively while delivering a seamless and frictionless customer experience, thus paving the way for superior customer experiences in billing inquiries and payments.

Customer Sentiment Analysis

Sentiment analysis constitutes a discipline within the domain of customer feedback, which takes into consideration the emotions, attitudes, and behaviors of customers. The resultant data is utilized to gauge their overall satisfaction, level of involvement, and loyalty to the brand. Within the realm of communication service providers, sentiment analysis assumes a pivotal role in endeavors aimed at customer retention.

Sentiment analysis plays a pivotal role across a diverse array of use cases, such as voice of the customer surveys, agent assist technology, and intelligent routing, among others. This process leverages AI to scrutinize customer feedback, social media posts, and reviews, allowing for a nuanced understanding of sentiment and the proactive addressing of concerns. Remarkably, AI and automatic processes are instrumental in responding to customer sentiment in real-time during interactions, enabling a strategic "rescue" of the engagement through appropriate measures or escalations.

Delving deeper into the realm of AI and process automation reveals their significant potential to revolutionize customer sentiment analysis within the communications and service provider sectors. Illustrating this transformation with examples from industry titans such as AT&T, T-Mobile, DISH Network, and Comcast sheds light on the evolving landscape.

Historically, the extraction and analysis of customer feedback posed substantial challenges due to the voluminous and qualitative nature of the data. Companies found it arduous to distill customer perspectives on their products, services, or brands across myriad channels.

The advent of AI-powered sentiment analysis has dramatically streamlined the process of understanding customer feedback, yielding clearer insights and actionable intelligence. This analytical approach encompasses several critical stages. The initial phase involves the collection of data, encompassing unstructured inputs from diverse sources, including emails, chats, social media, and phone interactions.

Subsequently, natural language processing (NLP) techniques are employed to decipher the context and connotations of the language used by customers. Following this, machine learning algorithms are applied to detect patterns, trends, and sentiments within the data.

Upon completing these stages, the process culminates in the categorization of sentiments as positive, negative, or neutral. AI engines typically assign a numerical score to these sentiments, using "tags" to illuminate key emotions and issues.

Finally, visualization tools enable agents and supervisors to view sentiment analysis outcomes on their screens, facilitating informed decision-making. While sentiment analysis can enhance intelligent routing, it is important to note that the visual representation of data is not an obligatory step but rather an optional tool for enhanced comprehension.

There are endless use cases for using sentiment analysis in the context of customer experience management.

An illustrative application of social listening involves the monitoring of brand mentions across social media platforms to identify customer concerns. Employing NLP and sentiment analysis enables the early detection of issues and the identification of trends and key influencers in social media dialogues.

Another pertinent example lies in the realm of smart ticketing, which grapples with the classification of inbound support tickets and their linkage to pertinent knowledge base suggestions, facilitating their seamless routing to suitable agents. Here, the application of NLP to scrutinize ticket content and ensure effective routing proves instrumental.

Furthermore, there exist notable use cases of sentiment analysis in the domain of product research, where understanding customer sentiments toward products and services is pivotal. This entails informed decision-making via the analysis of customer reviews, feedback, and social media comments to glean insights into product satisfaction through sentiment analysis, thus aiding strategic decision-making.

An extensively employed application of sentiment analysis is in fine-tuning customer support transactions. By leveraging sentiment analysis to curtail support times and elevate survey scores, the overall customer experience is significantly enhanced. This feat is accomplished through AI-driven sentiment analysis tools, aggregating diverse touchpoints such as voice calls, emails, surveys, support tickets,

Table 66: Benefits of AI-based sentiment analysis

AI-based sentiment analysis capability	Chief benefits
Measurement of customers' happiness	Improves subscriber retention
Feedback analysis	Addresses concerns more quickly and effectively
Action triggers on sentiment	Improves outcomes in real-time before it's too late
Feedback analysis	Streamlining provides better understanding and actionable insights
Visualizations	More timely aid to agents and supervisors
Monitoring brand mentions	Early warning detection of customer pain points
Smart ticketing	More effectively routes support tickets to the right agents
Product research	More informed decision-making
Optimized support transactions	Educes support times and improves survey scores
Brand reputation	Maintains a positive brand image
Reactive to proactive conversion	Better customer experiences and increased revenue

and reviews, thereby furnishing accurate and real-time customer experience trend data. Such data, in turn, facilitates the calibration of product roadmaps in alignment with prevailing customer sentiments.

You can also use sentiment analysis to manage your brand. This involves monitoring brand feedback for reputation, with a resolution that entails continuously analyzing social media posts, reviews, and customer interactions to address concerns promptly and maintain a positive brand image.

In summary, by utilizing AI and automation, companies can shift customer sentiment analysis from reactive to proactive, resulting in improved customer experiences and higher revenue. These strategies are applicable across the industry and benefit all types of communications service providers.

Complaint Resolution

Service providers must address customer grievances efficiently. This process includes listening to complaints, understanding their essence, and taking appropriate actions to resolve issues, such as fixing technical problems or correcting billing errors. The goal is to enhance customer relationships and make customers feel valued.

Effective complaint management helps CSPs build loyalty and maintain high service standards. The use of AI-powered chatbots has improved complaint handling by enabling efficient initial responses, quick acknowledgments, and appropriate routing. Real-time monitoring allows for the tracking of complaints and interactions, helping identify patterns for proactive problem resolution.

Addressing customer complaints efficiently is essential for maintaining customer satisfaction, especially when businesses handle large volumes of data across various communication channels. Manual processing can be time-consuming and error-prone, leading to delays and customer frustration. Incorporating AI and automation can streamline complaint resolution, improve response times, reduce manual labor, and enhance accuracy.

For instance, when a customer complains about an unexpected increase in their insurance premium via email, AI-enabled digital assistants can craft a personalized response, request additional information, and categorize the complaint for further action. AI can also analyze the emotional tone in live calls to detect varying emotional states, helping agents address concerns appropriately.

Moreover, AI-powered self-service chatbots manage initial complaints via chat interfaces, acknowledging and directing them to the right departments. Conversational commerce through messaging app bots on platforms like WhatsApp and Facebook Messenger allows

Table 67: Benefits of AI-enabled complaint resolution

AI-enabled complaint resolution capability	Chief benefits
Managing complaints with AI chatbots	Enables efficient handling of initial complaints, quick acknowledgments, and routing to appropriate departments, reducing response time and manual effort
Progress monitoring	Facilitates real-time tracking of customer complaints and interactions, helping in identifying patterns for proactive problem resolution
Escalating issues to human agents	Ensures complex or sensitive complaints are handled personally, maintaining a high level of customer service and satisfaction
Personalized responses	Improves customer experience through relevant and timely communication
Data extraction and reporting	Better decision-making and strategy development
Emotional insight	Timely interventions and escalation, enhancing customer interaction quality
Leverage popular messaging apps	Choice-based convenience and seamless communication and complaint escalation pathways
Pattern detection	Allows businesses to proactively address concerns and prevent escalation, improving customer retention

businesses to engage in natural language dialogues with customers, providing information or escalating complaints as needed.

In summary, real-time monitoring through AI helps identify patterns and resolve issues proactively, improving customer satisfaction and retention rates. Leveraging AI and automation for complaint resolution enhances the overall customer service experience.

Automation Of Billing Queries And Disputes

Communication service providers have been at the forefront of leveraging advanced technologies to optimize customer billing inquiries and resolve disputes. This includes deploying AI, machine learning algorithms, and other software solutions to precisely respond to billing queries and rectify potential inaccuracies. Such technological integration enhances overall efficiency and customer satisfaction by delivering prompt and consistent responses, standardizing billing management procedures and improving customer service experiences.

Manually handling billing queries and disputes can be time-consuming and error-prone due to the high volume of inquiries and the complexity of billing information. By employing AI and automation, companies can streamline billing processes, ensure quicker query resolution, reduce manual effort, and minimize errors, leading to an enhanced customer experience.

AI-powered virtual assistants can manage initial customer interactions, utilizing natural language processing to comprehend queries and accurately provide billing details and payment histories without human intervention. Automated dispute resolution systems can efficiently handle disputes by verifying charges against contract terms and escalating unresolved issues to human agents, thus reducing backlog and enhancing efficiency.

Predictive analytics can analyze historical payment patterns to forecast potential payment delays, enabling proactive communication with customers.

Automated invoice validation employs an AI rules engine to compare invoice data against predefined criteria, flagging discrepancies and streamlining the validation process through automated approval or rejection, thereby minimizing errors and reducing manual effort.

Integration with CRM and ERP systems provides a comprehensive view of customer interactions, facilitating better-informed decisions and improved collaboration across departments.

These technological advancements address the challenges associated with billing processes, establishing a new standard for efficient and effective management.

In summary, there is a shift toward automating billing queries and dispute resolutions within the service provider sector, using technologies like AI, machine learning algorithms, and bespoke software solutions. This approach aims to manage customer billing inquiries, streamline dispute resolution, and reduce inaccuracies, significantly decreasing manual processing and improving operational efficiency and customer satisfaction.

Table 68: Benefits of automated billing and dispute queries

Billing queries and dispute automation capability	Chief benefits
Virtual assistants	Due to no wait times, it elevates customer service experience
Streamlined billing processes	Quick resolution of queries; reduces manual effort; minimizes errors
Natural language processing	Understands customer queries without human intervention; ensures accuracy
Automated dispute resolution	Reduces dispute backlog; automates the handling process
Predictive analytics	Predicts payment delays; improves cash flow and financial stability
Automated invoice validation	Minimizes billing errors; streamlines validation through automation
CRM and ERP integration	Provides a comprehensive view of customer interactions; enhances decision-making

The deployment of AI-powered virtual assistants and the integration of process automation and predictive analytics promise changes in billing management, leading to quicker resolution of queries, minimized errors, and an enhanced customer experience. These technological advancements support more efficient management of billing processes, establishing new standards in customer service and operational practice.

Customer Reminders And Notifications

Service providers pioneered the use of customer reminders and notifications along with the travel and hospitality industry. Here, automation systems can systematically send messages to customers to inform them about upcoming payments, service outages, and a variety of other issues that impact the customer experience. Popular amongst these notices are data consumption alerts, service interruption advisories, promotional offers, and updates on service terms and conditions. The primary goal is to enhance customer experience, reduce attrition, and increase operational efficiency using channels such as SMS, email, automated calls, or in-app alerts, based on customer preference and message content.

AI and automation advancements significantly improve customer reminders, service notifications, and alerts within the CSP domain. Key challenges include the timely delivery of updates, personalized notifications, and efficient management of large volumes of alerts. AI and automation help overcome these challenges, enhancing the customer experience.

In scheduled network maintenance or upgrades, AI-powered notifications automate alerts through multiple channels. Predictive analytics help schedule maintenance to minimize customer inconvenience, customizing messages based on location and service plan.

For unplanned service disruptions, real-time AI monitoring quickly detects outages and sends automated alerts explaining the issue and providing resolution timelines. AI-driven troubleshooting guidance enhances transparency and reduces customer support queries. Personalized automated payment reminders via SMS or email improve timely payments and reduce late fees by including direct payment links.

When introducing new plans or upgrades, AI segments customers based on engagement and sends targeted notifications. This precision marketing and automated order processing streamline the upgrade process, increasing service uptake and customer satisfaction.

In emergencies, geolocation-based alerts ensure advisories are relevant to the customer's location, using SMS, app notifications, and voice calls to enhance safety and awareness.

In summary, sending automated customer reminders and notifications informs subscribers about bill payments, data usage, and service updates. These communications via SMS, email, and app notifications enhance customer experience, reduce churn, and improve efficiency.

Table 69: Benefits of customer reminders and notifications

Customer reminders and notifications capability	Chief benefits
Alerts for scheduled maintenance or upgrades	Minimizes customer inconvenience and improves customer satisfaction
Real-time monitoring for service disruptions	Enhances transparency, sets realistic expectations, and reduces customer support queries
Personalized payment reminders	Improves timely payments, reduces late payment fees, and streamlines the payment process
Notifications for new plans and upgrades	Eases adoption of new plans/features, boosting sales, and enhances customer experience
Geolocation-based alerts for emergencies	Ensures timely delivery of critical information and enhances safety by providing localized emergency contacts and safety protocols; helps in community awareness and preparedness

With AI and automation, notifications become more effective, enabling predictive scheduling, real-time alerts, personalized reminders, and targeted promotions. AI helps manage large volumes of notifications efficiently and tailors communication to customer preferences, enhancing customer service for CSPs.

Handset, Gateway, And Device Upgrades And Upsell

Communication service providers can leverage AI for in-depth analysis of customer data, such as payment history, loyalty, account size, and number of lines. This approach aids in making informed decisions about equipment upgrades for their customers, especially with 5G technology.

AI-based contextual recommendations can enhance upselling opportunities, increase customer engagement, and yield returns on infrastructure investments. Identifying subscribers likely to upgrade without high marketing costs becomes easier with comprehensive customer history analysis, helping providers understand subscribers' preferences for services like Internet, phone, and entertainment.

Personalized communication is key to effectively presenting upgrade opportunities. Tailored messages explaining the benefits of network upgrades, such as faster speeds and improved video streaming, are more effective than generic promotions. AI support in upgrade scenarios includes suggesting upgrades based on loyalty and payment history and providing device compatibility information.

Automation and AI also optimize resource allocation by analyzing user data to offer relevant and timely upgrade options. This ensures that CSPs can provide personalized upgrade choices. Automated systems help manage upgrade eligibility, reducing customer service costs and improving financial stability. This was exemplified by AT&T's reduction in financial losses through advanced decision-making systems. Insights and personalized communication improve the effectiveness of device upgrades and upsell strategies, benefiting both subscribers and service providers.

In summary, when it comes to upgrading equipment and handsets, communications service providers have a significant opportunity to utilize AI for analyzing customer data. This includes payment

Figure 49: Handset upgrade decisioning scenario

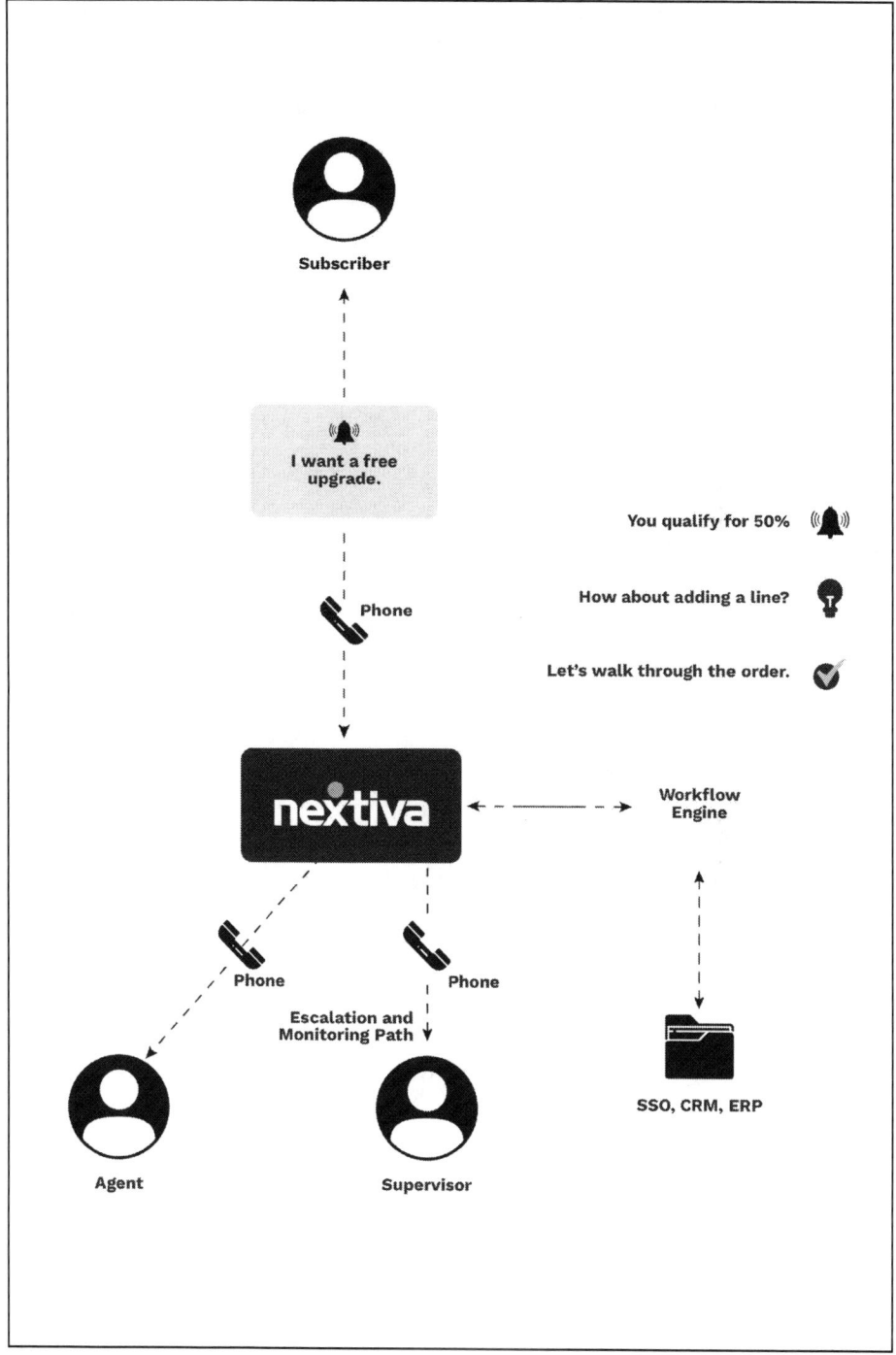

Table 70: Benefits of automated decisioning in device upgrades

Automated decisioning in device upgrades capability	Chief benefits
AI-based contextual recommendations	Maximizes upselling opportunities; elevates customer engagement; realizes substantial returns on infrastructure investments
Comprehensive analysis of customer history	Helps in identifying subscribers likely to upgrade; reduces marketing costs
Personalized approach in communication	Enhances effectiveness of device upgrades and upsell strategies
Automation and AI in upgrade scenarios	Optimizes resource allocation; ensures timely and relevant upgrade offers
Use of chatbots for providing upgrade information	Simplifies the process of informing subscribers about device compatibility and upgrades
Advanced decision-making systems	Minimizes financial losses from discretionary errors; improves customer experience and financial stability

history, loyalty, account size, and the number of lines. This analysis is crucial for identifying customers who may benefit from either no-cost or low-cost equipment upgrades. Additionally, AI can greatly improve the process of upgrading handsets, gateways, and devices, as well as help in developing upsell strategies for major CSPs.

While one challenge is motivating subscribers to switch to devices with better network performance, using AI to provide contextual recommendations can truly revolutionize customer engagement and unlock upsell opportunities. This approach has the potential to deliver substantial returns on infrastructure investments and pave the way for a brighter future for all involved.

Travel And Hospitality

THE TRAVEL AND hospitality industry includes a diverse range of businesses and services designed to cater to the needs of travelers and tourists. It covers accommodations such as hotels, resorts, vacation rentals, and dining options, including restaurants and cafés. Additionally, it includes transportation services like airlines, cruise lines, and car rentals, as well as travel agencies and tour operators that help with trip planning and coordination. Moreover, the industry includes entertainment and recreational services, such as theme parks, museums, and cultural attractions, all of which are a significant part of this sector.

Recently, the industry has shifted toward more personalized and experiential travel, reflecting a growing demand for distinctive and upscale experiences. This trend has led to specialized markets like eco-tourism and adventure travel. Additionally, the industry is embracing technological advancements, with digital platforms and mobile applications enhancing the consumer booking and travel experience. Overall, these trends emphasize the importance of "personalization" in the consumer relationship. The emergence of process automation and artificial intelligence enables this personalization but also presents some challenges that we will discuss later in this chapter.

Top Automation Targets In Travel And Hospitality

The implementation of automation in the travel and hospitality industry is leading to a paradigm shift in customer experiences through the targeted deployment of advanced technologies. One of the primary focus areas lies in the analysis of the voice of the customer (VOC) and sentiment, facilitated by AI-driven tools that assist businesses in deciphering customer sentiments from reviews, surveys, and social media. This empowers them to discern service enhancement opportunities and align their offerings with customer expectations. Furthermore, AI is playing a pivotal role in augmenting loyalty programs through the automation and personalization of customer engagements.

An additional area of substantial automation focus is personalization, where AI-powered chatbots and virtual assistants provide constant support, manage reservations, and deliver tailored suggestions. Predictive trip planning further enriches the travel experience by utilizing AI to propose personalized itineraries based on past behaviors and preferences. Self-service technologies, including automated check-ins, digital room keys, and intelligent room systems, optimize processes and enhance convenience, thereby ensuring a seamless and gratifying travel experience for customers. Collectively, these advancements are setting new benchmarks for customer engagement and satisfaction within the industry.

Voice Of The Customer And Sentiment Analysis

Within the hospitality industry, the application of AI extends beyond mere customer feedback analysis to the enhancement of loyalty programs. Hotels and travel companies leverage AI-driven tools not only to decipher customer sentiments from reviews, surveys, and social media but also to automate and personalize loyalty program engagements.

For instance, Radisson Hotel Group and Marriott have been pioneers in employing AI to sift through guest feedback from various channels. This approach aids them in identifying service improvement opportunities and aligning their offerings more closely with customer expectations. Similarly, Hilton's utilization of AI to delve into guest preferences showcases the industry's shift toward delivering bespoke experiences rooted in deep data-driven insights.

The evolution of loyalty programs through automation represents another strategic integration of AI within the sector. Automated systems are adept at tracking guest interactions across multiple platforms, thus ensuring that loyalty points and benefits are accurately and promptly awarded. This not only enhances operational efficiency but significantly elevates the customer experience, making loyalty programs more engaging and responsive.

Marriott Bonvoy, for example, leverages AI to customize rewards and offers, taking into account individual guest preferences and behaviors. This level of personalization fosters a deeper connection with customers, encouraging repeat business and fostering brand loyalty.

In essence, the utilization of AI in analyzing customer feedback and automating loyalty programs underlines the hospitality industry's commitment to leveraging technology to enhance service quality and customer satisfaction. By harnessing the power of AI, hotels and travel companies are not only able to address issues swiftly but also to create more personalized and rewarding experiences for their guests, setting a new standard in customer engagement and loyalty.

Personalization

In the dynamic travel and hospitality sector, we are witnessing a remarkable transformation underscored by the integration of sophisticated automation technologies. This evolution is primarily driven by the pursuit of enhancing guest experiences and optimizing operational processes. Central to this shift is the movement toward highly personalized guest services, marking a new era where convenience and customization converge to redefine industry standards.

A notable development in this realm is the increasing reliance on AI through the adoption of advanced chatbots and virtual assistants.

These AI-powered tools are not only operational around the clock, but they have also demonstrated remarkable proficiency in managing reservations, handling a wide array of inquiries, and delivering highly personalized recommendations. This extends to crafting offers meticulously tailored to guests' unique preferences and historical patterns, derived from their previous engagements and stays.

Furthermore, the advancements in AI extend beyond mere customer service automation. The industry is strategically embedding AI deeper into the very core of the guest experience by deploying AI-powered personalization engines. These cutting-edge technologies perform comprehensive analyses of data gathered from previous visits, individual guest preferences, and specific behavioral patterns to develop bespoke suggestions. Whether it's recommending dining experiences that resonate with individual guests, suggesting activities that align with their interests, or even proposing their preferred types of accommodations, the ultimate aim is to make each stay as unique and memorable as the guests themselves.

Building upon these innovations, predictive trip planning emerges as a significant facet of AI's influence on the travel sector. Utilizing advanced algorithms, AI analyzes a traveler's past behaviors, preferences, and prevailing trends to proffer personalized itineraries. This includes recommending destinations, activities, and accommodations that perfectly match the traveler's interests.

Self-Service

Recent advancements in the travel sector underscore its remarkable progress in enhancing traveler experiences through innovative technologies. The adoption of contactless and self-service solutions across airports, hotels, and car rental firms has streamlined processes, maintained hygiene standards, and facilitated a seamless travel journey, crucial in the post-pandemic world. Technologies like automated check-ins, digital room keys, and self-service kiosks have spearheaded these initiatives, focusing on efficiency and convenience.

Integration of artificial intelligence in customer service through virtual assistants and chatbots has revolutionized customer interaction, offering 24/7 support for inquiries, reservations, and service requests.

These AI-powered tools have reduced reliance on human labor while improving communication accuracy and effectiveness. Additionally, the shift toward automated booking and scheduling systems has enhanced operational excellence by minimizing manual errors, ensuring accurate customer data management, and improving the reliability of bookings.

Furthermore, the adoption of smart room technologies by numerous hotels through the Internet of Things (IoT) and related innovations has significantly enhanced guest comfort. Automated lighting, climate control, and entertainment systems, controllable via mobile apps or voice commands, not only improve guest experiences but also promote energy efficiency. These technological advancements reflect the travel industry's commitment to setting new benchmarks in customer service, convenience, and quality, marking a transformative era of efficiency, comfort, and sustainability.

In addition to customer-oriented automation targets, professionals in the travel and hospitality industry are embracing additional strategies such as revenue management and dynamic pricing. This entails an increasing reliance on AI and machine learning algorithms by hotels and airlines to analyze market demand, competitor pricing, and historical data for the purpose of optimizing pricing strategies in real-time. This practice is aimed at maximizing revenue and occupancy rates by adjusting prices based on prevailing market conditions.

Furthermore, industry practitioners are actively exploring the potential of AI for predictive maintenance and asset management. Through the integration of IoT sensors and AI, hotels and airlines are able to conduct real-time monitoring of their equipment and infrastructure, thus enabling predictive maintenance measures which, in turn, reduce downtime and repair costs while ensuring a seamless experience for guests and passengers. An illustrative example of this is the utilization of smart HVAC systems in hotels to forecast and address issues before they impact guest comfort and the deployment of similar technologies by airlines for more efficient aircraft maintenance.

In summary, the hospitality and travel industries are undergoing a significant transformation fueled by the integration of AI and sophisticated automation technologies. This shift is aimed at enhancing customer experiences through personalization and operational efficiency.

AI-driven tools are now central to analyzing customer feedback and optimizing loyalty programs, while the adoption of contactless and self-service technologies simplifies the travel journey, ensuring safety and convenience in a post-pandemic context.

Additionally, the application of AI extends to revenue management and predictive maintenance, where real-time data analysis and IoT devices are leveraged to optimize pricing strategies and maintain equipment, ensuring uninterrupted guest experiences and maximizing revenue. This evolution reflects a broader trend toward leveraging technology to meet consumer expectations and redefine industry standards.

Automation Challenges In Travel And Hospitality

Incorporating automation in the travel and hospitality industry comes with unique challenges. Balancing personalized services with privacy concerns is one major challenge, as collecting and analyzing large amounts of personal data raises privacy issues.

Managing fluctuating demand based on seasons, holidays, and events requires advanced AI systems. Integrating these technologies with outdated legacy systems can complicate digital transformation efforts. Additionally, addressing cultural and regional differences is crucial for providing seamless experiences to a global clientele. Real-time service delivery is another challenge, as guests expect immediate responses and solutions, requiring highly reliable AI systems. Let's take a deeper look at how these challenges affect the travel and hospitality industry.

Personalization With AI Versus Privacy Concerns

During a recent podcast, one partner at McKinsey and Company, Alex Cosmas, said: "Not only is travel and hospitality the world's largest sector, but it's actually the most intimate sector. That means the answer for each of us to what a good experience looks like—whether I'm traveling for leisure or for business—is, by definition, fundamentally different. And the promise of AI has been to take the pattern of history, take the pattern of millions, and boil that down to the individual response that is relevant to me as a segment of one."

In response to increasing consumer demand for personalized services, travel, and hospitality professionals are customizing recommendations for activities, dining, and accommodations based on individual preferences and past behaviors. However, this trend raises significant privacy concerns due to the collection and analysis of vast amounts of personal data. As awareness regarding data usage grows, consumers are expressing apprehensions about potential misuse or breaches of their information.

To successfully navigate these concerns, hotels and travel companies must prioritize transparency in their data practices and secure explicit consent from guests. Implementing robust data protection measures and ensuring compliance with privacy regulations are crucial steps in safeguarding personal information. Specifically, the application of AI-driven personalization must adhere to strict privacy protocols to maintain customer trust. The industry faces the critical challenge of balancing the delivery of tailored services with the imperative to address privacy issues effectively. Achieving this balance is essential for fostering consumer trust and loyalty in our increasingly data-centric world.

Seasonal Demand Fluctuations

The travel and hospitality industry frequently encounters the complex challenge of managing seasonal demand fluctuations. These fluctuations are influenced by a variety of factors, including holidays, school breaks, prevailing weather conditions, and specific events. This results in marked variations in peak times; for instance, beach resorts see heightened activity in the summer months, while ski resorts experience their peak during the winter season. Unlike leisure travel, business travel exhibits a downward trend during holiday periods.

Hoteliers must adjust room availability and pricing in near real-time. Airlines need to optimize flight schedules and fare structures for demand changes. Efficient seasonal demand management requires accurate workforce forecasting for both peak and off-peak periods.

The potential of AI within the travel and hospitality sector, particularly in addressing these challenges, is of significant interest. However, the integration of AI technologies is hindered by the prevalent reliance on legacy systems, necessitating substantive investments in both technology upgrades and comprehensive staff training programs.

Despite these obstacles, the strategic application of AI technologies stands as a pivotal factor in optimizing operational processes and substantially enhancing the overall guest experience in the face of seasonal demand variations.

Digital Transformation From Legacy Systems

In their ongoing work on the IDC advisory called "Retail Insights: Worldwide Hospitality and Travel Digital Strategies," researchers Dorothy Creamer and Leslie Hand emphasize the importance of digital transformation for travel and hospitality. They highlight the need for frictionless experiences and guest journeys, which are critical for success in the industry.

Many hotels and travel companies still rely on outdated legacy systems for their operations. Integrating advanced AI and automation technologies with these existing systems can be challenging, often requiring significant investment and technical expertise.

Examples of these legacy systems include:

- **Property Management Systems (PMS)** are essential for daily hotel operations, covering reservations, check-ins, room assignments, and billing. Legacy PMS platforms like MICROS-Fidelio and Hotel Information Systems (HIS), often lack flexibility and integration capabilities compared to modern solutions.
- **Central Reservation Systems (CRS)** manage bookings and inventory across various channels, crucial for both hospitality and airlines. Legacy CRS platforms, such as Pegasus CRS and SynXis CRS, can be cumbersome and slow, making real-time updates and smooth bookings difficult.
- **Global Distribution Systems (GDS)** connect travel agents with services like airlines, hotels, and car rentals. These systems can be complex and costly to maintain. Examples

include Sabre and Amadeus, which, despite updates, still face integration issues due to their legacy infrastructure.
- **Customer Relationship Management (CRM)** systems track guest interactions and preferences to enhance customer service. Older CRM platforms may not support advanced analytics or AI integration, hindering personalization. Notable legacy CRM systems include Siebel CRM and ACT! CRM, which often faces challenges in integrating with modern technologies.

Cultural And Regional Differences

In travel and hospitality, addressing cultural differences is crucial with AI integration. Serving a global clientele requires understanding diverse norms. For instance, Japan's "omotenashi" emphasizes anticipatory service, contrasting with the informal, efficient approach in the U.S. AI systems must recognize and adapt to these varied service standards for successful deployment.

AI systems need to accurately navigate numerous cultural norms and preferences, extending beyond mere language translation. They should offer recommendations respecting local customs and dietary needs—suggesting halal options in the Middle East or understanding vegetarian meal preferences in India—and recognize the significance of local festivals, holidays, and prayer times to enhance the travel experience through a deep understanding of cultural nuances.

Furthermore, effective communication, tailored to regional styles and expectations, is critical, highlighting the need for AI systems' adaptability. With global communication preferences ranging from direct to more nuanced and indirect styles, AI must feature advanced natural language processing capabilities and a comprehensive grasp of cultural contexts. This ensures meaningful interactions and engagement, providing personalized and respectful service that meets the needs of a diverse global clientele.

Real-Time Service Delivery

Real-time service delivery is crucial in the travel and hospitality industry, where guests' expectations for immediate responses and solutions are heightened. Delays can result in dissatisfaction and negative feedback, given the premium placed on efficiency in travel contexts. For instance, prolonged check-in times or delayed room service can mar the overall guest experience.

To address these expectations, the implementation of AI, including sophisticated chatbots and virtual assistants, is essential. These systems must offer round-the-clock support, handling tasks ranging from FAQ responses to booking management, and process inquiries swiftly to ensure guests receive prompt assistance. Achieving reliable and efficient AI system performance, particularly during peak seasons, demands a strong infrastructure and constant oversight.

Additionally, real-time service encompasses on-site technologies, such as smart room features enabled by the Internet of things (IoT), which allow guests to customize their stay via smartphones or voice commands instantly. This tech also involves AI in monitoring and promptly addressing maintenance needs to avoid adversely impacting the guest experience.

The core challenge is in maintaining the AI systems' reliability and efficiency, ensuring they can manage high demand and complex scenarios without fail. Continuous technological investment and improvement are necessary to keep up with travelers' growing expectations and to deliver a seamless, enjoyable experience.

In summary, the integration of automation within the travel and hospitality sector presents several complex challenges that must be meticulously addressed. The use of AI to enhance guest experiences through personalization is a double-edged sword; it necessitates the collection and analysis of extensive personal data, raising significant privacy concerns. Practitioners are tasked with maintaining a fine balance between offering customized services and protecting customer privacy. Equally critical is the ability to manage the ebb and flow of seasonal demand, which requires AI systems that can predict and adjust to changes with precision, considering variables like holidays and weather conditions.

Top Automation Use Cases In Travel And Hospitality

The journey toward digital transformation is underscored by the need to amalgamate cutting-edge AI technologies with aging legacy systems, a process that often demands considerable financial resources and technical acumen. Moreover, the global nature of the travel and hospitality industry means that AI systems must be sensitive to cultural and regional distinctions, ensuring that services are both seamless and culturally attuned. The industry's shift toward real-time service delivery amplifies the need for AI systems that are not only reliable but also capable of offering prompt resolutions to ensure guest satisfaction and uphold high standards of service. In the following section, we will explore some of the solutions available that rise up to these daunting challenges.

AI-Based Agent Assist For Concierges

In the hospitality industry, the integration of AI-powered virtual concierges is revolutionizing the way guest experiences are elevated. These virtual assistants are designed to offer guests a wide array of services, including making restaurant reservations and offering local recommendations, all accessible 24/7. This ensures that guests receive immediate, personalized assistance at any time of the day, making their stay more enjoyable and streamlined. For instance, guests can effortlessly book a table at a nearby restaurant or discover local attractions through the virtual concierge, with recommendations tailored to their preferences and past behavior, thus significantly enhancing their overall experience. This personalized service makes guests feel uniquely valued and well-cared for, fostering loyalty and satisfaction.

Moreover, automated check-in and check-out services, complemented by live agent support, significantly refine the guest's journey from arrival to departure. Utilizing a mobile app or kiosk for these processes allows guests to bypass traditional wait times, enabling a smooth transition into and out of their accommodations. Should any issues arise during these automated processes, live agents are promptly available for immediate assistance, ensuring any problem is swiftly

Figure 50: AI-based agent assist for human concierges

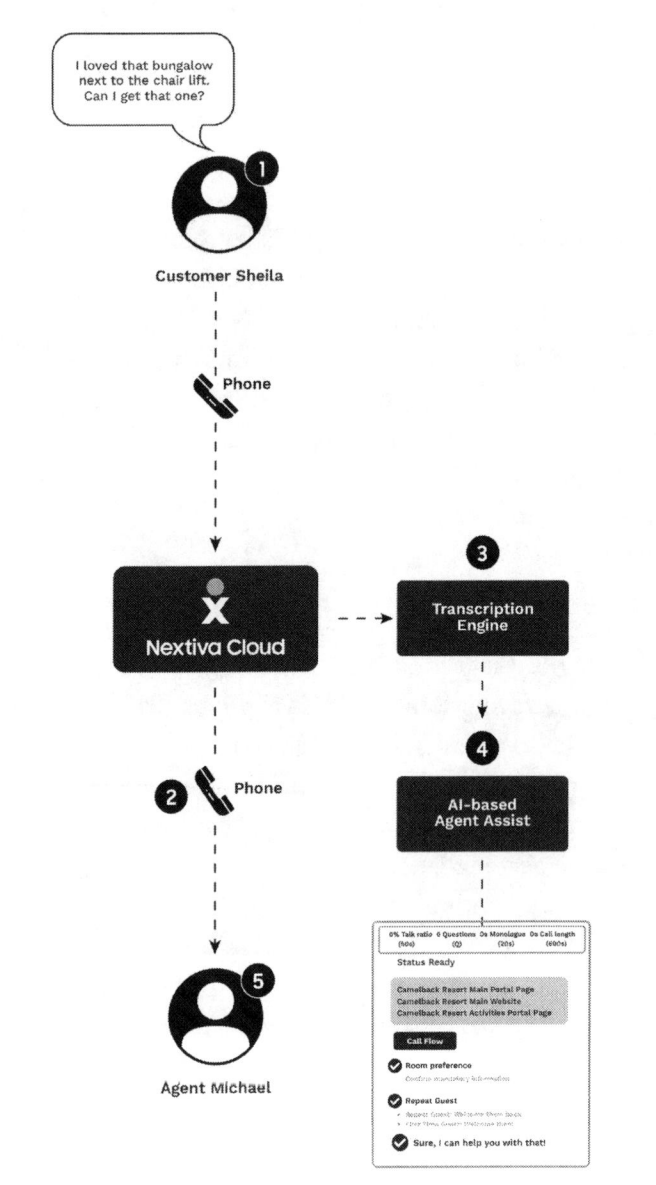

- ❶ Customer Sheila Brown calls for help with a water filter.
- ❷ Nextiva uses skills-based routing to connect the call to Agent Michael.
- ❸ Nextiva sends the transcribed text to MosaicVoice.
- ❹ MosaicVoice coaches the agent on adherence and best practices.
- ❺ Agent Michael stays on point and assists Sheila with her reservation.

resolved. This hybrid model not only streamlines operations but also significantly enhances guest satisfaction by reducing unnecessary delays and providing instant support when needed.

Enhancing the reservation experience, even live concierge professionals can leverage AI for real-time agent assistance, thereby improving efficiency and accuracy in customer interactions. For example, Travel Outlook, a concierge-based business process outsourcing (BPO) firm, utilizes real-time "top gun" agent assistance to enrich caller experiences. When a customer wishes to rent the same chalet as the previous year, AI systems quickly provide agents with relevant information, including availability and alternative options. This instant access to pertinent data enables agents to offer solutions seamlessly and suggests upselling or cross-selling opportunities based on the guest's history and preferences, thus amplifying revenue opportunities and enriching the customer experience.

Personalized itinerary planning is another facet where AI-driven services, combined with the expertise of live agents, present a deeply customized travel experience. AI algorithms can suggest activities, dining options, and attractions tailored to the guest's interests, while live agents can add value by making special arrangements or providing additional insights. This synergy ensures guests not only receive recommendations perfectly aligned with their preferences but also enjoy the benefit of personalized service, making their stay truly memorable.

The integration of artificial intelligence (AI) in customer service, utilizing virtual assistants and chatbots, has dramatically transformed the booking process, making it far more efficient and user-friendly. These AI-powered tools are available around the clock to assist with inquiries, reservations, and service-related requests, thus reducing the dependency on human labor significantly. This revolution in service allows guests to effortlessly make or modify their bookings through these chatbots, which are capable of handling numerous requests at once and providing instant booking confirmations. Furthermore, AI systems excel in managing scheduling changes effectively, ensuring that customer data is consistently accurate across all platforms, which greatly minimizes manual errors and enhances the reliability of bookings. For example, if a guest needs to make a change to their

Table 71: Benefits of AI-based agent assist for human concierge

Concierge services capability	Chief benefits
Historical guest preferences	Removes friction for the guest by pre-fetching historical information of previous stays
AI-based "top gun" agent assist	Agents are provided with coaching in real-time to reduce the time it takes to book a reservation
Real-time transcription	The dialog between the guest and agent can be quickly reviewed to reduce repeat questions from the agent to the guest, which makes for a smoother experience for the guest
Automatic summarizations with sentiment	Supervisors benefit from a normalized mechanism for capturing call summaries, saving many hours of listening and reading for QM assessment of agents

reservation, the AI system can rapidly adjust the booking details and notify the guest of these changes, thereby improving the overall customer experience.

In summary, the benefits of incorporating AI-based agent assistance to augment virtual concierges in the hospitality industry are manifold. They provide round-the-clock assistance, reduce wait times, and ensure a hassle-free experience from start to finish.

The use of real-time support and troubleshooting increases operational efficiency, reduces call handling times, and improves the accuracy of customer service interactions. Ultimately, the combination of automated services with the personal touch of live agent support facilitates an unparalleled guest experience, fostering loyalty and ensuring memorable stays.

AI-Based Concierge Services

Travelers often face challenges in accessing timely and personalized assistance during their stay at hotels or resorts. Traditional concierge services may not always be available 24/7, leading to delays in addressing guest inquiries and requests. This can result in a less satisfactory guest experience and may impact the overall perception of customer service.

An AI concierge can provide round-the-clock personalized assistance to guests, enhancing their stay by offering immediate responses to inquiries, managing reservations, and providing tailored recommendations for dining, activities, and local attractions. This AI-powered virtual concierge can handle a wide range of tasks, from recommending services to providing real-time support, ensuring a seamless and enjoyable experience for guests.

Automated concierge services aim to provide timely, personalized assistance to hotel guests, enhancing their overall travel experience with convenient services. Customers are motivated to receive assistance during their stay, with the intent to access concierge services 24/7 for inquiries, reservations, and personalized recommendations, ensuring a seamless stay.

Guests are focused on tasks such as making reservations for dining, activities, and local attractions. They also often seek personalized recommendations and assistance for a better trip experience. However, customers face challenges such as accessing concierge services outside regular hours and receiving timely and accurate responses to their inquiries and requests.

In this scenario, the use of both human and AI-based concierge are contemplated. An AI-based concierge bot can be programmed to deliver personalized assistance during the guest's stay and provide accurate information. It can be programmed to offer 24/7 concierge services, guiding and supporting customers with inquiries, reservations, and personalized recommendations. The AI concierge's main tasks include helping customers book hotels, restaurants, and activities, as well as providing personalized recommendations based on customer preferences.

Figure 51: AI-based concierge services

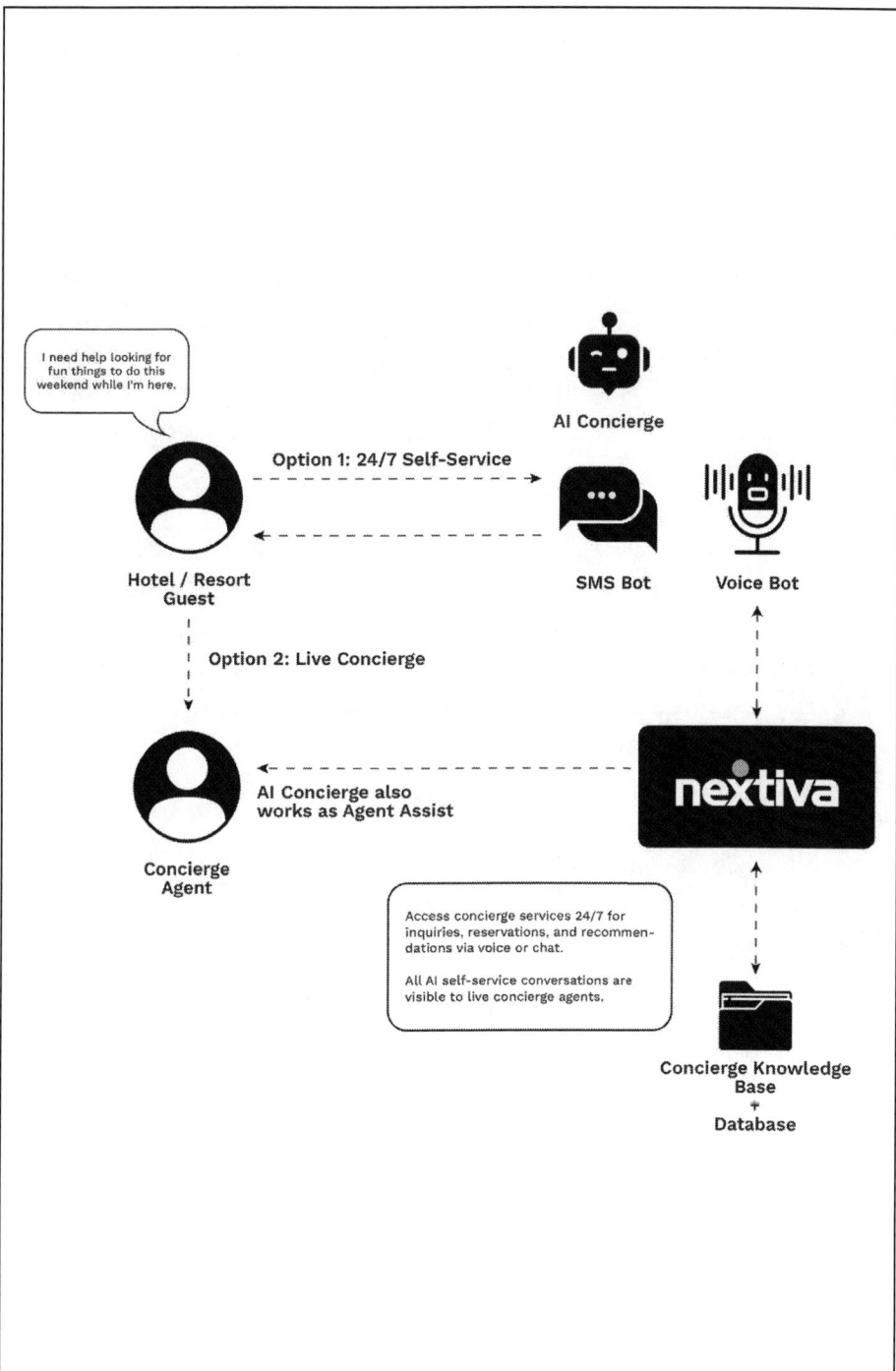

TRAVEL AND HOSPITALITY

Human concierges are motivated to provide excellent customer service by assisting guests with their inquiries and requests and offering timely assistance and recommendations. Their intent is to provide personalized recommendations and support to ensure guests enjoy their stay. Human concierges face challenges in maintaining a high volume of guest inquiries and requests while ensuring accurate and timely responses to guest needs to maintain great service.

The diagram depicts a travel and hospitality use case for an AI-based concierge system. This illustrates how a hotel or resort guest can receive assistance in finding activities for the weekend through two primary options: self-service and live concierge support.

First, a hotel or resort guest expresses the need for help in finding fun things to do over the weekend. This request is channeled into two service options. The guest interacts with an AI concierge comprising a voice bot and an SMS bot. These bots connect to the UCXM platform. The UCXM platform accesses the concierge knowledge base and database to provide information to the guest.

The guest can also choose to connect with a live concierge agent for assistance. The AI concierge supports the live agent by providing relevant information from the knowledge base. The UCXM platform is central to this process, seamlessly connecting with both the AI concierge and the concierge knowledge base and database to facilitate efficient service delivery.

The bottom right of the diagram outlines the service description, indicating that concierge services are accessible 24/7 for inquiries, reservations, and recommendations over voice or chat.

Additionally, all self-service conversations with the AI are visible to live concierge agents, ensuring a cohesive and integrated support experience. This setup demonstrates how the UCXM platform enhances customer service in the travel and hospitality industry by providing continuous support and integrating both automated and human assistance.

In summary, travelers often face challenges in accessing timely and personalized assistance during their stay at hotels or resorts. Traditional concierge services may not always be available 24/7, leading to delays in addressing guest inquiries and requests, which can result in a less satisfactory guest experience and impact the overall perception of customer service.

An AI concierge can provide round-the-clock personalized assistance to guests, enhancing their stay by offering immediate responses to inquiries, managing reservations, and providing tailored recommendations for dining, activities, and local attractions. This AI-powered virtual concierge can handle a wide range of tasks, from recommending services to providing real-time support, ensuring a seamless and enjoyable experience for guests.

Automated concierge services aim to provide timely, personalized assistance to hotel guests, enhancing their overall travel experience with convenient services. Guests focus on tasks such as making reservations for dining, activities, and local attractions and seek personalized recommendations and assistance for a better trip experience. However, they face challenges accessing concierge services outside regular hours and receiving timely, accurate responses to their inquiries and requests.

Table 72: Benefits of AI-based agent assist for human concierge

Concierge services capability	Chief benefits
An AI concierge provides round-the-clock personalized assistance	24/7 real-time availability ensures guests receive timely and accurate responses
AI concierge manages reservations and provides tailored recommendations	Personalized recommendations and ease of travel enhance guest satisfaction
AI concierge handles a wide range of tasks, from recommending services to providing real-time support	Operational efficiency through AI and automation increases competitive advantage and guest satisfaction
The human concierge assists with inquiries, reservations, and personalized recommendations	Ability to focus on more complex, higher-value interactions with full visibility into AI concierge recommendations

Combining human and AI-based concierge services can effectively address these challenges, providing continuous support and enhancing the overall guest experience. Human concierges can offer high-level personalized recommendations, while AI concierges can manage reservations and provide 24/7 support, ensuring guests have a seamless and enjoyable stay.

Pet Travel Virtual Assistant

Traveling with pets can be a stressful and complex process for pet owners. They often face challenges such as finding pet-friendly accommodations and transportation, ensuring their pets' safety and comfort, and accessing emergency veterinary services while on the go. These challenges can lead to a less enjoyable travel experience and can deter pet owners from traveling with their pets altogether. To address these issues, an AI-based pet travel assistant provides a comprehensive solution.

In this context, a hotel or resort guest traveling with their dog can receive assistance in two ways. Firstly, through the 24/7 self-service option, the guest can interact with an SMS bot or a chatbot. These bots are integral components of the pet travel virtual assistant system, which communicates with the UCXM platform. This platform accesses a pet travel knowledge base and database to provide the necessary information and services to the guest.

Alternatively, the guest can opt to interact with a live concierge agent. In this scenario, the AI system also functions as an agent assistant, supporting the concierge agent by providing relevant information and recommendations. The UCXM platform is central to this service delivery process, enabling access to concierge services around the clock for inquiries, reservations, and recommendations over voice or chat. All self-service conversations with the AI are visible to live concierge agents, ensuring a seamless and integrated service experience for the guest. This setup demonstrates the efficiency and effectiveness of combining AI and human support to enhance the travel experience for guests with pets.

Concierge agents are motivated to deliver efficient booking experiences for pet-friendly accommodation and transportation. They

Figure 52: AI-powered pet travel assistant

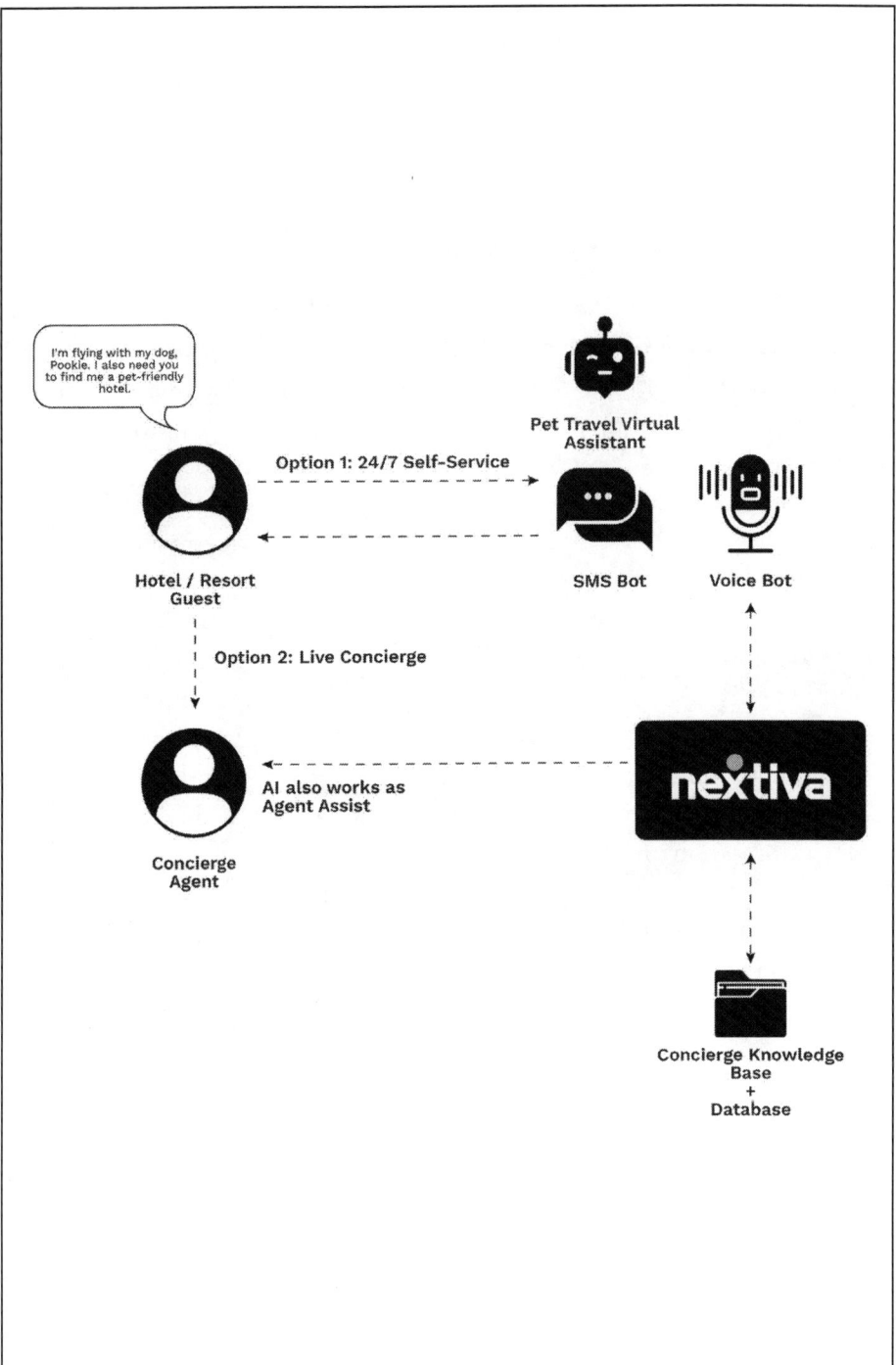

aim to provide accurate information and excellent customer service by assisting with pet and owner travel needs, ensuring a smooth travel experience for both. Their top tasks involve helping customers book pet-friendly options, providing information on pet policies, required documentation, travel tips, and offering personalized recommendations and support.

However, concierge agents face challenges such as ensuring the availability of pet-friendly options that meet customers' needs, keeping databases up-to-date and maintaining integration, and ensuring accurate and timely responses to customer needs and emergencies. They also need visibility into conversations between the bot and the customer to provide better support.

The solution is an AI pet travel assistant that provides 24/7 real-time support and personalized assistance. This assistant can book pet-friendly accommodations, transportation, and restaurants, offer recommendations for pet-friendly activities and services, and locate emergency veterinary assistance when needed. By leveraging AI, the assistant can offer tailored suggestions and immediate responses, ensuring a seamless and stress-free travel experience for both pets and their owners.

The benefits of a pet travel virtual assistant include booking pet-friendly accommodations, flights, and transportation, and providing details on airline pet policies and required documentation. It offers round-the-clock support and emergency assistance, enhancing the travel experience with recommendations for pet owners and their pets.

The assistant creates personalized travel itineraries, considering the pet's needs and preferences, and suggests pet-friendly routes, rest stops, and activities. The system allows real-time adjustments based on the pet's condition and the owner's preferences, ensuring a smooth journey.

In the event of a medical emergency, the assistant offers immediate access to veterinary services, providing directions to the nearest clinic and connecting with a live agent for further guidance and coordination. This ensures pets receive timely care, offering peace of mind to pet owners during travel.

Applications of this nature may be integrated into Android or iOS apps or executed through IVR (interactive voice response). In both scenarios, the interface and communication would resemble the Delta Virtual Assistant for pet travel.

By streamlining the process of booking pet-friendly accommodations, flights, and transportation, these virtual assistants handle routine inquiries and tasks efficiently.

Meanwhile, live agents are available to address more complex issues, ensuring a comprehensive customer experience. This blend of technology and human touch enhances operational efficiency and fosters customer loyalty by addressing the specific needs of pet owners, transforming the contact center into a hub of effective support.

A pet travel virtual assistant streamlines the process of planning a journey with pets. By providing interactive travel checklists, it enables owners to customize their preparations based on the unique needs of their pet and the specifics of their itinerary. This tool facilitates the packing of essential items such as food, water, medications, and comfort items, ensuring nothing crucial is forgotten. It also offers tailored advice on preparing pets for travel, including tips on acclimating them to their carriers or crates.

In addition to virtual assistance, the service collaborates with live agents to address any questions or offer extra recommendations.

This integrated approach ensures that pet owners receive comprehensive support, making the preparation process as stress-free as possible. The combined efforts of the virtual assistant and live agents guarantee that both pets and their owners are well-prepared, leading to a more comfortable and relaxed travel experience.

Customers are motivated by the desire to ensure their pets' safety, comfort, and well-being during travel. They aim to have a stress-free travel experience by easily finding and booking pet-friendly accommodation and transportation and accessing real-time support when needed. Their top tasks include booking pet-friendly accommodations and transportation, and planning and organizing pet-friendly options during travel. However, they face challenges such as finding reliable, pet-friendly options and services, and ensuring their pets' needs are met and emergencies are handled promptly.

In summary, the pet travel virtual assistant makes traveling with pets a lot easier for pet owners. It streamlines the process of finding pet-friendly accommodations, flights, and navigating airline policies,

Table 73: Benefits of a virtual pet travel assistant

Pet-oriented AI assistant capability	Chief benefits
AI pet travel assistant provides 24/7 real-time support and personalized assistance	Enhanced convenience for customers, ensuring they receive help anytime and improving their travel experience
Pet-aware travel checklists	Ensures all essential items are packed, providing peace of mind for the pet owner; aids in the preparation of a smooth journey
Book pet-friendly accommodations, transportation, and restaurants through the AI assistant	Personalized recommendations reduce the stress of planning and ensure pet-friendly options are available
AI assistant offers recommendations for pet-friendly activities and services	Customers enjoy a well-rounded, enjoyable travel experience with tailored suggestions
Locate emergency veterinary assistance when needed with the AI assistant	Provides peace of mind knowing that help is available in case of emergencies, ensuring pet safety

significantly enhancing the travel experience. Through personalized advice on hotels, restaurants, and attractions, it fosters customer loyalty.

Assistants like these are becoming more popular and they are available around the clock. This is comforting if a pet is ill and you need veterinary assistance. By accommodating adjustments and focusing on the specific needs of pets and their owners, it ensures a stress-free journey, highlighting its commitment to pet safety and owner satisfaction.

Voice Of The Customer Solutions

Voice of the customer (VOC) and sentiment analysis play key roles in understanding and responding to guest feedback in the travel and hospitality industry. Using AI and automation allows businesses to gather deep insights from reviews, surveys, and social media, offering a comprehensive view of customer sentiments. This approach helps pinpoint areas needing improvement and enhances customer loyalty through personalized service. Here, we explore use cases like real-time sentiment monitoring and predictive sentiment analysis.

Agent assist tools are crucial in customer service, providing real-time insights and AI-suggested responses to live agents. For instance, when feedback is identified as negative, an agent is notified to engage with a personalized response. SMS bots send instant notifications to customers, acknowledging feedback and ensuring follow-up by a live agent. This strategy ensures customers feel valued and leads to higher satisfaction and loyalty. Additionally, real-time sentiment monitoring helps detect trends in feedback, enabling businesses to make informed decisions about service improvements.

Table 74: Voice of the customer solutions benefits

VOC solutions capability	Chief benefits
VOC agent assist tools	Automation can aid agents in quickly addressing issues that may have produced negative feedback, which helps to prevent unnecessary escalations
Predictive sentiment analysis	Anticipates and addresses issues before they occur; with more personalized interactions, you can tailor recommendations and solutions based on predictive insights
Multichannel feedback integration	Helps to gain a more comprehensive view of customer sentiments across all touchpoints in order to home in on preferences and modes of communication that represent the least friction
Sentiment-driven service adjustments	Quickly adapts services based on real-time feedback; shows customers that their feedback is valued and acted upon

Sentiment-driven service adjustments involve analyzing feedback to identify areas needing improvement. Automated systems flag issues for review, and live agents make necessary adjustments. This approach shows a commitment to customer satisfaction by addressing feedback promptly. Interactive voice response (IVR) systems gather feedback directly from customers, and follow-up communications inform customers of specific changes made based on their input. This continuous feedback loop ensures services meet customer expectations and enhances customer loyalty.

Overall, integrating VOC and sentiment analysis in customer service helps businesses understand and address customer needs, resulting in improved satisfaction and loyalty.

In summary, the integration of AI, automation, and live agents in voice of the customer and sentiment analysis offers numerous benefits for the travel and hospitality industry. Real-time sentiment monitoring allows businesses to promptly address negative feedback and improve customer engagement. Predictive sentiment analysis enables proactive customer service by anticipating and addressing potential issues before they arise. Multichannel feedback integration provides a comprehensive view of customer sentiments, allowing for more informed and personalized responses.

Lastly, sentiment-driven service adjustments ensure that businesses can continuously refine their offerings based on real-time feedback, maintaining high service quality and customer satisfaction. Together, these use cases illustrate the transformative potential of combining advanced technologies with human touch to enhance the overall customer experience.

Personalized Guest Services

In the travel and hospitality industry, integrating live service and automation within contact centers is transforming traveler customization. AI-powered personalization leverages data from previous stays, feedback, and booking patterns to offer tailored recommendations and services, enhancing guest experiences and operational efficiency. This technology extends to theme parks, allowing for personalized itineraries. AI-driven chatbots and virtual assistants provide round-the-clock support, ensuring swift problem resolution and proactive service.

Combining AI with live agent support sets new standards for guest satisfaction, meeting modern travelers' expectations through intuitive service delivery.

The process involves sophisticated data collection and analysis to discern patterns and preferences unique to each guest. Hotels can offer recommendations thoughtfully aligned with guest interests. For instance, a guest with a history of enjoying spa services might receive similar recommendations or exclusive offers during their upcoming stay. AI also remembers guest room preferences, ensuring comfort.

Leveraging AI for personalized services marks a shift toward more responsive customer service. By offering experiences tailored to preferences, hotels boost guest satisfaction, foster loyalty, and achieve operational efficiency. This approach reduces staff burden by automating personalization processes, allowing more focus on other tasks. Consequently, this meets modern travelers' expectations, setting a new benchmark for customer service in the industry.

In theme parks, AI can help to craft tailored itineraries by analyzing visitor preferences and behaviors. Families preferring thrill rides can follow routes maximizing enjoyment and minimizing wait times. This customization extends to dining, shows, and events, aligning closely with visitor interests. For special dietary needs, AI identifies suitable dining options, enhancing the overall guest experience through thoughtful personalization.

Enhancing guest satisfaction in the travel and hospitality industry involves real-time AI support. Incorporating AI-driven chatbots and virtual assistants revolutionizes service delivery, providing 24/7 support and immediate responses, improving guest satisfaction. AI systems notify staff of issues promptly, ensuring quick and efficient resolution.

Combining AI with live agent support offers real-time issue resolution, preventing potential issues. For example, a negative review about room cleanliness can prompt AI to alert a live agent, who can then offer solutions. This proactive problem-solving addresses concerns effectively, fostering a sense of being heard and valued, leading to higher satisfaction and positive reviews.

Examples of this advancement include Marriott International and Hilton Hotels. Marriott uses AI-powered chatbots for real-time support, while Hilton's AI concierge, "Connie," provides information on amenities and local attractions, managing service requests. This shift toward real-time AI support transforms the industry, setting new service delivery standards and improving guest satisfaction. By ensuring prompt assistance and efficient problem resolution, these systems meet modern travelers' expectations, enhancing the guest experience.

In summary, the integration of AI-powered personalization in the travel and hospitality sector is revolutionizing the way services are rendered, vastly enhancing guest experiences. By analyzing data from past interactions, this technology enables customized recommendations and services, significantly boosting satisfaction and operational efficiency.

Table 75: Benefits of personalized guest services

Personalized guest services capability	Chief benefits
AI-powered personalization	Personalized services that meet individual preferences make guests feel special and valued, leading to higher satisfaction levels; tailored experiences encourage guests to return, fostering loyalty and repeat visits
Theme park tailored itineraries	Personalized dining and entertainment options ensure guests' needs and preferences are met, enhancing their overall experience; guests enjoy a more tailored and efficient visit, leading to higher satisfaction and more memorable experiences
Real-time support services	Requests are handled efficiently, ensuring they are fulfilled without delay
Real-time issue resolution	Higher satisfaction levels; quick and effective problem resolution leads to happier guests and positive reviews

Hotels and theme parks, like Disney with its MagicBand technology, are at the forefront of this change, offering tailored experiences that cater to individual guest preferences. Additionally, the incorporation of AI-driven support tools, such as chatbots and virtual assistants, offers round-the-clock assistance, streamlining service delivery and ensuring quick resolution of guest queries. Companies like Marriott International and Hilton are leading examples of this technological advancement, setting new standards in guest satisfaction and operational excellence.

Loyalty Program Automation

In the travel and hospitality industry, combining artificial intelligence (AI) with live agent support is transforming the management of loyalty programs. AI customizes rewards based on guest behavior, while live agents assist with enrollment and queries, creating a valuable experience. This hybrid approach enhances guest engagement and increases loyalty and satisfaction.

Managing loyalty programs manually can be time-consuming and prone to errors. Traditional loyalty programs often lack personalization, leading to lower engagement and satisfaction among customers. Additionally, manual processes can result in delays in tier adjustments and reward distributions, negatively impacting the overall customer experience.

Loyalty program automation leverages AI to customize rewards, automate tier adjustments, enhance guest engagement, and send notifications via SMS, in-app messages, or email. AI analyzes customer data to offer personalized rewards and experiences, making loyalty programs more engaging and effective. Automation streamlines the management of loyalty programs, reducing the workload on employees and improving operational efficiency.

For example, AI can offer personalized rewards that cater to individual preferences, ensuring guests feel uniquely valued. Live agents provide assistance with program enrollment and queries, helping guests understand and utilize rewards effectively. AI can identify frequent guests and offer special discounts, while live agents ensure these benefits are communicated clearly.

TRAVEL AND HOSPITALITY

Figure 53: Loyalty program automation

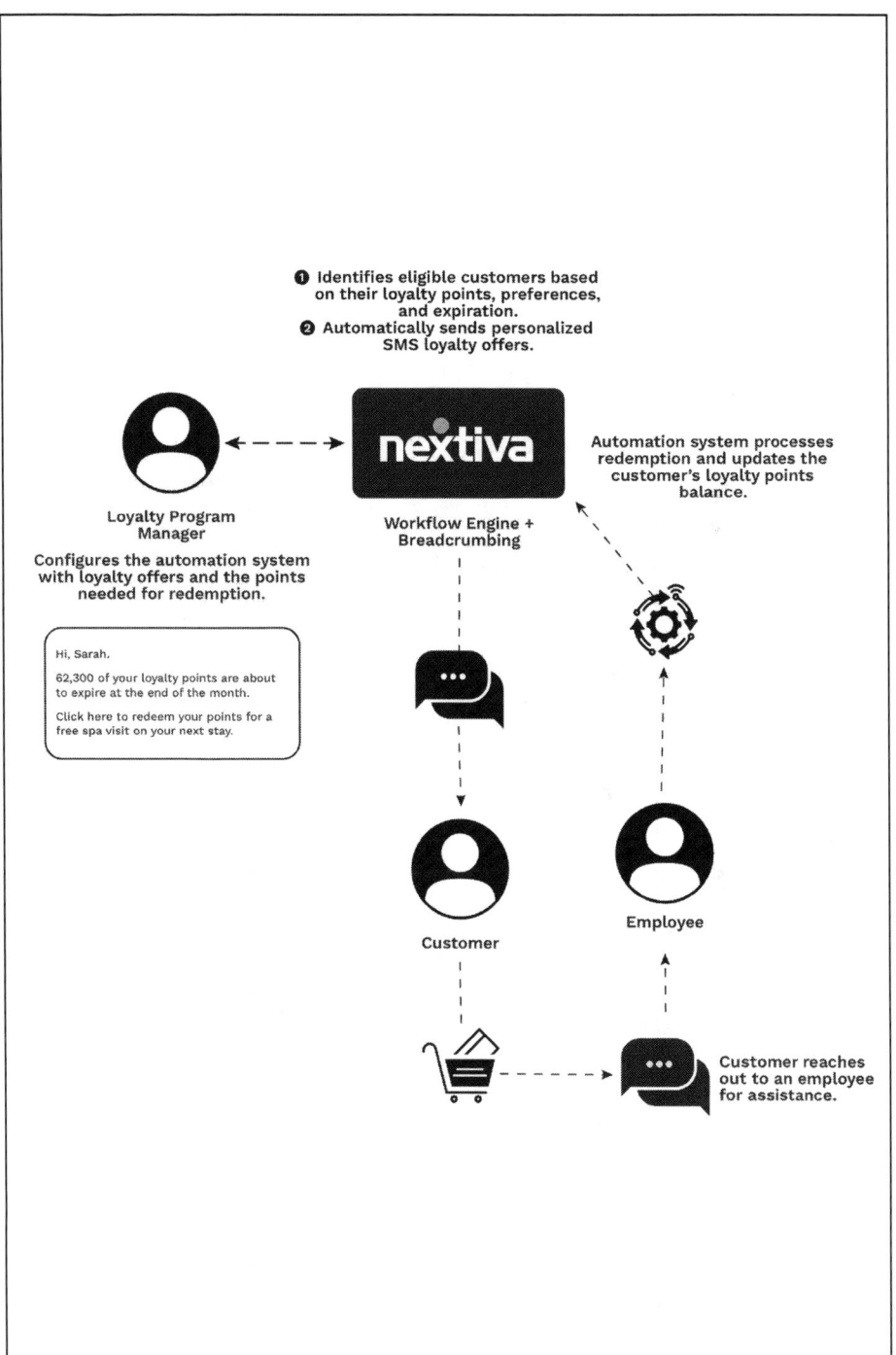

The automation of loyalty tiers through AI adds sophistication to loyalty programs. AI dynamically adjusts guest tiers based on real-time behavior, ensuring prompt recognition of loyalty. For instance, frequent bookings can trigger automatic tier upgrades, with live agents explaining new perks to guests. This approach boosts guest satisfaction and reinforces loyalty.

AI can also streamline the reward redemption process, offering flexibility and customization. A UCXM system can leverage AI to suggest rewards based on preferences and past behavior, while live agents ensure a seamless redemption experience. For example, AI recommending a free night's stay can be supported by a live agent facilitating the booking, enhancing guest satisfaction and loyalty.

Proactive engagement campaigns leverage AI to reconnect with guests. AI identifies inactive guests and initiates personalized outreach, with live agents delivering tailored offers and support. This approach rekindles guest interest and participation in loyalty programs.

AI in loyalty account management anticipates issues like expiring points, notifying live agents to preemptively address them. For instance, AI can alert agents about expiring points, prompting them to advise guests on using their points effectively. This proactive communication ensures guests maximize their loyalty benefits.

This integration of AI and live agent support enhances the efficiency of loyalty programs and ensures a personalized and proactive guest experience, fostering stronger loyalty and satisfaction.

A loyalty program manager sets up the automation system with various offers and required points. The UCXM platform identifies eligible customers based on their points, preferences, and expiration dates. It then sends personalized SMS offers to these customers.

For example, a message might read:

"Hi Sarah, 62,300 of your points will expire soon. Click here to redeem them for a free spa visit."

Customers can click the link to redeem the offer or ask employees any questions they have. Employees provide the necessary information to complete the redemption. The UCXM platform processes the redemption and updates points balances.

This automation process shows how AI-powered systems efficiently manage loyalty programs. It boosts customer engagement with personalized offers, ensures timely responses to queries, and smooths out redemptions. Using the UCXM platform helps businesses offer a seamless experience, enhancing customer loyalty and satisfaction.

Table 76: Benefits of loyalty program automation

Loyalty program automation capability	Chief benefits
Loyalty program automation leverages AI to customize rewards, automate tier adjustments, and enhance guest engagement	Leads to more frequent use of rewards and increased customer satisfaction
Automatic analysis of customer data to offer personalized rewards and experiences	Ensures loyalty programs are more engaging and effective, leading to higher customer retention and loyalty
Automation streamlines the management of loyalty programs	Reduces workload on employees and improves operational efficiency, allowing them to focus on more complex tasks
Personalized rewards that cater to individual preferences	Ensures guests feel uniquely valued, enhancing guest satisfaction and loyalty
AI dynamically adjusts guest tiers based on real-time behavior	Ensures prompt recognition of loyalty, boosting guest satisfaction and reinforcing loyalty
System suggests rewards based on preferences and past behavior	Offers flexibility and customization in reward redemption, enhancing guest satisfaction and loyalty
AI identifies inactive guests and initiates personalized outreach	Rekindles guest interest and participation in loyalty programs, increasing engagement
System anticipates issues like expiring points and notifies live agents	Ensures proactive communication and maximizes guests' loyalty benefits, improving customer satisfaction

In summary, integrating AI with live agent support enhances loyalty program management by customizing rewards based on guest behavior and assisting with enrollment and queries. This approach boosts engagement, loyalty, and satisfaction. Manual management is time-consuming, error-prone, and often lacks personalization, leading to lower engagement and delays in tier adjustments and reward distributions.

Automated loyalty programs use AI to tailor rewards, automate tier changes, enhance engagement, and send notifications. AI analyzes data for personalized rewards, improving efficiency and reducing employee workload. It adjusts tiers in real-time, ensuring timely recognition of loyalty. The combination of AI and live agents ensures seamless redemption and communication, ultimately enhancing program efficiency, loyalty, and customer satisfaction.

Final Thoughts

I HOPE YOU have enjoyed poring over "Winning the Customer Experience Race." Perhaps your head is swimming with ideas on how you can use AI, automation, and a solid UCXM platform to advance your customer experience initiatives. As we reflect on the many strategies and tools discussed, it's crucial to remember the essence of customer experience—empathy and understanding.

1. **Embrace a data-focused perspective.** You should strive to centralize customer interaction data for accuracy and accessibility. Clean, comprehensive data is vital for successful AI use. Nextiva exemplifies this and can offer advice on standardizing a data-driven method.
2. **Achieve a careful balance between efficiency and empathy.** Automation can indeed revolutionize your processes, but it should never strip away the human touch that defines exceptional service. Each chapter has highlighted the balance between efficiency and empathy and how you can leverage technology while still maintaining a personal connection with

your customers. High-volume, low-complexity, low-emotion tasks are ideal for automation. Examples include updating customer information, processing routine transactions, and managing simple inquiries. In contrast, tasks with high emotional stakes and complexity should remain with human agents who can provide empathy and understanding. Examples include handling sensitive customer complaints, providing personalized customer support, and managing crisis situations.

3. **Audit your current state of CX.** Start by analyzing your current workflow and identifying areas where automation can alleviate routine tasks. Consider developing pilot projects for high-volume and repetitive processes, such as data entry or appointment scheduling. These initial steps will not only streamline operations but also free up your team to focus on more complex and emotionally nuanced interactions.

4. **Embrace continuous improvement.** Training and development should not be overlooked. Equip your team with the skills to manage automated systems and understand when to intervene personally. This dual approach ensures that your customers always feel valued and understood, regardless of the method of interaction. Invest in tools that provide detailed analytics and customer feedback. By continuously monitoring the performance of your automated systems, you can make data-driven adjustments and improvements. This proactive stance will help you stay ahead in the fast-evolving landscape of customer experience.

5. **Don't try to automate everything.** Consider focusing on key intersections: transaction volume, complexity, and emotion. Automating scenarios with high emotional stakes and complexity can often lead to negative outcomes, diminishing the quality of customer service and potentially harming the customer relationship. For example, automating the process of handling an insurance claim for a sick family member removes the personal touch needed during such a sensitive time. Similarly, using a voicebot for funeral arrangements would fail to provide the necessary compassion and support. While

technology enables many automated workflows, it is crucial to assess the emotional and task complexity before proceeding. The key question to ask is, "Should you?" Automation should enhance customer experiences, not detract from them. Evaluating use cases by comparing transaction volume, complexity, and emotional stakes helps in deciding suitability.

6. **Engage and learn from industry peers.** Much of my knowledge comes from interacting with customers across various industries who excel in customer experience. By sharing your ideas and collaborating with peers, you can develop and refine best practices together. Join industry forums, attend conferences, and participate in webinars to stay updated on the latest trends and strategies. Networking with like-minded professionals will provide valuable insights and foster a culture of continuous improvement. The most successful companies are often pioneers who frequently share their insights and continually enhance their approaches.

7. **Explore additional resources.** Obtain a copy of the Nextiva Press book: "Mastering the Customer Experience." This resource provides a comprehensive step-by-step guide on approaching and thoroughly evaluating automation candidates. The eight-step plan outlined in the book assists in categorizing all current transactions and positioning them on the previously mentioned complexity scales. This proven methodology will enable you to identify appropriate automation opportunities and establish a strategic path for achieving success.

In addition to the step-by-step guide, the book includes case studies and real-life examples that demonstrate the practical application of these strategies. These examples provide valuable insights into how other organizations have successfully implemented automation, highlighting both the challenges they faced and the solutions they devised. Furthermore, the book offers tools and templates that you can use to streamline your evaluation process. These resources are designed to help you gather and analyze data, make informed decisions, and develop a clear and actionable automation roadmap.

Lastly, "Mastering the Customer Experience" emphasizes the importance of continuous improvement. It encourages you to regularly review and refine your automation efforts, ensuring that they continue to meet your evolving business needs and customer expectations. By adopting a mindset of continual optimization, you can stay ahead of the curve and maintain a competitive edge in the ever-changing landscape of customer experience.

Conclusion

In conclusion, I urge you to strike an appropriate balance between high-touch human interaction and automation. While automation and AI can streamline processes and enhance efficiency, it is essential to preserve the human element in customer engagements.

By harmonizing technology with personalization, you can ensure that customer experiences are both efficient and empathetic. Adopt a measured approach. Focus on implementing one initiative at a time to ensure clarity in ROI and success metrics. Many automation and AI projects fail due to unclear objectives. Establish a clear business case, secure adequate funding, and build momentum by concentrating on a single use case before progressing to the next.

—Edwin Margulies, editor-at-large

About The Editor

EDWIN MARGULIES IS a distinguished leader in the customer experience (CX) industry, bringing over 40 years of expertise in launching and scaling high-tech companies. His main focus has been on creating innovative and collaborative systems aimed at enhancing the customer experience. Margulies is the author of 20 published books and possesses a keen interest in usability and human factors. He has conducted numerous audits and benchmarks for automation systems and websites. Additionally, he supports open architecture standards and has initiated and developed several industry-recognized programs.

Throughout his career, he has meticulously documented the ever-evolving landscape of customer experience. Some of his notable publications include "Client Server Computer Telephony," "Understanding the Voice Enabled Internet," and "Mastering the Customer Experience." His latest work, entitled "Winning the Customer Experience Race," serves as an homage to his esteemed customers and industry practitioners who have tirelessly worked to develop applications and services that delight customers.

Made in the USA
Middletown, DE
18 October 2025

19291574R00190